George Park Fisher

The colonial era

George Park Fisher

The colonial era

ISBN/EAN: 9783337150105

Printed in Europe, USA, Canada, Australia, Japan

Cover: Foto ©ninafisch / pixelio.de

More available books at **www.hansebooks.com**

THE AMERICAN HISTORY SERIES

THE COLONIAL ERA

BY

GEORGE PARK FISHER, D.D., LL.D.

PROFESSOR IN YALE UNIVERSITY

WITH MAPS

NEW YORK
CHARLES SCRIBNER'S SONS
1898

COPYRIGHT, 1892, BY
CHARLES SCRIBNER'S SONS

TROW DIRECTORY
PRINTING AND BOOKBINDING COMPANY
NEW YORK

DEDICATED

AS A TOKEN OF AFFECTION

TO

GEORGE WHARTON PEPPER

PREFACE

This work is the first of a series of four, which, although distinct in authorship, and each complete in itself, are designed to furnish in a brief but readable form a connected history of the United States from the discovery of the Continent to the present time. The present volume, on the Colonial Period, carries the narrative down to the year 1756, the date of the Declaration of War between England and France. It embraces, therefore, the beginnings of the decisive struggle of the two nations for dominion in America, or of what used to be called the "Old French War." The record of the remainder of the Colonial Period may conveniently find a place in connection with the era of the Revolution, of which it was the prelude.

Until we reach the point where the narrative in this volume ends, it is expedient, at least in a work of no larger compass than the present, to trace the history of the Colonies one by one. It is true that the English Colonies from the beginning were moving slowly towards the goal of political unity. In the American Union the federal and national elements are combined in the way so concisely stated in a passage from the pen of Madison in *The Federalist*, where it is said: "Our system is neither a national nor a federal system, but a composition of both. In its foundations, federal, not national; in the sources from which the ordinary powers of government are drawn, partly federal and partly national; in the operation of these powers, national, not federal; in the extent of them, again, federal, not national; and finally, in the authoritative mode of introducing amendments, neither wholly federal nor wholly national." Albeit the system was, " in its foundations, federal, not national," yet from the start, prior to any organic connection of the Colonies, save their common relation to the British Crown, historical forces were in action that were destined to create a national factor of not less power than the federal element in shaping our civil polity. But in the space traversed by the present volume the Colonies were predominantly distinct communities, so that with the exception of the group of them comprised in New England they can best be treated separately. Yet the English Revolution of 1688 is so important a landmark, that it appeared to me advisable to break the narrative into two parts. By this arrangement the attention is not kept fastened on each Colony by itself through the entire course of the history, while the others are in the main left out of sight. It also seemed a little more conducive to unity of impression to take up the several Colonies in a different order in the second Part, from that adopted in the first.

While it has been my aim in the composition of this book to consult brevity, I have not been willing to reduce the narrative to a bare sketch. Political events must necessarily have a prominent place; but manners, customs, and phases of intellectual progress are not left unnoticed.

It need not be said that there is often controversy, and sometimes heated controversy, respecting events in the past and the merits of actors who have long ago passed off the stage. In this particular our early American history forms no exception. As to the judgments expressed in the following pages on persons and things that are still the subject of debate, all I can say is that they have not been hastily formed, and that I have given heed to the familiar, but never trite. injunction to hear both sides—"Audi alteram partem."

While I have spent much time in the study of the original sources, with special painstaking on doubtful points, I have received aid from many writers who in later times have explored the field of our early history, or particular sections of it. There are three of the comparatively recent works to which I am bound to make special acknowledgments. These are Winsor's "Narrative and Critical History of America," Doyle's "English Colonies in America," and Palfrey's "History of New England." A brief estimate of the character of these works will be found in the Bibliographical Note at the end of the volume.

NEW HAVEN, February 26, 1892.

CONTENTS

PART I.

FROM THE DISCOVERY OF AMERICA TO THE ENGLISH REVOLUTION OF 1688

CHAPTER I.

PAGE

PHYSICAL GEOGRAPHY, ... 1

The Pacific Coast—The Atlantic Coast—The Appalachian Ranges—The Forests.

CHAPTER II.

THE INDIANS, ... 5

Their Languages—The Peruvians—The Mexicans—The Red Men—The Mound-Builders—The Indians Classified—Indian Traits—Their Manners—Their Occupations, Food, and Dwellings—Tribal Arrangements—Their Religion—Their Moral Qualities—Their Number.

CHAPTER III.

DISCOVERIES AND SETTLEMENTS PRIOR TO THE FIRST PERMANENT ENGLISH COLONY, ... 12

The Renaissance—New Inventions—Maritime Enterprise—The First Voyage of Columbus—"The Indies" Allotted to Spain and Portugal—Columbus Discovers the Mainland—

Voyages of the Cabots—Spanish Voyagers—Florida Discovered—The Mississippi Discovered—De Soto—Spanish Settlers in Florida—Rise of New France—Champlain Founds Quebec—English Voyages of Exploration—Gilbert and Raleigh—Gosnold.

CHAPTER IV.

VIRGINIA UNTIL 1688, ... 30

James I. and his Policy—Incentives to Colonization—The Virginia Company—Constitution of its Two Branches—The London Company—The Settlement of Jamestown—John Smith—The New Charter—Delaware—Dale—Argall—The Third Charter—The House of Burgesses—Growth of the Colony—Annulling of the Charter—Spanish Intrigues—Harvey—Berkeley—Under the Commonwealth—Navigation Laws—Arlington and Culpepper—Bacon's Rebellion—A Royal Province—Negro Slavery.

CHAPTER V.

MARYLAND UNTIL 1688, ... 62

The First Lord Baltimore—Avalon—Grant of Maryland—The Maryland Charter—Religion in Maryland—Toleration—Clayborne's Settlement—The Maryland Colony—Conflict with Clayborne—Period of the Commonwealth—Non-conformists in Maryland—Act of Religious Freedom—Puritan Ascendency—Baltimore Regains His Province—Fendall—Slavery—Dispute with Penn—End of Proprietary Government—Society in Maryland.

CHAPTER VI.

THE CAROLINAS UNTIL 1688, ... 70

Grant of Carolina by Charles II.—The Two Settlements—"The Fundamental Constitutions"—North Carolina—Civil Disturbances—Sothel—Ludwell—South Carolina—Slavery—Scotch-Irish and Huguenot Immigrants—Civil Disturbances.

CHAPTER VII.

NEW ENGLAND TO THE PLANTING OF CONNECTICUT IN 1636, 82

The Plymouth Company—The Popham Colony—John Smith in New England—The Council of New England—Puritanism in England—Religious Parties in Elizabeth's Reign—The Independents—The Scrooby Congregation—The Pilgrims in Holland—The Voyage of the Mayflower—The Settlement at Plymouth—The Government at Plymouth—Growth and Character of the Colony—Towns—Mason's Grant of New Hampshire—The New Puritan Emigration—Endicott at Salem—The Charter of the Massachusetts Company—The First Congregational Church—Alleged "Intolerance" of the Puritans—Transfer of the Massachusetts Company to New England—John Winthrop—The Great Emigration to Massachusetts—Sufferings of the Colony—Its Form of Government—Congregationalism—Roger Williams—Williams Founds Providence—Vane—Mrs. Ann Hutchinson—Winthrop again Chosen Governor—Heroic Spirit of the Colony—Council of New England Surrenders its Charter—Roger Williams and his Colony—Settlement of Rhode Island—The Settlements in New Hampshire—Gorges' Settlement in Maine.

CHAPTER VIII.

NEW ENGLAND FROM THE PLANTING OF CONNECTICUT IN 1636 TO 1688, ... 126

The Early Settlers in Connecticut—The Migration to Hartford—The Government of the Three Towns—The Founding of New Haven—Its Government—The Fiction of the "Blue Laws"—Settlement at Saybrook—Saybrook Joined to Connecticut—The Pequot War—The New England Confederacy—Commission for the Management of the Colonies—Samuel Gorton—War of the Narragansetts and the Mohegans—Acts of the Confederacy—The Cambridge Synod—John Clarke—Maine and Massachusetts—The Quakers in Massachusetts—The Navigation Law—The Charter of Connecticut—Union of New Haven and Connecticut Colonies—The Royal Commission—King Philip's War—Annulling of the Massachusetts Charter—Royal Government in New England—Andros—Revolution in Massachusetts—Society in New England.

CHAPTER IX.

NEW YORK TO 1688, ... 177

Hudson's Discovery—Block's Exploring Voyage—The "New Netherland" Company—West India Company Chartered—The Dutch at Manhattan and Albany—Purchase of Manhattan Island—The Patroons—Van Twiller Succeeds Minuit—The Swedish Settlement—Trouble with the Indians—Peter Stuyvesant—Treaty with Connecticut—Attack on the Swedes—Delaware Purchased—Religious Contests—Demand for Popular Franchise—Relations to Connecticut—Holland and England—Conquest of New Netherland by the English—The New Government—War between England and France—Lovelace—New Netherland Retaken by the Dutch—Restored to the English—New York Described by Andros—Dongan—Charter of Liberties—New York a Royal Province—The Revolt of Leisler.

CHAPTER X.

NEW JERSEY TO 1688, ... 194

Grant to Berkeley and Carteret—Settlement at Elizabeth—Settlement at Newark—East Jersey—West Jersey Acquired by Penn and His Associates—Sale to Penn of Carteret's Rights—Scottish Emigration to East Jersey—Effect of the Revolution of 1688.

CHAPTER XI.

PENNSYLVANIA TO 1688, ... 199

Early Life of Penn—Grant to Him by James II.—Penn's Charter—His Constitution—The Body of Laws—Penn's Treatment of the Indians—Emigration to Pennsylvania—Religion in the Colony—Penn in England—Disorder in the Colony—Pennsylvania Described.

PART II.

FROM THE ENGLISH REVOLUTION OF 1688 TO 1756

CHAPTER XII.

THE EFFECT ON THE COLONIES OF THE REVOLUTION OF 1688, ... 207

Result of the Revolution of 1688—King and Parliament—The Colonial Governments—Spirit of the Colonial Houses of Delegates—Navigation Laws—French and Indian Wars—French Explorations—French Claims to Louisiana—Movements in the Direction of Colonial Union.

CHAPTER XIII.

NEW ENGLAND FROM 1688 TO 1756, ... 216

Board of Trade and Plantations—French and Indian Attacks—Unsuccessful Attempt on Canada—Massachusetts Fails to Regain her Charter—The New Charter of Massachusetts—The Witchcraft Delusion—The Government of Phips—Bellomont—Inroads of French and Indians—Separation of New Hampshire from Massachusetts—Rhode Island under Bellomont—Dudley—Queen Anne's War—Rhode Island under Dudley—Connecticut—Shute—Explanatory Charter of Massachusetts—New Hampshire and Connecticut—The "Great Revival"—Belcher—Connecticut and Rhode Island—Burnet—Shirley—Renewal of Hostilities with France—Capture of Louisburg—The Albany Congress—Military Expeditions—New Hampshire and Connecticut.

CHAPTER XIV.

NEW YORK FROM 1688 TO 1756, ... 241

Leisler's Insurrection—The Assembly called by Sloughter—Fletcher's Ecclesiastical Measures—Bellomont—Cornbury—Trial of Mackemie—Hunter—The "Palatines"—Burnet

—Cosby—The Liberty of the Press—Independent Spirit of the Assembly—"The Negro Plot"—Clinton's Struggle with the Assembly—The Albany Convention—Johnson's Victory—Paper Money—Character of the Middle States—Society in New York —Education—Ruling Families.

CHAPTER XV.

NEW JERSEY FROM 1688 TO 1756, ... 255

New Jersey after the Revolution—New Jersey a Royal Province — Cornbury and the Assembly — Hunter — Burnet — New Jersey Separated from New York—The Elizabethtown Claimants—The Revival in New Jersey—Social Life.

CHAPTER XVI.

PENNSYLVANIA AND DELAWARE FROM 1688 TO 1756, . . 260

Charges Against Penn — Disorder in Pennsylvania — "The Counties" — George Keith — The Proprietary Displaced — Penn Regains his Province—He Befriends Negroes and Indians—New Charter of Privileges—The Two Parties—Evans—Evans Recalled—Gookin—The Assembly against Logan—Death of Penn—Administration of Keith—Gordon—Anti-Quaker Party—Opposition to the Proprietaries—Franklin—Society in Pennsylvania—Physicians—Tradesmen—Philadelphia—Intellectual Life.

CHAPTER XVII.

MARYLAND FROM 1688 TO 1756, ... 272

The Revolution in Maryland—Overthrow of the Proprietary Government—Intolerance in Maryland—Nicholson—Proprietary Government Restored—Maryland in 1751.

CHAPTER XVIII.

VIRGINIA FROM 1688 TO 1756, ... 277

The Revolution in Virginia—The Governors and the Burgesses—William and Mary College—James Blair—Governor

Spotswood—His Dispute with the Burgesses—His Journey over the Blue Ridge—New Immigrants—The Churches—Slavery—The Rich Planters—Dinwiddie—The Ohio Company — English and French Claims — Dinwiddie and the Burgesses — George Washington — An Adjutant-General: A Messenger to the French: At Great Meadows: An Aid of Braddock—Defeat of Braddock—The Retreat—Washington at Winchester—Washington Visits Boston.

CHAPTER XIX.

THE CAROLINAS FROM 1688 TO 1756, ... 292

North Carolina—Conflict of Parties—Indian War—Increase of the Colony — A Royal Province — Immigrants — South Carolina—Archdale—Charleston—Indian War—War with the Yemassees—Hostility to the Proprietaries—End of the Proprietary Rule—Nicholson—The Governor and the Assembly—Indian Troubles—Revolt of Slaves—Trade and Emigration—Glen—Society in South Carolina.

CHAPTER XX.

GEORGIA FROM ITS SETTLEMENT TO 1756, ... 303

Oglethorpe—His Career—His Plan for a Colony—Grant of Territory—The Settlement—Immigrants from Salzburg—The Colony Reinforced — State of the Colony — Trials — John Wesley — Charles Wesley — Expedition against St. Augustine—Spanish Attack Repelled—Whitefield in Georgia —Surrender of the Charter—The New Government—Social Condition.

CHAPTER XXI.

LITERATURE IN THE COLONIES, ... 313

The Writings of John Smith — Sandys — Whitaker — Early New England Writers—Winthrop—Mather's "Magnalia"—Hubbard—Prince—The New England Divines—Their Ideas of Providence—Absorption in Religion and Theology—The Bay Psalm-Book—Anna Bradstreet—"The Day of Doom" —Franklin and Edwards—Legists.

APPENDIX

		PAGE
I. CHRONOLOGICAL TABLE,	. . . . . .	321
II. BIBLIOGRAPHICAL NOTE,	. . . . . .	325

INDEX, ... 337

LIST OF MAPS

1. PHYSICAL MAP OF THE UNITED STATES, . . *Frontispiece*
2. ORIGINAL GRANTS, ... *Page* 30
3. THE AMERICAN COLONIES IN 1755, . . *End of the volume*

PHYSICAL MAP OF

THE COLONIAL ERA

PART I.

FROM THE DISCOVERY OF AMERICA TO THE ENGLISH REVOLUTION OF 1688

CHAPTER I.

PHYSICAL GEOGRAPHY

The Pacific Coast—The Atlantic Coast—The Appalachian Ranges—The Forests

THE Western continent differs from the Eastern in having a length from north to south far greater than its width. The isthmus that forms the connecting link of its two grand divisions reaches down almost to the equator. North America, stretching as it does from the Polar Sea to the region of perpetual summer, includes all varieties of climate. It was on the eastern shore, and within the temperate latitudes, that the colonies were planted which were destined to develop into the thirteen original States of the Federal Union. In America, in contrast with Europe and Asia, the direction of the mountain ranges is from north to south. The complex mountain system on the Pacific side of North America—the system named the Cordilleras, the continuation of the

Andes—extends so near to the coast as to leave room only for a narrow seaboard. Down the western slopes, so abrupt is their decline, the rivers flow in a swift and tumultuous current into the ocean. Moreover, the Pacific coast is so little indented south of Puget Sound that it furnishes very few harbors. There is one at San Diego and another at San Francisco. Besides these two havens there are left, within the bounds of the United States, only Puget Sound and the broad estuary of the Columbia River—an estuary which it is impossible to enter without the aid of expert pilots. The signal advantage afforded to San Francisco by its commodious harbor would avail of itself to explain the growth of that flourishing city. Even if the Pacific shore had looked toward Europe instead of Asia, its lack of bays and other inlets, taken in connection with the nearness and height of the adjacent mountains, would have presented great obstacles to colonization. On the Atlantic side the natural features were quite different, and in a high degree favorable. There the distance of the coast from Europe is only half that which parts California from Asia. The Appalachian ranges that stretch in broken masses from Maine to Georgia and Alabama are comparatively low. Their slopes are, moreover, much farther from the ocean, thus affording space for a seaboard generally from one hundred to two hundred miles in width. From these mountain ranges, and from the numerous plateaus which are formed by them, the rivers find their way to the Atlantic, or, on the south and southwest, to the Gulf of Mexico. North of the thirty-fifth parallel the coast is broken by numerous indentations. Among the inlets are several large bays, as Massachusetts Bay, which is partly encircled by an arm of Cape Cod, Delaware Bay, into which pours the river of the same name, and the Chesapeake, which receives the waters of the Susquehanna and the Potomac. Along the coast, above the thirty-fifth parallel, there are many harbors where vessels can safely cast anchor or load and discharge their cargoes. Below that line the number of convenient havens is small. "Scarcely any continent," says Professor Shaler, "offers such easy ingress as does this continent to those who come to it from the Atlantic side. The valleys of the St. Lawrence, the Hudson, the Mississippi, in a fashion, also, of the Susquehanna and the James, break through or pass around the low-coast mountains, and afford free ways into the whole of the interior that is attractive to European peoples." The break made by the Hudson led up through the valley of Champlain to the St. Lawrence, and formed a natural line of communication between New York and Canada. One might pass from the Hudson to the northwest, up the valley of the Mohawk and thence into the region of the Mississippi and its tributaries. In the south there was another pathway to the same region through the Cumberland Gap. It was long before pioneers of English descent explored beyond the natural barriers of the mountain ranges. In that vast field of the interior the French were their forerunners.

Of the two parallel ranges that form the Appalachian system the eastern may be traced from Eastern Canada to Alabama. The western, or Alleghany range, begins near Albany and has the same terminus in the south. *The Appalachian ranges.* Between these two ranges, from New Jersey to Georgia, is a "broad, elevated, somewhat mountainous" valley, of exceeding fertility. The Hudson cuts through the ranges, and below the Hudson the intervening valley is reached from the east by crossing the South Mountain of Pennsylvania, the Blue Ridge in Virginia, and the Black Mountain of North Carolina.

When the English settlers planted themselves on the

border of the Atlantic coast, the whole territory from the St. Lawrence to the Gulf of Mexico, and from the ocean to the central plains beyond the Appalachians, was woodland, except here and there a small patch of ground which had been cleared by storm or flood, or by the "girdling" of the trees by Indian hatchets and the burning of the undergrowth. Wherever the emigrants went, they found themselves enclosed by the sombre, boundless forest. The trees included nearly three hundred species. Even the trees which belonged to genera that had been familiar to the eyes of the settlers in the Old World were mostly of new species.

The forests.

CHAPTER II.

THE INDIANS

Their Languages—The Peruvians—The Mexicans—The Red Men—The Mound Builders—The Indians Classified—Indian Traits—Their Manners—Their Occupations, Food, and Dwellings—Tribal Arrangements—Their Religion—Their Moral Qualities—Their Number.

THE Western continent, at the time of its discovery, was inhabited by a great number of tribes and peoples. Concerning their relationship among themselves we have a limited amount of knowledge. On the question of their affinities with races on the Eastern continent, numerous theories have been broached, but it would be unsafe at present to pronounce a confident judgment. The languages of these tribes and peoples in both North and South America were generally, *Their languages.* although not exclusively, of one essential type. Their tongues were mostly of the *polysynthetic* class. That is to say, they formed conglomerate words by a peculiar incorporation of syllables, of such a character that a single word might be made to do the work of a sentence. In fact, the word comprised definitions of the elements that entered into it, and so might be prolonged indefinitely. Even the tongue of the Eskimos, distinct as they were in their physical characteristics, did not differ in its fundamental structure from the languages *The Peruvians.* of most of the other American peoples. Peru and Mexico were semi-civilized nations. Peru under the sway of the Incas had a kind of theocratic govern-

ment, the ruler being held to be of divine descent, and being possessed of absolute sovereignty. The Peruvians were acquainted with the art of writing. They were cultivators of the soil, of which every individual possessed a portion. They had good roads, with post-houses, were skilful builders, and expert potters and workers in metals. Their chief divinity was the Sun. Another people, the Mayas of Central America, in their ruined cities left behind striking proofs of architectu-
The Mexicans. ral taste and skill. The Mexicans had a less despotic form of government than the Peruvians. They had invented a system of picture-writing. Except in those mechanical arts which have been referred to, they were in advance of the Peruvians. Their religion was not destitute of beneficent elements, yet its ritual included human sacrifices. They were fierce in the treatment of enemies, of whom the Tlascalans, their unsubdued neighbors, were the most formidable. The Pueblo race, whose remains are found in New Mexico, in Arizona, and in Southern California, are to be distinguished from the Mexican Aztecs. A portion of the Pueblos built their dwellings on high plateaus that were almost inaccessible; others built in the cliffs of the cañons. Their houses were of stone or sun-dried brick, in size huge, and made to contain hundreds of inmates, who lived in a communal way. The Pueblos made cloth and pottery, but, on the whole, they appear to have been not so far advanced
The Red Men. as the Aztecs. The red men have kept the name of "Indians," which was given to native Americans under the idea that the newly discovered regions of the West were a part of India. They are called
The Mound-builders. "red" from their bronze or cinnamon color. They were preceded by the prehistoric race of "mound-builders," whose earthworks, which are all that is left of their forts and temples, are found in the

valleys of the Mississippi and of the Ohio. The remains of mechanical art that have been dug out of these mounds show that their builders, whoever they were, had made considerable progress on the road to civilization. It is quite probable that they were the ancestors of modern aboriginal races, who were their inferiors in taste and skill. The Indians with whom the English settlers of North America were brought into contact are classified under several grand divisions, or families of tribes. The principal of these was the great Algonkin family. It spread from Hudson's Bay and the Eskimos of Labrador as far south as North Carolina, and from the Gulf of St. Lawrence and the Atlantic west to the Mississippi. Their language "was the mother-tongue of those who greeted the colonists of Raleigh at Roanoke, of those who welcomed the Pilgrims to Plymouth." But the territory of the Algonkins enclosed, or nearly enclosed, within itself, the lands of an alien group, that of the Iroquois, comprising the Five Nations, which became the "Six Nations" when their kinsmen, the Tuscaroras, joined them in 1713. They dwelt on the south of Lakes Erie and Ontario and of the St. Lawrence. To them the name of Iroquois is generally applied ; but the Hurons, to the north of them, were a branch of the same ethnical division. South of the Tennessee River, and spreading to the Mississippi and to the Gulf, were the tribes of the Muskogee family, of whom the Creeks were the most powerful. To this group belonged, also, the Cherokees, Chickasaws, Choctaws, and Seminoles.

The Indians classified.

We have no knowledge of the Indians prior to their intercourse with the whites. In judging of them we must take into account modifications of character and manners. which resulted from such intercourse. In general their traits were such as are found usually in savage races of the more vigorous

Indian traits.

type. Among themselves, while their main characteristics were the same everywhere, there were not wanting marked tribal peculiarities. For example, some tribes were not so resentful and implacable as others, and were less formidable as enemies. The remarks which follow, although in general applicable to all, are especially descriptive of the tribes with which the Northern Colonies, whose contests with the Indians were the most severe and prolonged, came into contact.

In stature the Indians were quite up to the ordinary height, and were well formed. They had high cheek-bones; long, coarse, jet-black hair; scant beard, and small eyes. They clothed themselves in the skins of wild animals. In summer the men went almost naked, wearing only an apron of deer-skin. The feet were protected by moccasins made of the same material, or of the hide of the moose. They tattooed themselves, and were fond of other sorts of barbaric decoration, taking special delight in feathers and gay colors. They were alert, swift of foot, and capable of energetic action, which was followed, however, by lassitude. They showed no aptitude for persevering industry, and wilted down under any employment that required long-continued exertion.

Their manners. They were reserved, indisposed to smile or to weep, and bore physical suffering, however intense and protracted, with stoical indifference. In negotiations of importance they exhibited a certain grave courtesy. But among themselves their sedate manner often gave place to a low jollity. They entered into their festivities with glee. Dancing was a favorite pastime. Among their customary sports were various games, especially foot-ball and quoits. They were adepts in whatever pertains to wood-craft. In making their light canoes, their bows, their hatchets of stone, and their pipes, and in dressing skins for their clothing, they

Their occupations, food, and dwellings.

evinced no small degree of skill. They were good marksmen. They had no flocks or herds, and no domestic animals except a dog of a wolfish breed which sometimes attended them. The women tilled the soil, while the men were engaged in war, or in hunting and fishing. They raised nothing but maize, which they knew well how to cultivate, and a few other vegetables. Fish, where fish could be obtained, were a great article of food among them. Their relish for oysters is proved by the deep beds of oyster-shells which were found by the white settlers on the southern shores of Connecticut. The money of the Indians was *wampum*—pieces of sea-shell, laboriously shaped in a particular form and strung on a thread. Their habitations, or *wigwams*, were circular or oblong in shape. They were constructed of branches of trees stuck in the ground, and bending toward the centre, a hole being left at the top for the smoke to escape. They were sometimes lined with mats and covered with the barks of trees, or daubed with mud. The Indians generally had but one wife, but this was the effect of no law, and there was no restraint if they chose to discard their wives. Touching examples are on record of strong parental and filial affection among them; but this cannot be said to have been a pervading characteristic. The Indians dwelt in villages. Each tribe had its chief, whose office descended, but by no means invariably, in his family. Within the tribe or confederacy there existed that sort of clanship which is found so frequently among savage races, and bears the name of *totemism*. Each clan had its own *totem*—the wolf, the tortoise, or whatever it might be, and was distinguished by a corresponding symbol. The chief of the tribe, or sachem, might not of necessity be the leader in war. Subordinate sachems, or "sagamores," were consulted in grave emergencies. But the organization of the

Tribal arrangements.

natives was loose. Except on urgent occasions, or under the inspiration of some remarkable warrior, it was hard for them to combine in large numbers. In popular assemblies any who were respected or gifted in speech might declare their counsel. The Indian harangues were highly ornate, being stored with metaphors drawn from natural objects. The Indian tongues lack words to denote the things of the spirit. The figurative style of their speakers, which is occasionally somewhat impressive, partly accounts for the exaggerated ideas of the intellectual capacity of the red men which have been diffused by poets and romance-writers. Their religious notions were like those of many savage peoples in other parts of the world. They clothed the various objects and activities of nature with a distinct personal life. They had their fetiches and incantations. But it is quite doubtful whether, independently of all instruction, they arrived at any clear conception of one "Great Spirit." Their "medicine-men" were conjurers. A religious significance was attached to their dances. But the Indians had no temples, no rites of worship, no priesthood. The vices that are most often laid to the charge of the Indians are treachery and cruelty. In common with uncivilized peoples generally, it was one of their "ruling ideas" that the wrongs done by an individual were to be avenged on the clan or race. There is no doubt that the Indians were sly, suspicious, stealthy in their ways of compassing their ends, and adepts in dissimulation. These tendencies were naturally called into activity in their dealings with the whites. There are not wanting among them in our early history striking instances of fidelity to promises, and steadfast loyalty in friendship. Their worst trait was the spirit of revenge, and the merciless cruelty which made them delight in indiscriminate slaughter, and in inflicting tortures on their

Their religion.

Their moral qualities.

enemies and captives. To count up as many scalps as possible was the ambition of the Indian youth. This kind of success was the highest title to honor.

There has been an exaggerated impression of the number of savages at the time when our country began to be settled. How many there were it is impossible to estimate with any approach to exactness. Bancroft judges that the total number on the whole area east of the Mississippi, now covered by the United States, was not far from one hundred and eighty thousand.

Their number.

CHAPTER III.

DISCOVERIES AND SETTLEMENTS PRIOR TO THE FIRST PERMANENT ENGLISH COLONY

The Renaissance—New Inventions—Maritime Enterprise—The First Voyage of Columbus—"The Indies" Allotted to Spain and Portugal—Columbus Discovers the Mainland—Voyages of the Cabots—Spanish Voyagers—Florida Discovered—The Mississippi Discovered—De Soto—Spanish Settlers in Florida—Rise of New France—Champlain Founds Quebec—English Voyages of Exploration—Gilbert and Raleigh—Gosnold.

THE fifteenth century was the age of the Renaissance, the reawakening of learning and art from a long slumber. The mediæval era in its distinctive character was giving place to a new order of things. Compact monarchies were growing up on the ruins of feudalism. Europe was astir with a fresh intellectual life. New inventions were appearing to accelerate the advance of civilization. In the middle of the fifteenth century, gunpowder was brought into use. Fire-arms were now to displace, to a large extent, the old weapons of war. About the same time, printing by movable types was first devised, an art that spread with marvellous rapidity. The mariner's compass, which in China had long served the purpose of guiding land-carriages, began to be used by Europeans on the sea. Vessels were no more obliged to cling to the coast, but could venture out into the mid-ocean. These inventions were conspicuous signs and effects of that spontaneous outburst of intelligence and energy which made this epoch a turning-point in history. A great stimulus was given to maritime exploration by Prince Henry of Portugal—Henry the Navigator, as he was styled. At the outset of his career he was a gallant soldier, but he turned from brilliant deeds of arms to the eager study of astronomy and geography. He was bent on finding a path by the sea to Arabia and the regions of the farther east. The discoveries made under his auspices on the western coast of Africa increased the interest that was felt in maritime enterprises. In 1466, the Azores were occupied by Portugal. The Canaries were acquired and subdued by Spain. The strongest desire was roused to discover an ocean path to the countries of Eastern Asia. This was the goal which ambitious seamen set before them. It was while in pursuit of this object that Christopher Columbus made his great discovery. The Norse sagas relate that centuries before his time, as early as the year 1000, Scandinavian explorers, who had previously occupied places on the western shore of Greenland, planted a colony in "Vinland," which has been supposed by many to be near the coast of New England. But the fact of the existence of such a settlement for any considerable time lacks verification. Where it was precisely is uncertain, and it soon came to naught. That different landings on the American shore were made by hardy seamen from Greenland is very probable. The opinion that the earth is round had been held by Plato, Aristotle, and other ancient writers. It was revived in the middle ages by Averroes, a Spanish-Arabian philosopher, was adopted in the time of Columbus by inquisitive men of science, and was embraced by Columbus himself. He felt sure that the eastern coasts of Asia could be reached by sailing westward. Ten years, full of struggle and disappointment, elapsed before he embarked from Palos

Henry the Navigator. 1394–1460.

The Norse sagas.

Columbus.

in the three little ships, two of which were only half-decked, that were furnished him largely by the bounty of Isabella, the Queen of Castile. Guided by a sea-chart which Toscanelli, a Florentine astronomer, had sent to him, he passed the Canaries and would have reached the coast of Florida or Virginia had he not been persuaded by one of his companions, Pinzon, to turn to the southwest, the direction which a flock of pigeons was observed to take. Just as a mutinous spirit was ready to break out among his discouraged sailors, he reached the island of Guanahani, in the Bahamas. But for the change in his course, the descendants of Spanish Roman Catholics, instead of English Protestants, might now possess our Atlantic seaboard. When Columbus carried home the report of his discoveries, it seemed likely that difficulties would spring up between Spain and Portugal. It was considered that to the popes belonged the right to dispose of all lands inhabited by the heathen. About a half century before, Nicholas V. had granted to the Portuguese their conquests on the west coast of Africa, but in terms so broad and general that they were inclined to dispute the claim of the Spanish sovereigns to any portion of what was called "the Indies." To make the latter secure in their possessions, and to prevent a conflict between the two rival pioneers on the sea, Pope Alexander VI., on May 3–4, 1493, issued two bulls to determine their respective rights. The second defined in particular what was bestowed in the first. It gave to Ferdinand and Isabella, their heirs and successors, all lands that might be discovered west and south of a line drawn from the North to the South Pole, at the distance of one hundred leagues west of the Azores and Cape Verd Islands. This gift was made as a reward of their Christian zeal, which, it was said, had been lately manifested in the conquest of Granada. In

June, 1494, by a convention at Tordesillas, it was settled that the imaginary line should run three hundred and seventy leagues west of the Cape Verd Islands. This gave the most of Brazil to the Portuguese. The intent was that Portugal should prosecute her voyages of discovery by the eastward path, and Spain by the westward. In 1498 a Portuguese navigator, Vasco da Gama, succeeded in finding a way to India by sea. He doubled the Cape of Good Hope, and on May 20th sailed into the harbor of Calicut. By this achievement the course of European commerce with the East was changed. The routes overland and through the Mediterranean to Venice and other cities were gradually forsaken. It was still left, however, to explore for other ways, perhaps shorter, to the same regions. *Da Gama doubles the Cape of Good Hope.*

In the same year that the Portuguese made their memorable discovery, Columbus, on his third voyage, entered the mouth of the Orinoco, and on August 1st saw the mainland of the southern division of the Western continent. He died, however, as he had lived, in the unquestioning belief that the territories which he had found pertained to the land that was called by the ancients India. A designation given to Brazil, owing to its discovery by Americus Vespuccius in 1501, resulted in the attaching of his name to the Continent. *Columbus discovers the mainland of South America. Vespuccius.*

More than a year before Columbus beheld the South American coast the mainland of North America was seen by the leader of an English exploring expedition. England had no disposition to acquiesce in the bestowal of all territories west of the Atlantic upon Spain. Without interfering with Spanish discoveries, there was room for seeking a passage to India on the northwest. In 1496 Henry VII. granted to John Cabot, a Venetian, resident in Bristol, and to his three sons, a *Voyage of the Cabots.*

patent, by which they were authorized to seek out, subdue, and occupy, as vassals of the king, any regions which had been hitherto "unknown to all Christians." John Cabot, with one small vessel, set sail in 1497, and reached the coast of Labrador, if not also Newfoundland and Nova Scotia. There is some reason for the opinion that his son, Sebastian, accompanied him in this voyage. A second patent was granted to John Cabot on February 3, 1498, but he did not accompany his son in the fleet of six vessels which left Bristol in the following May. This is the last that we hear of the senior Cabot. He probably died about the time that the expedition started. He believed that by sailing southward from the places which he had discovered he could find the land of jewels and spices. But the expedition of the younger Cabot attempted to reach Cathay by the northwest passage. Being forced by the blocks of ice and the cold to turn his prows in a southerly direction, he sailed along the coast as far as the Chesapeake, landing at different places, always, however, in quest of a way by water to the Indies.

In 1501 Gaspar Cortereal, a seaman in the service of Manouel, King of Portugal, explored the coast of North America for six or seven hundred miles southward from the mouth of the St. Lawrence. His ships carried back to Portugal more than fifty Indians, who were sold into slavery.

Voyage of Gaspar Cortereal.

The spirit of chivalry, zeal for the propagation of the Catholic religion, and greed of gold conspired to prompt the Spanish to embark in schemes of conquest and settlement in the New World.

In 1513 an old soldier, Ponce de Leon, left Porto Rico with three ships and discovered the coast of Florida. He failed afterwards in an attempt to colonize the territory which he had obtained a commission to govern.

Ponce de Leon discovers Florida.

DISCOVERIES AND SETTLEMENTS 17

On September 25, 1513, Balboa, a daring discoverer, at the head of an expedition which had left Darien, from the summit of the range of mountains on the isthmus, looked down on the Pacific. Descending to the shore, he took formal possession of the ocean in the name of his sovereign. *Balboa discovers the Pacific.*

In 1521 an expedition sent out by Vasquez de Ayllon from St. Domingo, landed on the coast of South Carolina, which was called Chicora. The captain sailed off treacherously with a throng of natives whom he had enticed on board his ships. *Vasquez at Chicora.*

It was in 1519 that Cortez departed from Cuba on his memorable expedition, and within two years he conquered Mexico. In 1526, Vasquez came in person with a commission to subdue and govern Chicora; but after having wasted his fortune, besides losing many of his men, he failed in his attempt. Gomez was sent out by Charles V., 1524, to search for a northern passage to Cathay. Having touched at different points along the coast as far north as Newfoundland, he went back to Spain with a cargo of furs and of Indians for the slave-market. *Cortez.*

In 1519, Pineda, commanding four ships, with pilots on board, explored the northern coast of the Gulf of Mexico to a point beyond the Rio Grande. The outlet of the Mississippi was marked by the pilots on the maps which they drew. *Pineda.*

Another effort to colonize Florida was made in 1528 by Pamfilo de Narvaez. His followers were from the higher class, and some of them the sons of nobles. He landed at Tampa Bay, and took possession anew of Florida in the name of his sovereign. Eager, like so many others, to find the precious metals, and deceived by the natives, who were glad to be freed from his presence, he led his companions into the in- *Narvaez.*

2

terior, where they travelled up and down, undergoing infinite labor and suffering, struggling through miry swamps and thick forests, until they were forced to turn back to the coast. There, as they had parted from their vessels, they had to construct boats, on which they managed to reach the mouth of the Mississippi. Four survivors, one of whom was Cabeza de Vaca, the treasurer, who was next in command to Narvaez, at last landed somewhere on the coast of Texas. All that they had suffered up to this time was but the beginning of their hardships. Directing their course inland, they wandered for eight long years. They lived much with the Indians, but worked their way across Texas and through an extensive region which cannot now with certainty be identified, to Culiacan, on the Gulf of California, where they arrived in May, 1536. There they found countrymen, and were escorted with honor to the city of Mexico.

Cabeza de Vaca.

For a long time reports were rife among the Spanish conquerors of Mexico that far to the north lay cities abounding in wealth. The natives related that a few hundred miles north of the capital there were seven such great and wealthy cities. A succession of attempts were made to find Cibola, the name attached to the place where the untold riches lay. In 1539, a messenger despatched by Coronado, Governor of New Galicia, came back with the story that he had seen Cibola, and found it a more splendid city than Mexico. Coronado organized an expedition, consisting of three hundred Spaniards, some of them mounted, and all of them well equipped. He penetrated to the seven cities, but discovered them to be the stone-built towers of the Pueblo Indians. The tales of their wealth turned out to be fabulous. But Coronado, moving toward the northeast, prosecuted his explorations for three years longer.

The search for Cibola.

He found no opulent cities, but he "portrayed the country north of Sonora, from what is now Kansas on the one side, to the chasm of the Colorado on the other." In 1542, he returned to Mexico.

Ferdinand De Soto was a Spaniard, poor, but of good birth, who rendered much effective aid to Pizarro in the conquest of Peru, and carried a fortune back with him to Spain. Appointed by Charles V. Governor of Florida, a name attached by the Spaniards to the whole region between the Atlantic and the Mississippi, he landed, in May, 1539, with his enthusiastic band of six hundred men, at Espiritu Santo Bay. It was the strongest and best furnished of all the exploring expeditions that Spain had sent out. It shared, however, the common fate. After long and miserable wanderings in the regions north of the Gulf, in quest of another Peru, or of mineral treasures which their deceitful Indian guides constantly promised that they should find, early in 1541 they reached the Mississippi. Ascending that river on the west side, they at length bent their course toward the northwest. Soto displayed the greatest fortitude and perseverance, but he treated the natives with atrocious cruelty. Baffled and nearly worn out, the party followed the Washita down to its junction with the great river. Here, on May 21, 1542, Soto died and was buried beneath its waters. His men, resolved to make their way to Mexico, first attempted to do so by land, but had to come back to the Mississippi and slowly to construct frail barks, in which the survivors of the party descended to its mouth, and proceeded along the coast until they reached Panuco.

Up to this time the Spaniards had gained no permanent foothold in America north of the Gulf and beyond the limits of their conquests in Mexico. They had shown an astonishing bravery and endurance, and had wasted

De Soto.

many lives. But the ruling motive in their expeditions had been the passion for gold and plunder. Even at the close of the next century the only Spanish settlement within the bounds designated above was St. Augustine.

The French very early made themselves acquainted with the fisheries of Newfoundland. It was their fishermen and sailors who gave its name to Cape Breton. In 1524, John Verrazano, who was a Florentine by birth, but, in the service of Francis I., distinguished himself by capturing treasure-ships of Spain, made a voyage to America to look for a way to Cathay. He sailed up the coast, stopping at different points, from Cape Fear, in North Carolina, to Newfoundland. In 1534, Jacques Cartier, a Breton sailor, left the port of St. Malo for the coast of Labrador. He entered the Bay of Chaleurs, and also the estuary of the St. Lawrence, without being aware of its relation to the river. He did not give up the search for a way to the Indies. In 1535, he returned to the same coast, and ascended the St. Lawrence as far as Hochelaga, the site of Montreal, stopping on his way at the island afterward named Orleans. It is a mistake to suppose that he was the first to give to the whole region the name of New France. Subsequently Francis I. associated with Cartier a nobleman, the Lord of Roberval, whom he made Governor of New France, Cartier being Captain-General, subordinate to him. Cartier was the first to sail. He left France in May, 1541. He built a fort not far from Quebec, and visited Hochelaga. About the time that Roberval arrived with reinforcements, Cartier left for France, carrying with him quartz crystals, which he mistook for diamonds. The two leaders failed to act in concert, and nothing substantial was accomplished. Roberval's effort to plant a colony on the St. Lawrence failed.

Verrazano's voyage.

Cartier.

Among the French the Huguenots were the first to attempt to found colonies within the present limits of the United States. Under the patronage of the famous Protestant leader, Coligni, Jean Ribaut crossed the ocean with two ships. He discovered the St. John's River, in Florida, which he called the May, and sailing northward he entered, in 1562, an inlet which he named Port Royal. There, on an island, he built Fort Carolina, so named for Charles IX., the king of France. The territory adjacent subsequently received the same designation. The few colonists whom he left abandoned the place, and when on their way home in a bark which they had themselves built, were picked up by an English ship. Two years later Laudonnière, who had been a companion of Ribaut, brought over another colony to the May River, where a fort was built which was also named Carolina. When their store of food was consumed, the colonists were relieved by Sir John Hawkins, an English captain, explorer, and slave-trader. Just then, as they were about to return to France, Ribaut arrived with a reinforcement of colonists and supplies for the settlement. The Spaniards were not disposed to tolerate the intrusion into Florida of a company of French heretics. Philip II. committed the work of extirpating them to a fit instrument, Melendez de Aviles. On September 1, 1564, Melendez entered a harbor which he named St. Augustine. Having discovered the situation of the French fort, he attacked it by land and put the whole garrison to the sword, "not," he said, "as Frenchmen, but as Lutherans." Two years after, Dominic de Gourges, a French soldier, anxious to avenge this barbarous act, with three ships sailed to Florida, captured two of the Spanish forts which had been constructed by the followers of Melendez, and not being able to take home his prisoners, hanged them upon trees, doing it, he said in the inscription over them, "not as unto Spaniards or mariners, but as unto trait-ors, robbers, and murderers." St. Augustine, the oldest town in the United States, east of the Mississippi, was left in the hands of Spain.

<small>Spain holds St. Augustine.</small>

France would have taken a much more active part in colonization had it not been for the turmoil of the civil wars that lasted from about 1560 until near the close of the century. In 1594, the terrible struggle ended in the accession of Henry IV., and, in 1598, the edict of Nantes secured freedom of worship for his Protestant subjects. There was a revival of commerce, and the fur-trade, which had gradually sprung up, created an increasing interest in the northern parts of America. In 1598, the Marquis de la Roche, a nobleman of Brittany, received a commission to conquer Canada. But the forty men whom he left on the Isle of Sable, near Nova Scotia, were convicts taken from the jails. For a long time it was imagined, not in France alone, but generally in Europe, that people who were good for nothing else were fit to become colonists. Criminals, idlers, and vagabonds were despatched to the American coast to found social communities. All but twelve of de la Roche's men perished in their miserable abode. These twelve had the good fortune to get back to France. In 1603, De Monts, a Calvinist, a man of high character, was appointed Governor of Acadia, with authority over all inhabitants as far south as the latitude of Philadelphia. After cruising along the coast as far as Cape Cod, he finally placed his colony at Port Royal—afterwards named by the English Annapolis—where there were already some French settlers. After two years De Monts lost his monopoly of the fur-trade, and his colonists returned to France. The settlement was renewed by Poutrincourt. It was almost, but not wholly, extinguished by Argall, the

<small>The rise of New France.</small>

<small>De Monts.</small>

leader of two expeditions from Virginia to break up the French colonies. In 1611, Jesuit priests from France ascended the Kennebec and made friends with the tribes between that river and the Penobscot. When the monopoly granted to De Monts was revoked, a company of French merchants was found to carry on the fur-trade. They executed their plans through the agency of Samuel de Champlain, the most eminent of all the leaders in French colonization in America. Champlain was a man of talents, education, and wide experience. In 1608, he founded Quebec, and led an invading party against the hostile Iroquois. He visited the lake which bears his name. The religious orders, especially the Jesuit Society, sent out their missionaries in an increasing number. The history of the Jesuit missionaries in the "New Land" is a record of almost unexampled devotion and fortitude. France was laying the foundations for what bade fair to be a widespread and lasting dominion. *Champlain founds Quebec.*

After the voyages of the Cabots, Henry VII. was desirous of avoiding a conflict with the pretensions of Spain. When Edward VI. ascended the throne Sebastian Cabot was an old man. He was made governor of a company of merchants who were to seek for the coast of China by the northeastern route. An expedition was sent out under Sir Hugh Willoughby. One of the vessels reached the harbor of Archangel. The only result of the enterprise was the opening of commercial communication with Russia. As long as Henry VIII. acknowledged the papacy, he had felt bound to respect the Pope's grant to Spain. When he threw off the papal authority, and broke with Charles V. on account of the discarding of Queen Catharine, the Emperor's aunt, he was more free from restraint. There was still faith in the possibility of finding a northwestern passage to the *English voyages of exploration.*

land of spices, and the fisheries of Newfoundland grew more and more attractive. On the accession of Elizabeth, the antagonism of England to Spain became intense. The spirit of maritime adventure and exploration grew into a passion. Even when the nations were nominally at peace, English sea rovers lost no opportunity to intercept and capture the Spanish vessels, laden with treasure, which they met with, or hunted for, on the ocean. Elizabeth connived at these breaches of public law, which were prompted to a considerable extent by patriotic feeling, in retaliation for wrongs inflicted on English subjects who fell into the hands of the Inquisition. They were agreeable to her as bringing gold and silver into her coffers. Repeated voyages of Martin Frobisher to the northern coast of America led to geographical discoveries of value, notwithstanding the partial diversion of these expeditions from their design by the fancied discovery of gold and the consequent transportation to England of cargoes of worthless soil. Sir Francis Drake, in the course of his memorable voyage around the world, was one of those who explored the northwest coast. There sprung up a class of zealous students of geography and active promoters of discovery and colonization. Richard Hakluyt is a typical example of this class. From early youth, fascinated by geographical studies and accounts of voyages, he gave all his time at the university to these researches, and accepted the post of chaplain to the English ambassador at Paris for the express purpose of informing himself respecting the discoveries and colonial enterprises of the French and Spanish. Afterwards, in addition to his personal connection with such undertakings, he published copious historical accounts of enterprises, especially English enterprises, of this character.

Two names which are conspicuous at this period in maritime undertakings are Humphrey Gilbert and Walter Raleigh. Gilbert was the half-brother of Raleigh, and was thirteen years older. Gilbert's untimely death prevented him from doing what he might have done, but he lived long enough to merit the high place which he holds in the catalogue of explorers. Raleigh was one of the ablest men of that day, and as versatile as he was able. He was a soldier, taking his first lessons in war from the Huguenots in France, to join whose army he left his studies at Oxford when he was only seventeen, and in whose battles he fought during the next seven years. He became, likewise, the foremost English seaman, as skilful and daring in naval encounters as he was in contests on the land. He was an orator, also, and a leader in the House of Commons; a courtier too, displacing rivals and winning in a remarkable degree the personal regard of Elizabeth, who showered on him estates and monopolies, the usual rewards bestowed on her favorites. Lastly, he was a literary man, a friend of Sidney and of Spenser. He beguiled his prison hours at last in the composition of a history of the world. If Raleigh had great faults, he had great merits. They were the characteristic merits and faults of his time and country. One thread runs through all his career. He cherished an undying antipathy to Spain and Spanish rule. He fought Spain in the Low Countries; in Ireland, where he took part in the conflict and massacre at Smerwick; in the harbor of Cadiz, where he was in the van in the attack on the Spanish fleet; and wherever on the seas a Spanish ship could be assailed. He had large plans for wresting from Spain all her American possessions, and, even if that could not be done, for building up a rival English dominion in the New World. With broad schemes

Gilbert and Raleigh.

of this nature he no doubt had an eye, also, to the advancement of his own private fortunes.

In 1578 Gilbert, who had been knighted for services in Ireland, parted with his patrimony and sold his estates <small>Gilbert's first expedition.</small> to get the means to fit out a great expedition. Letters-patent were given him to conquer and possess any heathen lands not already in the hands of Christians. The selfishness and folly of some of his associates reduced his force of men and vessels. He sailed, however, on November 18, 1578, with seven ships, one of which was commanded by Raleigh. The destination of the fleet was not revealed, and now is not known; but it was apparently intended for an attack on the Spaniards somewhere. It returned the next summer, after an encounter in which one of the ships was lost. Not disheartened by this experience, Gilbert, in June, <small>Gilbert's second expedition.</small> 1583, embarked on a second voyage with five ships. He landed on the coast of Newfoundland, and took possession of that island in the name of the Queen. He explored the coast southward for a certain distance, but at last had to turn his course homeward, with only two ships, the remnant of his fleet. On the return voyage, the frigate in which Gilbert sailed was wrecked, and the brave commander perished. In 1584, Raleigh obtained a charter from Eliza- <small>Raleigh sends out two vessels.</small> beth, and fitted out at his own cost two vessels, under the command of Philip Amadas and Arthur Barlow, the latter of whom wrote the history of the voyage. They sailed southward along the shores of Carolina. Barlow's narrative, which contained a glowing description of the newly found region, was presented by Raleigh to the Queen. About this time he received the honor of knighthood. To the regions which his captains had visited, the Virgin Queen gave the name of Virginia. It shows what profit Raleigh gained from his monopoly in the sale of wines, and from other benefits conferred by his royal mistress, that he was able to fit out another fleet of seven vessels, at the same time that he aided Davis, one of his friends, to undertake a voyage to the northwestern coast. Raleigh's vessels, which carried out one hundred and eight colonists, had for their naval commander a brave seaman, Sir Richard Grenville, and carried, as governor of the prospective colony, a soldier of repute, Ralph Lane. They reached Roanoke, where they established themselves. They examined, however, the neighboring coast southward to the Secotan, and northward as far as the Chesapeake, and pushed for some distance into the interior. They were charmed with the scenery and with the products of the country. They quickly turned to their use three of the indigenous products of America—tobacco, maize, and potatoes. Through the agency of these colonists of Raleigh, tobacco was introduced into England. By his personal example he did much to make the use of it common. The potato he was the first to cultivate, planting the tubers on his Irish lands near Cork. Lane shows his enthusiasm in a letter to Elizabeth's Secretary of State, Walsingham: "All the kingdomes and states of Chrystendom theyere comodytyes joyeyned in one together, doo not yealde ether more good or more plentyfulle whatsoever for publyck use ys needeful or pleasinge for delyghte."

<small>Raleigh's colony at Roanoke.</small>

Nevertheless provisions began to fail. The colonists were homesick, and when Sir Francis Drake touched at Roanoke on his way home, and when the bark and the boats which he proposed to leave for their use were swept away in a sudden storm, they were glad to be transported by him from this earthly paradise to England, leaving fifteen persons behind to hold the place and wait for newcomers. Time had been wasted in journeys in quest of gold and pearls, and the Indians had been offended by harsh treatment. In 1587, Raleigh's last colony was sent out, comprising in it wives and families, and instructed to settle on the Chesapeake. The fifteen men who had been left at Roanoke had perished. There John White, the leader of the new company, was obliged to stay—as he alleged, on account of the refusal of the pilot to explore the coast. The settlers suffered from the hostility of a tribe of Indians. Other troubles existed, so that White went back to England in the returning vessel to seek for reinforcements and supplies. But England was now completely absorbed in the preparations to beat back the Spanish Armada. There was no room for thought of anything else. Yet in the spring of 1588, Raleigh sent White with two vessels containing supplies for the colonists at Roanoke. Both ships, owing to an encounter with French men-of-war, put back to England. Raleigh had now spent £40,000 in his efforts to colonize Virginia. To secure the prosecution of the work, still retaining his charter, he made a company of adventurers and merchants sharers in the benefits of the patent which he had granted to the Roanoke settlers. In 1590, White returned to Roanoke, but found no traces of the colonists. They had either perished or been incorporated among the Hatteras Indians. Evidence of some weight has been gathered in support of the latter theory. Among the lost was White's daughter, Eleanor Dare, and his grandchild, the first child born of English parents within the limits of the United States.

In 1602, Bartholomew Gosnold, without authority from Raleigh, set out from Falmouth in a small bark for the New World. Instead of taking the common route by the way of the Canaries and the West Indies, he sailed directly across the Atlantic by the course which had been taken by Verrazano, from whose letter he may have derived the suggestion. He visited the coast of Maine, sailed southward, rounded Cape Cod, and on one of the Elizabeth islands his men built a house roofed with rushes. But they fell into a dispute among themselves, and abandoned the island—if indeed they had ever proposed to remain there—and went back to England with a freight of sassafras and cedar. This voyage led to other expeditions. In 1603, Martin Pring came over to the coast of New England, entered Massachusetts Bay, and the harbor where Plymouth is situated. His two vessels remained long enough for an acquaintance to be made with the Indians, and also for gathering cargoes of sassafras, which was the object that Pring had in view. In 1605, George Weymouth was the leader in an expedition which was sent out by the Earl of Southampton and Lord Arundel. Weymouth had previously explored the coast of Labrador. He now sailed northward from Cape Cod to the mouth of the Kennebec and up that river. Weymouth's reports directed the attention of Sir Ferdinando Gorges to the advantages of the Maine coast, which so abounds in good harbors. The co-operation of Popham, the Lord Chief-Justice of England, was secured by Gorges. The result was that the harbors and rivers of that coast were more carefully examined by a vessel that Popham sent out.

Pring.

Weymouth.

When the seventeenth century dawned, England had planted no permanent settlement in the New World. Spain and Portugal, which had been the pioneers in the work of discovery and conquest, had acquired extensive possessions over which they ruled. The Spanish monarchy had begun to decline in vigor, but was still strong and formidable. The time had now come when England was to succeed in laying the foundation of permanent colonies on the American continent. The circumstances were somewhat, if not altogether, propitious.

CHAPTER IV.

VIRGINIA UNTIL 1688

James I. and his Policy—Incentives to Colonization—The Virginia Company—Constitution of its Two Branches—The London Company—The Settlement of Jamestown—John Smith—The New Charter—Delaware—Dale—Argall—The Third Charter—The House of Burgesses—Growth of the Colony—Annulling of the Charter—Spanish Intrigues—Harvey—Berkeley—Under the Commonwealth—Navigation Laws—Arlington and Culpepper—Bacon's Rebellion—A Royal Province—Negro Slavery.

In 1603, James I. succeeded to the English throne, thus uniting the crowns of England and of Scotland. The long and splendid reign of the last of the Tudors was followed by the ignoble rule of the Stuarts. The proud spirit of independence and self-reliance which had characterized both Elizabeth and her people gave way to a truckling policy in the dealings of the government with Spain, which was prompted by a desire to avoid war. There was nothing sinful in such a desire. Elizabeth had been driven to contend with a conspiracy against her throne and her life. The son of Mary Stuart was differently situated. He might naturally feel that he was not called upon to take up the contest which had been forced upon his predecessor in consequence of the denial of her title to the crown. James may be pardoned for indulging the hope that peace could be restored with the Catholic powers, and even with the Pope, and that a way might be found for a cessation of the conflict of the European nations, one with another.

ORIGIN

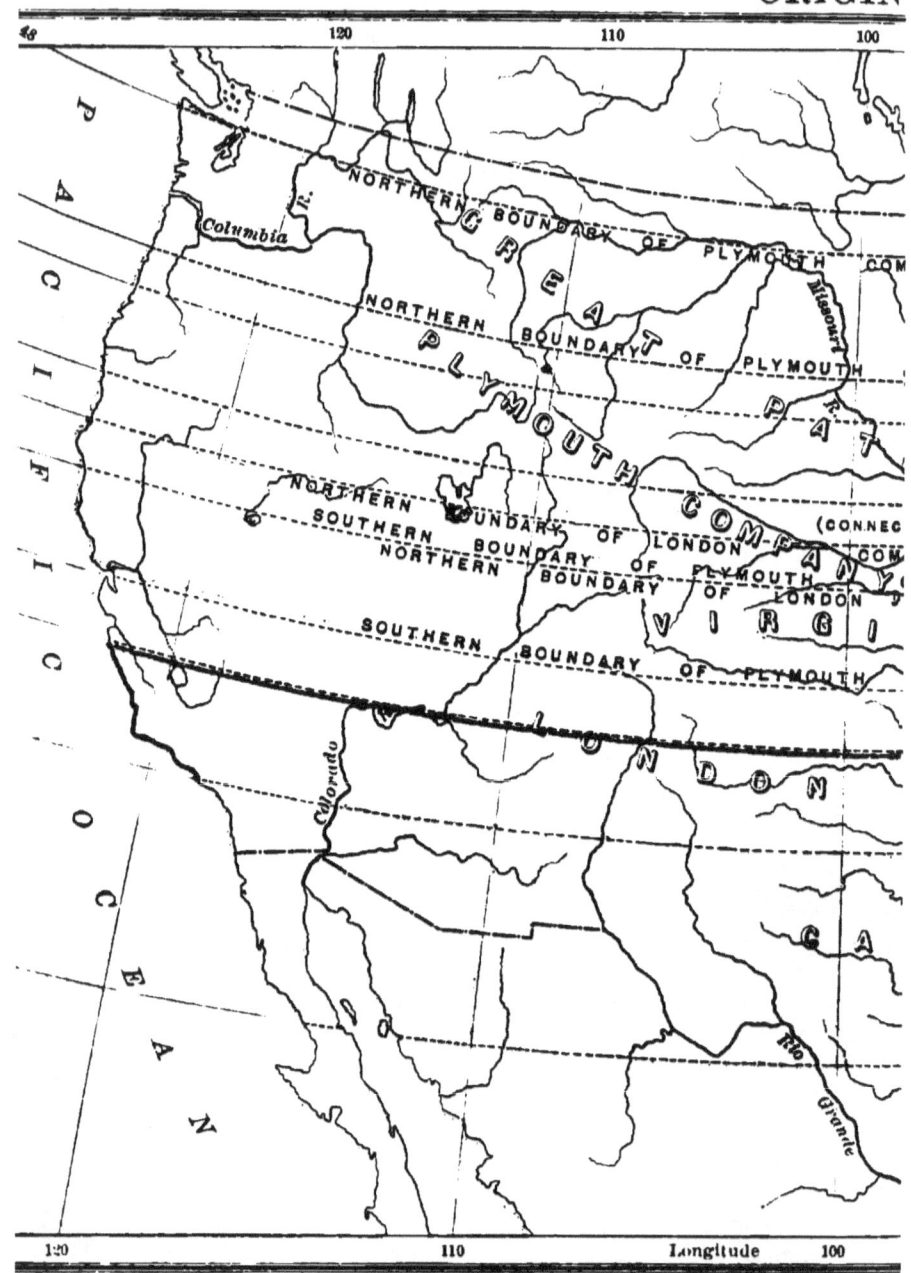

The grants of 1606 extended 100 miles inward from the coast;
the grants of 1609, 1620, 1629, and 1665, from "Sea to Sea."

GRANTS

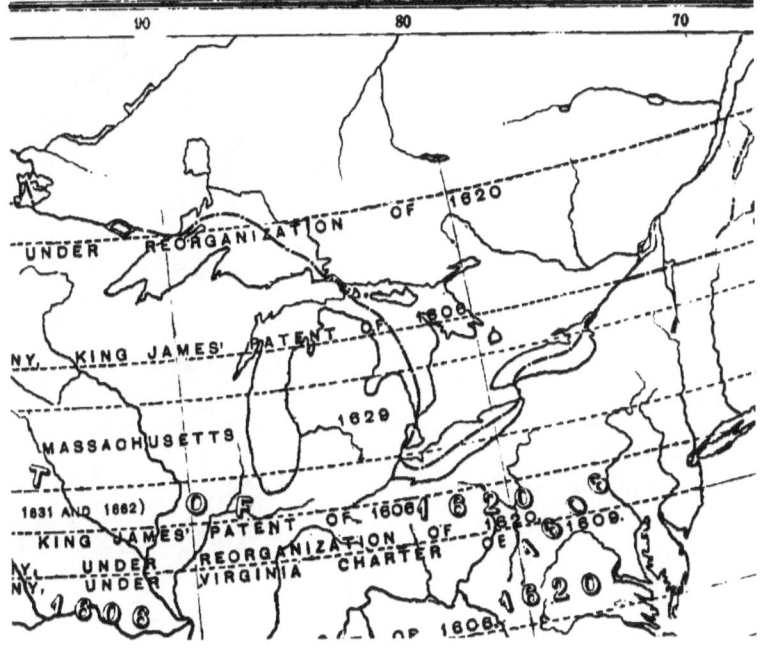

His fault lay in the conceit and presumption which led to his being outwitted by Spain, and still more in his consenting to the humiliation of England for advantages that were trifling in comparison with the price that was paid for them. The result of his policy was that England sunk in the estimation of foreign powers, while the lukewarm Protestantism of the king, and his contempt for popular rights, were building up within the kingdom the great Puritan party, and planting the seeds of civil war, to bear their harvest in the next reign. On the accession of James there were fresh incentives to colonization. All through the sixteenth century there had been a complaint in England of a redundancy of population. Such were the relations of classes and the state of industry that the peasant class had to endure much poverty and distress, and the conviction spread that some relief must be found. Crimes multiplied to a fearful extent, and were not checked by the cruel character of the penal laws. Under Elizabeth, in the protracted conflict with Spain, and in the wars in the Netherlands, there had been an outlet for surplus energy, employment for the restless and adventurous. Now, with various other sorts of idlers, there were not a few disbanded soldiers from the Low Countries; for James, in his first year, suspended hostilities with Spain, and in the year following signed a peace with that country. The day for the exploits of heroes like Drake and Raleigh was over. After the period of discovery, and of voyages prompted largely by dreams of sudden conquests and dazzling riches, the time had come for more sober and better contrived plans of emigration. Imagination was still alive, for the New World was yet to a great extent a mystery. But plentiful experiences of disaster and failure had not been wholly in vain. The proceedings of Gosnold, of Gorges, and of Popham indicated an

Incentives to colonization.

altered spirit in connection with such enterprises. They were felt to be too large and expensive for single individuals to undertake. It was organized companies on whom was to devolve the difficult task of establishing permanent settlements on the Atlantic coast, and of thus laying the foundations of great commonwealths. The organization of the East India Company, in 1599, had afforded an example of corporate societies of this general character, although that company was established simply for purposes of trade.

On April 10, 1606, King James granted to Sir Thomas Gates, Richard Hakluyt, Edward Wingfield, George Popham, and others, the first charter of Virginia. It provided for the establishment of a company, or of one company in two branches. The southern, or London Company—or "Colony" as it was called—was to have the authority to occupy lands between the thirty-fourth and forty-first degrees of north latitude. The second, or Plymouth Colony, having its head-quarters at that place, was to occupy the lands between the thirty-eighth and forty-fifth degrees. The two grants overlapped each other, but each company was prohibited from placing a settlement within a hundred miles of a previous settlement planted by the other. Each company was to have a hundred miles of sea-coast, half to the north and half to the south of its colony, with the islands for a hundred miles eastward, and the territory to the same distance westward. The extent of America westward was then quite unknown. In the letters of the time Virginia is often spoken of as an island.

Charter of the Virginia Company.

Each company was to have a resident council of thirteen members, to be appointed and removed as the king should direct. There was to be a superintending Council of Virginia, consisting of fourteen persons, and appointed by the king, with full

Constitution of the two companies.

authority to manage and govern, subject, of course, to his direction. The two subordinate councils were authorized to coin money, and to mine for the metals, it being stipulated that one-fifth of the gold and silver obtained should be paid to the sovereign. The patentees were empowered to exact duties, the rate of which was fixed, on goods imported by Englishmen and by foreigners. Lands assigned by the resident councils were to be held " in free and common socage "—that is, by the same tenure as lands in England. The colony has been styled "a vast joint-stock farm, or collection of farms." Each colonist was to be supported from the common earnings, and to have a certain share in the profits. The colonists and their children were to have "all liberties, franchises, and immunities," "to all intents and purposes," of native-born subjects of the king—a guarantee to which in subsequent times there was frequently occasion to appeal. If any attacked or robbed the vessels of other nations with which England was at peace, and, when proclamation of the wrong had been made in any of the ports of the realm, should refuse to make just reparation, the offenders were to be deprived of protection and left to the vengeance of princes and others whom they had injured. This ordinance, which was to prevent piracy, no doubt sprung especially from the desire to avoid occasions of quarrel with Spain.

About six months later the superior council was nominated by the king. Sir John Popham, the Chief-Justice, was one of the members, Sir Ferdinando Gorges, who became very prominent in connection with American affairs, was another. The council was soon enlarged by the addition of eleven new names, one of the additions being Sir Edwin Sandys, whose influence, after a time, became predominant in the London Company. For this company, which was to send out the first col-

The Royal Council.

ony, a set of instructions to serve as a constitution was framed, and was issued by the authority of the king. The council in England was to nominate the resident council, whose president was to be a layman chosen by itself. The Church of England was to be maintained. It was enjoined to treat the natives kindly, and "to use all proper means to draw them to the true knowledge and love of God." Persons accused of heinous offences, which were specified, were to be tried by jury. Minor offences were to be punished by the council at their discretion. The council might pass laws provisionally, but in order to continue in force they must be ratified either by the colonial Council in England, or by royal authority. But such enactments must not affect life or limb. The local council was to appoint a Treasurer or Cape Merchant, to regulate trade. The products of the labor of the colony were to be gathered into magazines prepared for the purpose, from which supplies were to be given out to the settlers.

The Constitution of Virginia put all power into the hands of the crown. It made the king, in relation to the colony, an absolute sovereign. It was fortunate for liberty in America that it did not remain the permanent system of government.

The fleet which the London merchants provided for transporting the emigrants—one hundred and five in number—was placed under the command of a competent *The Virginia* and tried seaman, Christopher Newport. It *colony.* sailed on December 19, 1606. Into the hands of Newport, and of two others, Gosnold and John Ratcliffe, who were associated with him in command, there was given a sealed paper, to be opened on their arrival in Virginia, containing the names of the resident council. In another paper minute directions were given as to the selection of a site, the exploring of the region, the treatment of the natives, and other topics. The number of colonists who were to accompany Newport in his journeys of exploration was fixed. His main objects were to be the search for the precious metals and for a way to the South Seas. Among the colonists who sailed with Newport were Gosnold, whose previous voyage has already been mentioned; Wingfield, who was a merchant; Hunt, who went out as chaplain; and the renowned John Smith, who had had abundant experience in different countries as a soldier and adventurer, and was led through his acquaintance with Gosnold to join the expedition to a land where his courage and capacity were to prove of essential value. Not much less than one-half of the colonists were "gentlemen," with no experience in manual labor; there were not many laborers; there were a few mechanics; but most of the emigrants were soldiers and servants. Before the fleet reached Virginia there was dissension on board, and for some unknown reason John Smith was placed under arrest. On opening the sealed paper his name was found to be on the list of the council. This body chose Wingfield for its president. On May 13, 1607, contrary to Gosnold's judgment, Jamestown was pitched upon as the place of settlement—the name being given to the place in honor of the king. It was on the north of the James River, thirty-two miles from its mouth. The site chosen for the settlement was then a low peninsula.

Jamestown.

On May 21st Captain Newport, with a party of twenty-three companions, started up the river in the shallop on an exploring tour. From a "gentleman" of the party we have a detailed account of what they did and saw. They went as far as the site of Richmond. They were hospitably treated and faithfully guided by the Indians. Among them was a chieftain who was a namesake and perhaps a son of a

Newport's exploring party.

more powerful potentate, Powhatan. The garden of the subordinate chief was on the bank of the river. There, the "Diary" informs us, "he sowed his wheate, beane, peaze, tobacco, pompions, gourds, hempe, flaxe, etc." "Were any art," it is added, "used to the naturall state of this place, it would be a goodly habitatyon."

On the return of the party, on May 27th, they learned that the settlers had been obliged to repel a formidable attack by two hundred savages. Newport completed the palisade about the fort, gave the colonists the best advice, insisting on the importance of harmony and good conduct, and, on June 22d, sailed for England. The chronicler quoted above has this record: "21, Sondaye.—We had a comunyon. Capt. Newport dyned ashore with our dyet, and invyted many of us to supper as a farewell." The sacrament was administered according to the forms of the English Church, under the shelter of a sail stretched from one tree to another. Newport's good counsels did not avail to secure peace. As soon as he had gone, disputes broke out. Gosnold, the most influential man, died. Wingfield was unpopular, fell out with several of his associates in the council, and was deposed from the office of Governor. Ratcliffe took his place, but succeeded no better. He exchanged blows with one Reed, and Reed for his offence was sentenced to die. He charged one Kendal with plotting a mutiny, and Kendal was hanged in Reed's place.

Divisions and disputes.

Half of the colonists died during the summer. Autumn came and brought supplies of wild-fowl and of maize. Early in December, Smith went with a party up the Chickahominy to explore the river and to trade for corn. Ascending as far as he could in his barge, he left his company, and with two Indian guides and two Englishmen, proceeded farther up the stream. He landed, leaving his two companions in the canoe.

John Smith a captive.

They were attacked and slain by hostile savages, and Smith himself, who had only one Indian guide with him, was captured. He amused his captors by showing them a pocket compass. He was conveyed by them from village to village, and was at last brought to the great Powhatan, whom he calls the "Emperor," by whom he was kindly received and sent to Jamestown in peace and safety. Such, in substance, is the account which Smith gives in his "True Relation of Virginia," which was written at the time and printed in 1608. In a subsequent work, which he edited, the "Generall Historie," which was published in 1624, he relates the familiar story of his salvation from imminent death by the intercession of the chieftain's daughter, Pocahontas. Not only is this tale inconsistent with the "True Relation" of 1608; it is not found in a later publication, the tract of 1612, the appendix to which was written by Smith's companions; and it is wholly wanting in the "Discourse of Virginia" by Wingfield, who was then at Jamestown, and tells us the story of Smith's capture and release. In his publication, issued sixteen years after the event, Smith amplified the original account by this addition, possibly to please the readers to whom Pocahontas, then the wife of an Englishman, John Rolfe, had become a romantic personage. The preface and other parts of the "General History" may seem to indicate that he had a taste for this sort of adornment. Pocahontas was a child twelve years old when Smith's marvellous deliverance is said to have occurred.

On the return of Smith he encountered the hostility of Ratcliffe, who proved to be a foolish and incapable governor. Ratcliffe preferred against him groundless accusations. He was delivered from danger by the timely arrival of Newport with fresh supplies. Disorder arose in the colony in consequence of the fancied discovery of a gold mine. For seven weeks, Smith was engaged in exploring the shores of the bay and the Potomac River. The confusion which he found to exist on his return was quieted by the removal of Ratcliffe from office. About this time there was a fire at Jamestown which consumed a part of the provisions. Smith was now made president. He departed again to continue his exploration of the bay; but his narrative of what he undoubtedly accomplished is decorated with more apocryphal incidents. In September a band of new-comers was brought over by Newport. In this period it was to the energy and tact of Smith that the salvation of the colony was due. He was active in all directions. He taught the "gentlemen" to use tools and to till the ground. It was encouraging that two women and eight Polish and German mechanics were among those who came with Newport.

Smith becomes president.

But at the moment the prospects of the colony were dark. The company complained to Smith of the smallness of their profits. He showed them in a temperate letter that their complaint was unreasonable. Their spirit is seen in their instructions to Newport to find either a lump of gold, a way to the South Seas, or news of Raleigh's lost colonists. Wingfield and others who had returned to England spread reports of the misfortunes and contentions of the colonists. The new settlement began to provoke ridicule. The fact was overlooked that "the air of Virginia could work no charm to turn idle spendthrifts into hard-working settlers." But the condition of the colony had the effect to arouse in England a new zeal in behalf of the enterprise. Pamphlets were written on the importance of it. Unhappily, one of the considerations urged was the need of a place abroad for idlers and scapegraces. The pulpit added its exhortations. On

Complaints of the company.

May 23, 1609, a new charter was issued to the company, which was now greatly enlarged, and received all the privileges of a corporation. At the head of the long list of persons who were to be the nucleus of the company is Robert Cecil, the Earl of Salisbury, whose name is followed by six earls besides, and by an imposing array of other representatives of the nobility, and members of the various professions and trades. Among these is the name of Francis Bacon. The Treasurer was to be the chief executive officer. There was to be a council in England, the vacancies in which were to be filled by the company, by whom the Treasurer, also, was to be chosen. This council was to appoint a local governor, to supersede the local council, which had heretofore ruled the colony, and to govern with unchecked authority. All legislative power was vested in the council. It was to be exempt from paying duties, except the five per cent. customs, for twenty-one years; but it might exact duties on exports and imports, the rate of which was fixed. The territory of the company was to extend two hundred miles to the north and two hundred miles to the south of Point Comfort, and over "all that space and circuit of land," from "sea to sea, west and northwest." This last term in the definition of boundaries founded the claim of Virginia to the territory northwest of the Ohio. For seven years the company was to be a "joint-stock farm, or collection of farms," and at the end of that time each shareholder was to receive a due allotment of land. An emigrant entering into the service of the company was to own one share. Whether the private ownership of farms to any extent, or private trade, up to that limit of time, was to exist, is left doubtful. It would seem as if the system of management ordained for a period was to be much like that of a penal settlement.

A new charter.

Lord Delaware, a man of worth and of eminent qualifications for the post, was appointed Governor. Unfortunately he did not come out at once. A body of emigrants, five hundred in number, was sent before him, but the vessel in which the three leaders embarked was cast on the Bermudas, so that most of them arrived at Jamestown in advance of their chiefs. The new emigrants appear to have brought no strength or advantage to the settlement. Smith describes them as "unruly gallants," sent out by their friends to save them from "ill destinies." Smith himself soon after was hurt by an accident, and returned to England. Some "misdemeanors" were laid to his charge, which cannot have been of a serious nature. He thought, however, that his services were not duly appreciated, and he did not return afterward to Virginia. After he left, there was nothing but anarchy and distress in the colony. Some of the settlers were killed by the Indians, and many died of disease. In the spring of 1610, Lord Delaware arrived, just in season to prevent the miserable remnant of the people from sailing away for Newfoundland in the pinnaces, in which they had already set out. The arrival of Lord Delaware brought in cheerfulness and order. The local council was organized, a roof was placed on the church, and new forts were erected. One hundred and fifty settlers accompanied Delaware, and some effort had been made to secure persons of good character. He ruled well, although with considerable pomp and show. In less than a year, in consequence of failing health, he returned to England. He was succeeded in authority by Sir Thomas Dale, in the character of "High Marshal," Delaware being still Governor-General. Dale proceeded with vigor in the administration of the government. He brought with him a system of martial law which had been framed in the Netherlands.

Delaware.

Dale: harsh code of law.

The enactments were of astonishing severity. Non-attendance upon Sunday services was made a capital offence. One guilty of blasphemy for the second time was to "have a bodkin thrust through his tongue." Other offences not connected with religion were to be punished with equal rigor.

In August, 1611, Sir Thomas Gates arrived, with three hundred fresh emigrants, together with a hundred cows and other cattle. On him the government now devolved. A new settlement was formed at Henrico, and another at Bermuda. Alexander Whitaker, a godly clergyman and missionary, ministered at these places. He had come over with Gates. 1612 is the date of the beginning of the systematic cultivation of tobacco, which is attributed to John Rolfe. The cultivation of this plant was so lucrative as to become the predominant and all-controlling occupation of Virginia. It was not only the principal form of agriculture; it kept out manufacturing. "Its influence," says Brock, a recent Virginia writer, "permeated the entire social sphere of the colony, directed its laws, was an element in all its political and religious disturbances, and became the direct instigation of the curse of African slavery." Whitaker labored to convert the Indians. At Henrico, a college was planted for the education of the natives. But the rights of the Indians were sometimes disregarded. The capture of Pocahontas enabled the English to conclude a peace with Powhatan, which became permanent in 1614, on the marriage of the young princess to Rolfe. The Chickahominies agreed to be the subjects of King James. In 1613, Captain Samuel Argall, an unscrupulous man, was sent by Dale on a voyage northward to destroy the settlements of the French, which were considered an invasion of the territorial rights of

Virginia. He expelled a Jesuit colony from Mount Desert Island. The next year he again left Jamestown and burned the deserted houses at Port Royal.

In 1612, a third charter was granted to the Virginia Company, which gave to it the islands for a distance of three hundred leagues from the coast. Thus it acquired the Bermudas, which, however, were soon disposed of to a separate corporation formed by a portion of its own members. The new charter authorized lotteries in England for the benefit of the company, by which a large sum was procured. Gates, returning to England, urged that "honest laborers" might be sent out. A more wise policy was introduced respecting the possession of land. Liberal bounties in land were offered to new emigrants. In 1615, every freeman became the owner of fifty acres in his own right. These changes, with the gains from the culture of tobacco, tended to inspirit the settlers. When Argall, in 1617, was sent out as Deputy Governor, through the influence of the faction in the company which was subservient to the Court, he found the streets and "all other spare places" in Jamestown planted with tobacco. After two years, the arrogance, cruelty, and greed of Argall became unbearable and he was driven out of the colony. When he fled, its condition, notwithstanding all that had been done for it, was far from being prosperous. There were only three ordained ministers within its limits.

A third charter.

But a new era now began. Yeardley succeeded Argall, and at his coming there were introduced the most important alterations in the method of government. The laws of England took the place of Dale's iron code. The first representative body of legislators that ever existed in America was now constituted. Its first meeting was held on July 30, 1619, in the chancel of the church at Jamestown. It consisted of twenty-

Yeardley.

two burgesses, who were elected by the eleven towns, plantations, and hundreds—this last term designating, as in England, a political division. The burgesses sat with the council, and they formed, together, one legislative body. *A House of Burgesses.* It was clothed with judicial as well as legislative authority. The provision in the charter for the security of the equal rights and immunities of the colonists was referred to in a petition to the company that the stipulation might not be violated. The authority of the Church of England in the colony was confirmed. Attendance on church twice on Sunday was required. Measures were passed looking toward the founding of a college. Each settlement was directed to see to the education and religious instruction of the natives. In accordance with the political ideas of that period, laws were enacted to prevent extravagance in dress; also, the price at which tobacco should be sold was prescribed. Tobacco was made the legal currency. It became the custom to fix the amount of taxes, fines, stipends of every sort, at so many pounds of tobacco. In this very year, when the earliest popular Assembly was convened, and within a month after it met, the first negro slaves were introduced by a Dutch man-of-war. *Negro slaves introduced.* In this year, along with twelve hundred settlers, there were sent one hundred convicts to become servants. An apprentice system was introduced. Boys and girls who were picked up in the streets of London were shipped to Virginia to be bound during their minority to the planters. It is more agreeable to record that generous gifts were made in England of money and land to the college at Henrico.

In July, 1620, the population of the colony was estimated at four thousand. The quantity of tobacco exported increased rapidly from year to year. But, in 1621, England set up a monopoly in trade with the colonies. Tobacco could no longer be exported directly to the Netherlands. The trade with the Dutch was cut off. Two leaders in the Virginia Company, Sir Edwin Sandys and Nicholas Ferrar, were especially active in promoting emigration. The liberation of the planters from their service to the company, and the ownership of the land by them, increased greatly the happiness and thrift of the colony. More than a thousand persons annually joined it. The discovery was at last made that only on the basis of family life could a stable and prosperous community be founded. Ninety young women of good repute were shipped to Virginia at the expense of the company, and they were followed later by another band, sixty in number.

<small>Growth of the colony.</small>

The advent of Sir Francis Wyatt, as Governor, in 1621, is memorable for the reason that he brought with him a written constitution of government. It was framed on the model of the English system. The Governor and the Council were to be appointed by the company. For the acts of the Assembly the sanction of the company was required; the orders of the company, in turn, required the concurrence of the Assembly. The Assembly was to meet annually. The right of veto upon its enactments was given to the Governor. The right of trial by jury was confirmed. We have here, in its main outlines, the form of government that was to be established in the American colonies generally.

<small>Wyatt: a written constitution.</small>

The new political life gave a fresh impulse to agriculture. A beginning was even made in manufactures. The great interests of education and religion attracted more attention. Fear of the natives was passing away. The settlers commonly dwelt not in hamlets, but in dwellings apart from one another. The large farms extended along the banks of the rivers, where the soil was adapted to the growth of the tobacco plant. Powhatan, the friend of the English, was now dead. While the colonists were growing careless and unsuspicious, the natives were becoming jealous and inimical. Occasions of quarrel were not wanting. At noon on March 22, 1622, the Indians, who were banded together in a secret conspiracy, fell upon the whites and slew three hundred and forty-seven persons of both sexes and of every age. There were all the circumstances of barbarity that commonly attend an Indian massacre. The result was that many of the plantations were abandoned. Some of the colonists returned to England. Where there had been four thousand inhabitants only twenty-five hundred were left. *Indian massacre.*

This crushing blow was followed in about two years by what appeared to be a dire calamity, the annulling of the charter. This catastrophe was in a great degree the result of the intrigues of Spain. These began much earlier than 1612, the date that has been assigned for their beginning. The archives of Simancas reveal the fact that from the inception of the Virginia Colony the eyes of the Spanish Government were upon it, and its efforts directed to the prevention of the movement and the destruction of the infant settlement. The Spanish ambassador in England, Zuñiga, obeyed his instructions to watch the enterprise and to use all exertions to move the king actively to discountenance it. On January 24, 1607, Zuñiga wrote to Philip III. informing him of the projected settlement in Virginia. He judged that the design of it was piracy. It was intended to provide the means of capturing his Christian Majesty's merchant ships. This inference was excusable, considering what an amount of this sort of privateering there had been in the past, and in view of the circumstance that the colony was to be *Annulling of the charter; Spanish intrigues.*

composed of men only. On October 8th he wrote again, that, as he had been directed, he had seen James, who said that he "had not particularly known what was going on." He did not like explicitly to prohibit the planting of the settlement, as it would be taken as a recognition of the Spanish king as lord of all the Indies, which he was not prepared to go so far as to concede. James was conciliatory, but not very definite. If anything wrong were done by English emigrants, Spain might punish them, and they would not be protected. On October 16th Zuñiga wrote: "It will be serving God and Y. M. [Your Majesty] to drive these villains out from there, hanging them in time which is short enough for the purpose." The colonists had landed at Jamestown on May 13th. The ambassador constantly prods his master, urging the expediency of immediately destroying the new settlement. Thus, on April 12, 1609, he writes: " I hope you will give orders to have these insolent people quickly annihilated." Spain sent spies to Virginia, but when they were arrested there, demanded and procured from the English Government their release, falsely asserting that they were innocent of the charge made against them. But no open attack was made on the colony. This was not deemed to be politic. The Spanish Government thought that it was likely to perish of itself. At a later time, when it was James's ambition to marry Prince Charles to a Spanish princess, Gondomar, then the ambassador of Spain, found that his intrigues against the Virginia Company found favor in the English Court.

Besides the desire to please Spain, James did not relish the resistance that was offered to his attempts to control the action of the company, especially in their not appointing as officers the persons whom he took it into his hands to nominate. His displeasure was heightened when Sir Edwin Sandys, who belonged to the Parliamentary opposition, was elected as their treasurer, and when the Earl of Southampton, who was equally obnoxious, was made his successor, at the expiration of Sandys's term. There was a controversy with the king occasioned by the rapidly increasing importation of tobacco. James's hostility to the company. James demanded more than the five per cent. to which he was entitled. The prohibition of the sale of this product to the Dutch was an incident in this dispute. There came to be two parties in the company, the Court party and their antagonists. Parties in the company. The meetings grew to be scenes of angry debate. Whatever was unfortunate and unpromising in the condition of the colony was made to serve as an argument for abrogating the charter. Especially the lack of missionary labor for the conversion and education of the Indians—which was partly due to the ill-success of iron-works in the colony, the proceeds of which were to be applied to that purpose—was made a ground of reproach and accusation. Commissioners were sent to Virginia to hunt up materials of attack. The company fought steadily against the endeavor of the Court to wrest from it the charter, and availed itself of whatever legal weapons it could lay hold of. But the judges were subservient to the Crown, and, on June 16, 1624, the charter was annulled by a judicial decree. Virginia passed under the immediate, absolute control of the king. The company was reduced to a powerless trading corporation. Southampton took the precaution to have the records copied, and these authentic monuments of its honorable history are now in the Library of Congress.

The process by which the Virginia Company was robbed of its charter was marked by the sort of knavery that characterized James's method of government, and which was styled king-craft. Iniquitous as the act was, and seemingly disastrous, it really operated to strengthen rather than to hinder the development of popular government in the colony. Probably it was left more to manage its own affairs than it would have been had it remained subject to an English corporation.

<small>Effect of the annulling of the charter.</small>

In 1625, Charles I. issued a proclamation by which two Councils were constituted, one in England and one in Virginia. The Governor and the Councils were to be appointed by the king. Arbitrary as the new form of government was in theory, there was in fact not much interference with the local Assembly. There was a rapid increase in prosperity. In 1629, the population rose to the number of five thousand. In 1630, Sir John Harvey was appointed Governor. He had been one of the commissioners sent out to the colony, and on that account was unpopular. A dispute concerning boundaries arose, in consequence of the claim by the founder of Maryland to the territory on which were the trading posts established by William Claiborne. Harvey gave great offence by taking sides with Maryland. Such was the resentment of the people that the Council took away from him his office, and sent him to England to answer the charges against him. The king decided in his favor, and after an absence of a year and a half he resumed his station He was superseded, in 1639, by Sir Francis Wyatt. Wyatt was succeeded in 1642 by Sir William Berkeley. Berkeley was instructed to keep out innovations in religion. By a law passed in 1623, absence from church was punished by a fine of a hogshead of tobacco. But the people themselves were generally opposed to dissent from the established faith and order. In 1642, in compliance with an earnest request, signed by seventy-one persons belonging to several parishes, three Congregational ministers were sent to Virginia from Boston.

<small>Harvey.</small>

<small>Wyatt: Berkeley.</small>

They reported a considerable measure of success, but an act of the Assembly expelled them from the colony. The use of the Prayer Book was required in every church. Opposition to the established religion was put down by imprisoning and banishing all Non-conformists. They found refuge in Maryland. *Non-conformists expelled.*

After the execution of Charles I. loyal messages were sent to Charles II. in Holland. Acts were passed attaching penalties to all expressions of disrespect to the late king, or disputing the right of his son to inherit the Crown. Parliament sent commissioners in a fleet to bring the refractory colony to terms. The commissioners had no difficulty in coming to an agreement with the Governor and Council and the House of Burgesses. There was to be no punishment inflicted for loyalty to the fallen house in the past, no abridgment of territorial rights, no restriction of commercial rights which was not likewise imposed on English-born subjects. The Burgesses, it was further agreed, should elect the Governor and Council, although it was allowed to the commissioners to nominate a Governor and Secretary—their act, however, not to serve as a precedent. Richard Bennet was chosen Governor, and Clayborne Secretary. There was no manifestation of ill-will or excitement on either side. *Virginia submits to the Commonwealth.*

After the abdication of Richard Cromwell, Berkeley was re-elected Governor by the Assembly, but under such conditions as preserved its prerogatives. This body was now, to all intents and purposes, clothed with sovereignty. On the restoration of Charles II. a royal commission was transmitted to Berkeley. Humble petitions were sent to the king to pardon the submission which, under compulsion, had been yielded to the Commonwealth. It was ordained that the anniversary of his father's death should *1660. Recognition of Charles II.*

be observed with prayer and fasting. The local rulers in the interval between Berkeley's retirement and his re-election had been men of Puritan proclivities. The enactments against dissent from the Church of England were now sharpened. A tax was levied on every one for its support. The control in ecclesiastical matters was put in the hands of twelve vestrymen in each parish, who were to fill their own vacancies. Non-conformists were forbidden to teach. The form set forth in the Prayer Book must be used at every marriage. Even Quakers were subjected to a fine for not attending the Established Church. Heavy fines were imposed on shipmasters who should bring Quakers into the colony, and on all persons who should "entertain them" in or near their houses "to teach or preach."

In 1661 the English Navigation Law was made more restrictive. Laws limiting foreign trade had been passed as early as the reign of Richard II. It was ordained at that time that no merchandise should be shipped out of the realm, except in English vessels, on pain of forfeiture. There were enactments of a like character under Henry VII. and Elizabeth. It was maintained by Virginia that her charter authorized her to trade freely with foreign nations. The Navigation Act, the passage of which marks an epoch in American colonial history, was passed in 1651, under Cromwell. In the time of James I., when the English naval strength fell to the lowest point, the Dutch developed their power on the sea, and not only inflicted there heavy blows on Spain, but absorbed the carrying trade which, under other circumstances, would have been enjoyed by England. When Cromwell became the head of the government, the old ambition which the heroes of Elizabeth's time had cherished, of making England the mistress of a great naval dominion, revived. The law of 1651 prohib-

English Navigation Laws.

ited the carrying of the products of England to the colonies except in English or colonial vessels, which, moreover, must have an English captain and crew. This new policy brought on war between the English and their Dutch neighbors. The issue of the struggle was that Cromwell dictated the terms of peace. In 1660, the first Parliament of Charles II. passed an act which added two new clauses to the law of 1651. Enumerated articles—sugar, tobacco, indigo, and others—were to be shipped to no country but England. No alien was allowed to establish himself as a merchant or factor in the colonies. Finally, in 1663, it was enacted that European products should not be received in the colonies from foreign vessels. The complete monopoly of commerce with the colonies was thus given over to English merchants. The effect was almost to destroy the trade of Virginia.

In 1671, Berkeley made answer to a series of inquiries which had been sent to him respecting the condition of the colony by the Commissioners of Foreign Plantations. In this document he describes the condition of Virginia as it was in 1670. The population was forty thousand. There were two thousand negro slaves and six thousand white servants. The freemen were drilled in military exercises once a month, in their respective counties, and were thought to be "near eight thousand horse." There had never been an engineer in the country, and the five forts on the rivers were ill-constructed. Every man, according to his ability, taught his own children. There were forty-eight parishes, and the ministers were well paid. "The clergy," adds the Governor, "by my consent, would be better if they would pray oftener and preach less. But of all other commodities, so of this, the worst are sent us. . . . But, I thank God, there are no free schools nor printing, and I hope we shall not have these hundred years." Learn-

The condition of Virginia (1671).

ing and printing Berkeley pronounces the patrons and promoters of heresies and sects, and of libels on government. As late as 1682, one Buckner, who ventured to print the laws of 1680, was put under bonds "not to print anything thereafter until His Majesty's pleasure should be known."

In the first year of the reign of Charles II., as titular king, he showed his good-nature and lack of conscience in a characteristic way by making a grant of a portion of Virginia, amounting to one-third of its territory, to certain of his followers. Their attempt to take possession of the territory was, for various reasons which are not fully known, given up, and the grant was restored to the king. But he proceeded, in 1673, to give all Virginia, for the term of thirty-one years, to two unworthy favorites—Lord Arlington and Lord Culpepper. The patentees were empowered to make grants of land, with the reservation of quit-rents. Land-surveyors and sheriffs were to be appointed by them. All the Church patronage was placed under their control. By the terms of this reckless grant all the existing titles to land were rendered insecure. The colonists resisted, and a compromise was made, in which it was conceded that their titles should stand. They sent a deputation, composed of three persons, to England, to look after their imperilled rights and interests. The colony had a fair prospect of obtaining a charter, when news arrived of serious disturbances in Virginia. There were a number of grievances of which loud complaint was made. One was the revival of a law which confined the suffrage to landholders and householders. After 1660, there was for a long period no election of burgesses, but the legislature was kept in existence by being prolonged from time to time.

<small>Grant to Arlington and Culpepper.</small>

In 1674, there were signs of a revolt, but the disaffection was for the moment appeased by some concessions. The troubles with the Indians became threatening. The legislation of the colony respecting them had been just and humane. In 1676, however, difficulties sprang up between certain planters and the Doegs, a tribe on that river. In the fighting that followed, there was a flagrant instance of bad faith in the treatment of six chiefs, who were killed near an Indian hut at the head of the Potomac. The hostility of the savages spread, but no efficient measures were taken by Berkeley to protect the lives of the people, many of whom were slain in attacks which they could not foresee or guard against. At last, in 1676, the Assembly declared war against the Indians, but when a force of five hundred men, which had been raised, was on the point of marching against them, the troops, by order of the Governor, were suddenly disbanded. The people, left defenceless, and finding their petitions disregarded, although murders were constantly committed by their wily, incensed foes, found a leader in the person of Nathaniel Bacon, Jr. Bacon was connected with the celebrated English family of that name, and on coming over to Virginia had been made one of the Council. He was a rich planter, courageous, and eloquent in speech. If he needed any special stimulus to action, it was found in the fact that his overseer and one of his favorite servants were killed by the savages on his plantation near the site of Richmond. Being denied a military commission from Berkeley, he put himself at the head of five hundred volunteers, and went against the enemy. He and his men were proclaimed as traitors by the Governor. Bacon responded in a declaration, in which Berkeley, in turn, was denounced as a tyrant and a traitor. The revolt became general in the lower counties. A new Assembly was convoked. Bacon was elected as

Troubles with the Indians.

Bacon's rebellion.

a member. On his way to Jamestown he was arrested, but was set free on parole. He presented a confession and apology to the Assembly, was pardoned, and was again received into the Council. The reform measures passed by the Assembly are the best disclosure we have of the aims of Bacon and his party. There were laws against illegal and excessive fees to officers, and requiring the yearly election of sheriffs and their assistants. The act limiting the franchise was repealed. To the Assembly was given the exclusive right to levy certain taxes which the county magistrates had imposed. Bacon believed that the Governor had formed a plot against his life. Accordingly he left Jamestown, but came back in a few days, with a force of four hundred men to sustain him. Berkeley found it impossible to rally the militia to withstand him. The Governor then gave him a commission, the Assembly made him general of their forces, and he marched once more against the Indians. Once more he was proclaimed as a traitor. Once more he returned, and Berkeley fled to Accomack. Bacon called together a meeting of the principal gentlemen of the colony for the purpose of adopting means for resisting the tyranny of Berkeley, and of subduing the Indians. In reply to the proclamation of the Governor he published a spirited vindication of his proceedings. Again he set forth to make war upon the Indians. Hostilities now began between the supporters of Berkeley and the party of Bacon. In the absence of the latter, some advantages were gained by the Governor. When Bacon had succeeded in his expedition, he came back to Jamestown; but, probably for the reason that he was not strong enough to hold it, he burned the statehouse and the few dwelling-houses which constituted the village. At this critical juncture Bacon fell sick and died. The insurgents lost heart, and their forces were broken up. It is possible that an impression that Bacon's movement was advancing too far, and was likely to bring on a conflict with the mother country, may have already thinned their ranks. Berkeley was now dominant. He had the support of a regiment of troops which arrived on February 29, 1677. *Defeat of Bacon's party.*

Berkeley associated with himself two commissioners to try the rebels. He was sustained by the Assembly which was elected at the beginning of the year. "Bacon's laws" were repealed, although many of them were at a later time re-enacted. The Governor was unsparing in the infliction of punishments on the insurgents. Many were thrown into prison. Not less than twenty-three were executed. To Drummond, the principal counsellor of Bacon, the vindictive old Governor said : "Mr. Drummond, you are very welcome ; I am more glad to see you than any man in Virginia ; you shall be hanged in half an hour." When the news of the insurrection reached England, three commissioners with five hundred soldiers were sent to the colony. They immediately found themselves in collision with the Governor, who was obstinately bent on carrying out his severe measures, which the Assembly deprecated and protested against. He had requested to be recalled, and finally yielded to the summons to carry out his request. Soon after his return to England he died. In the last two years of his official service, his despotic temper, embittered apparently by the recollection of the mortification he had suffered at the triumph of the anti-royalist party, and by his opposition to the popular will, effaced the impression which had been made by him at an earlier time. How far Bacon was disposed to carry the rebellion, whether he had thoughts of making Virginia independent, and to what extent his measures sprung from his own brain, or were inspired by abettors, possibly wiser than himself, are problems not yet solved. *Recall of Berkeley.*

After Berkeley's recall, the office of Governor was held for a short time, first by Sir Herbert Jeffreys, and then by Sir Henry Chichely. Early in 1680, Culpepper assumed the office to which, in 1675, he had been appointed for life. The franchise was to be again limited. Assemblies were to be summoned only by the Crown, and were to have no power in the making of laws, except to reject or accept enactments submitted to them, after they had been framed and approved by the Governor and Council, and by the king. It was ordained that there were to be no appeals to the Assembly, and none to the king in Council, except in cases where the value of one hundred pounds was involved. Culpepper made it clear that his main end was to enrich himself. The people were restless; he grew weary of his office and returned to England. The iniquitous grant to Arlington and Culpepper was revoked, and in July, 1683, Virginia once more became a royal province. The successor of Culpepper, Lord Howard of Effingham, had his faults, with none of his virtues. He asserted that he had the right to annul the acts of the Assembly at his discretion. He was directed to allow no printing-press in Virginia. In 1685, after the accession of James II., the Assembly was dissolved by royal proclamation, for questioning his right to negative the repeal of laws, and to restore the laws which were thus abolished. One of the members was imprisoned and put in irons for using expressions that were pronounced treasonable. In April, 1689, by order of the Council, the accession of William and Mary was proclaimed in Virginia, and a new era in its history began.

The subject of negro slavery in Virginia demands a more particular notice. It was from humane motives, however delusive, that the first Africans had been brought to America. Las Casas, the devoted and benevolent missionary bishop, sanctioned the bringing of negroes to Hispaniola to take the place of Indians, who were quickly worn out by the exhausting toil in the mines. He lived to see the error that he had committed and to repent of it. Indians were frequently seized by slavers on the American coast. "There was hardly a convenient harbor on the frontier of the United States which was not entered by slavers." Scruples were seldom felt in regard to the kidnapping and enslavement of Africans, and such was the force of cupidity that they were smothered when they arose. Sir John Hawkins brought over from Guinea to the West Indies three cargoes of blacks, the first in 1562, and the third in 1567. Reference has been made to the first introduction of negroes into Virginia, in 1619. Says John Rolfe, in Smith's "General History:" "About the last of August came in a Dutch man-of-warre that sold us twenty Negars." It was long before slaves became numerous in the colony. It was not until about 1650 that the number of them began to increase rapidly. The stimulus to this increase was furnished by the tobacco-culture. The overproduction of tobacco was attributed to the undue importation of slaves. It was enacted in 1662 that, contrary to the English law as to serfdom, children should follow the condition of the mother. The consequence was that mulatto children were slaves. The idea had long been cherished in Christendom that heathen, but not Christians, might be reduced to servitude. In 1667, the Virginia Assembly ordained that conversion and baptism should not operate to set the slave free. To kill a slave by severity of punishment was to subject the master to the charge of felony, as the intent to kill in such a case could not be presupposed. Civil disabilities were imposed on free negroes. In 1682, the slave-code became more stringent. No slave could leave a plantation without a written pass from his master. Slaves were forbidden to carry arms, or to use force against a Christian, even in self-defence. A runaway slave who refused to surrender might be shot. In 1687, it was discovered that a negro plot was brewing. Then followed enactments of extreme severity, verifying the maxim that cruelty is the offspring of fear. These codes do not imply, however, that slaves, as a rule, were ill-treated or cut off from sources of enjoyment. The amalgamation of the races was forbidden under heavy penalties.

When we seek to ascertain the social condition of the Southern colonies we are embarrassed by the dearth of contemporary literature. The contrast with New England in this respect is very marked. The natural advantages possessed by Virginia, the leading colony among them, from its noble rivers, its ample harbors, its fruitful soil, its varied and beautiful scenery, and its agreeable climate, were such as to make the outward conditions of life all that could be desired. The means of subsistence were easy to be procured. Few who had once established themselves within its limits desired to spend their days elsewhere. Although vagabonds and convicts had been sent over to the colony from time to time, they, after all, constituted but a minor fraction of the people, who, as a body, were of good English stock. The convicts themselves were, some of them, political offenders, who might not be tainted with vice, or lack the qualities of most value in emigrants. Such as were of a different character, according to a familiar experience in settlements, might do well when transplanted to a new country. The tendency was to eliminate the hopelessly idle and depraved. The circumstance that tobacco was the staple product, owing to the ease with which it was cultivated and the profits derived from its production, had a very great, and, in many respects,

Society in Virginia.

Effect of tobacco-culture.

a deleterious influence on civilization in Virginia. The fields on which this plant grew were soon worn out, and it was easier to transfer its cultivation to new lands than to fertilize the old. The culture of tobacco being so profitable, the diversifying of industry was prevented. The cereals were raised only so far as was absolutely necessary for the subsistence of the inhabitants. Efforts to prevent the over-production of tobacco, by what was called a "stint"—that is, a limiting of production for single years—were in the main unsuccessful. The result, on the whole, was that Virginia was kept from becoming what it might have been, one of the richest of agricultural communities. The planters lived by themselves on their estates, and became more and more fond of this sort of life. There was no urban life. Jamestown remained a petty village; Williamsburg, when it became the capital, contained few dwellings. The house of the chief magistrate was dignified by the name of the "Governor's Palace." The Government undertook to found towns by legal enactments, but they amounted to little more than "paper towns." At best they were insignificant hamlets where the courts were held. Reference has already been made to Berkeley's account of the colony in 1671. We have a realistic description of it, ten years later, which is attributed to the pen of Lord Culpepper. He represented commerce, manufactures, education, and government, both civil and ecclesiastical, as in a miserable condition. Merchants were more prosperous than any other class, but they were compelled to sell on credit, and to carry on "a pitiful retail trade." The planter could send out yearly in a ship his yield of tobacco, and receive back at his door, by the same means, everything that he could not raise, and even common household utensils. Work that absolutely required the labor of mechanics at home, was done on his own farm.

Virginia in 1681.

frequently by negroes. The Governor discharged multifarious offices. He was Commander and Vice-Admiral, Lord Treasurer, Lord Chancellor, and Chief Justice, with certain powers, also, that belong to a Bishop. The councillors, whom he could generally control, held a similar variety of offices. The County Court was composed of eight or ten gentlemen, having no education in law, and receiving annually their commissions from the Governor. The General Court, a court for the trial of the most important causes, and for the hearing of appeals, was composed of the Governor and Council as judges. Thus the judicial and executive offices were blended in the same body. The taxes for the support of the church and of the poor were assessed each year by the vestry; the county taxes by the justices of peace; and the public levy by the Assembly. The parishes, since they paid the ministers, claimed the right of presentation, and could exercise it, despite the Governor, since they could refuse to pay the salary. But the vestries, as we have seen, contrived to avoid presentation altogether by hiring the ministers from year to year. The ministers were thus made subservient to the will of those who employed them. There were good men among the ministers, but their character on the whole was not such as to command or deserve respect. It need not be said that they were the champions of the intolerant spirit that prevailed toward Dissenters. The number of parishes was twice as great as the number of the clergy. Lawyers were not held in esteem, and the condition of the medical profession was quite low.

<small>The parishes.</small>

The distinguishing element which merits attention in Virginian society was the aristocratic class. They were far from being always thrifty. By lavish expenditures and by anticipating their profits, they often needlessly allowed themselves to become

<small>The aristocracy.</small>

involved in debt. They were men of virile character, capable of energetic exertion, with the spirit and the manners to be expected in a class accustomed to command. To possess numerous horses, and horses of a choice breed, and—few and bad as the roads were—showy equipages, was a prevalent ambition. The loneliness of the life of the rich planters on their estates, and their love of social intercourse, led to the frequent interchange of visits among themselves, and to the exercise of a liberal hospitality to strangers. The blending of high-bred courtesy with a temper impatient of an affront is natural to such a class. Where there was no town life, the means of intellectual cultivation were scanty. Yet there is evidence that, even in the seventeenth century, libraries, larger or smaller, were found in some of the planters' houses. There was one subject—politics—from which the minds of the aristocratic class were seldom withdrawn. In political discussions and struggles the intellect of the leaders of society was exercised and disciplined. "The Virginia planter was essentially a transplanted Englishman in tastes and convictions, and imitated the social amenities and the culture of the mother country. Thus in time was formed a society distinguished for its refinement, executive ability, and a generous hospitality for which the Ancient Dominion is proverbial." If we understand by "Englishman" the ordinary type of English country gentleman, and make due allowance for the effect of remoteness from the direct influences of English society, the preceding remarks of a recent Virginian historical writer hold good. It must not be understood that there was no middle class in Virginia. There were the tradesmen, and there were the proprietors of smaller farms, who were possessed of fewer slaves. These were separated by an imperceptible line from the richer and more powerful landowners.

CHAPTER V.

MARYLAND UNTIL 1688

The First Lord Baltimore—Avalon—Grant of Maryland—The Maryland Charter—Religion in Maryland—Toleration—Clayborne's Settlement—The Maryland Colony—Conflict with Clayborne—Period of the Commonwealth—Non-conformists in Maryland—Act of Religious Freedom—Puritan Ascendency—Baltimore Regains His Province—Fendall—Slavery—Dispute with Penn—End of Proprietary Government—Society in Maryland.

THE names of George and Cecilius Calvert, the first Lord Baltimore and his son, who inherited the title, are inseparably associated with the planting of Maryland. George Calvert sprung from a respectable family in Yorkshire. He was educated at Oxford. He early made the acquaintance of Sir Robert Cecil, and became his private secretary. After the death of Cecil he was advanced by the special favor of King James I., and in 1617 was raised to the honor of knighthood. He supported the Spanish policy of James, and was a prominent leader of the monarchical party in Parliament. In 1619, he was appointed one of the principal Secretaries of State. Two years later he received a grant from the king of a manor in the County of Longford, Ireland, and later obtained a place on the roll of the Irish peerage under the name of Lord Baltimore. His moderate temper and habitual courtesy caused him to be generally liked, although his political course had been distasteful to the popular party in the House of Commons. Perseverance in carrying out his plans, with no display of enthusiasm, characterized him through life. In 1625, he was converted to the Roman Catholic faith. For years he had participated in the growing interest that was felt in schemes of colonization. He had been a member of the Virginia Company, and in 1622 became one of the eighteen members of the Council for New England, which succeeded the Plymouth Company. He sent out colonists to a plantation in Newfoundland, and by the charter which he obtained in 1623 he acquired a palatinate, or almost royal authority, in Avalon, his province in the southeastern part of that island. Twice he visited his American dominions. He repelled, bravely and successfully, attacks of the French. But a personal experience of the hardships of a winter in Avalon convinced him that the rigor of the climate was too great to permit the hope that a permanent and prosperous settlement could be established there. In a letter to Charles I., in 1629, he states that nothing prevents him from giving up for the future "all proceedings in plantations," except his natural inclination to "these kind of works." Leaving Avalon, he embarked for Virginia, whither his wife had gone before him; but there his creed stood in the way of a gracious welcome, and since he declined to take the oath of supremacy, because the terms of it were repugnant to his conscience as a Roman Catholic, nothing was left for him but to return to England. What he desired was "a precinct" of land in Virginia. This he obtained. He died two months before the charter passed the seal, and the grant was made to his son Cecilius, in 1632. The territory thus bestowed was named Maryland, in honor of the queen, Henrietta Maria. Its northern limit was the southern boundary of the Plymouth Company's grant, the fortieth parallel; on the west its limit was the most distant fountain of the Potomac.

Avalon.

Grant of Maryland.

Thence the line descended southeast on the right bank of the Potomac to a specified place, Watkin's Point, whence it ran due east to the Atlantic. The charter was modelled on that of Avalon, and was of the most liberal character. It made Baltimore and his heirs the proprietaries of the territory, which was to be a palatinate, like the see of Durham in England. That is to say, the prerogatives of the proprietor were well-nigh regal. He was simply bound to pay to the king a yearly rent of two Indian arrows, in acknowledgment of his feudal subordination, and a fifth portion of whatever gold and silver might be found in the province. He was to own the soil; to exercise the powers of a sovereign, both civil and military; to levy taxes; to confer titles and dignities, under a system of sub-infeudation; to constitute courts, from which there was to be no appeal; and to make laws with the assent of the majority of freemen, or of their representatives. His subjects were exempted from taxation by the crown. It was stipulated that on doubtful points of interpretation the charter should be construed in the sense most favorable to the proprietary.

<small>The charter of Maryland.</small>

Only two references to religion are to be found in the Maryland charter. The first gives to the proprietary the patronage and advowsons of churches. The second empowers him to erect churches, chapels, and oratories, which he may cause to be consecrated according to the ecclesiastical laws of England. The phraseology of these passages is copied from the Avalon patent that was given to Sir George Calvert when he was a member of the Church of England. Yet the terms were such that the recognition of that church as the established form of religion does not prevent the proprietary and the colony from the exercise of full toleration toward other Christian bodies. It was well understood by the recipient of the charter, and by those who

<small>Religion in Maryland.</small>

granted it, that, although the instrument says nothing on the subject, such toleration was to be practised, and that adherents of the Roman Catholic faith were not to be molested in its profession and in the use of their customary rites of worship. Baltimore had nothing of the zeal of a propagandist. Sincere in his beliefs, he was lukewarm as regards the diffusion of them. It has been said that the toleration which he adopted was a defensive provision, and there is truth in the statement. Any attempt to proscribe Protestants would have speedily proved fatal to the existence of the colony. In a document which emanated partly from Baltimore himself, it is declared to be evident that the distinctive privileges "usually granted to ecclesiastics of the Roman Catholic Church by Catholic princes in their own countries, could not possibly be granted here [in Maryland] without grave offence to the king and state of England," etc. It must be remembered that from the beginning a large majority of the settlers were Protestants, and the proportion of Protestants was constantly increasing. Nevertheless, the statement that the policy of toleration was unavoidable is only a fraction of the truth. It fails to do full justice to the spirit of the founders of Maryland. There is no reason to think that Cecilius Calvert, any more than his father, would have yielded to any demand, had it been made, to deprive their fellow-disciples of the Roman Church of religious liberty; nor can it be shown that, under any circumstances, they would have felt disposed to withhold an equal toleration from Protestants. The truth is, that the younger Baltimore—and in this respect he closely resembled his father—while he aimed to provide a safe asylum for adherents of his own creed, was mainly concerned to build up a lucrative and flourishing colony, whatever might be the creed of its inhabitants. Tolerant spirit of the Lords of Baltimore.

From the outset the project for a settlement within the limits by which Virginia was bounded in her charter, although that charter had been revoked, was withstood by all who were specially interested in that colony. Baltimore's patent described the territory which it proceeded to define, as heretofore unsettled—*hactenus inculta*—and inhabited only by savages. William Clayborne had established a trading settlement on the island of Kent in the Chesapeake, and thus within the boundaries of Maryland. The purpose of this settlement was to carry on a traffic in furs with the Indians. Whether it could be considered as anything more than a trading depot, whether or not it had the character of a permanent plantation, was a matter of dispute. The trading enterprise which led to his occupation of th Kent island was sanctioned by three Governors of Virginia, and was pursued, also, under a license from the kin_. The people there sent a delegate to the Virginia House of Burgesses. Clayborne, who had been a member of the Virginia Council and Secretary of State in that colony, had a strong support there in his refusal to permit the jurisdiction of Maryland to be extended over his island. The Privy Council decided that both colonies must help one another, and that the disputed question must be left to the course of law.

<small>Clayborne's settlement.</small>

Baltimore had intended to go out himself with his colonists; but he saw that it was necessary to remain at home to resist the busy assailants of his scheme and his charter. In fact, he never saw the land in the settlement of which he was so generous and efficient an agent. His brother, Leonard Calvert, was sent out in charge of the emigrants, and to represent him as the head of the colony. About twenty gentlemen, and two or three hundred laborers, set sail on November 22, 1633. Most of the company were Protes-

<small>Leonard Calvert: the Maryland colony.</small>

tants, but the major part of the gentlemen were Roman Catholics. At the Isle of Wight they took on board Father White and another Jesuit father, whom Baltimore had engaged to accompany them. The priests were strictly charged by him to abstain, on the voyage, from all obtrusive religious manifestations that might give offence to the Protestants with them in the ship. Arriving at Point Comfort, the emigrants were welcomed by Harvey, the Virginia Governor, who continued to favor their cause. He thus drew on himself the hostility of the Virginians, who resented what they deemed an encroachment on their territorial rights. On the St. Mary's, a branch of the Chesapeake, *St. Mary's.* they found an Indian town, which they purchased from the friendly inhabitants, who were about to emigrate from it. The relations of the new-comers with the natives continued to be amicable and cordial. There they founded the town of St. Mary's. The largest wigwam was consecrated by the Jesuit priests as a church. Soon an armed conflict began with Clayborne, *Conflict with Clayborne.* who refused to give up his claims to Kent. In this encounter he was worsted, and left for England, there to prosecute his suit for redress. The government of Maryland was extended over the island, and Clayborne failed to get any satisfaction from the Commissioners for the Plantations. At first the Maryland legislature consisted of the whole body of *The Legislature.* freemen. Then settlers who could not come to the meetings voted by proxy. For a time the delegates sat with such as preferred to attend in person. In 1650, two bodies were by law constituted, the Councillors, appointed by the proprietor, and the Representatives, elected by the people. A provision in the charter for creating an order of nobility was never carried into effect. The proprietary framed a body of laws, which, however, the legislature declined to accept, as being unsuited to the condition of the colony; and the code which the legislature took the initiative in framing he in turn declined to ratify.

The third Assembly, in 1639, formally acknowledged the allegiance of the colony to the king, and at the same time affirmed the prerogatives of the Lord Proprietor. It declared that "Holy Church shall have and enjoy all her rights, liberties, and franchises, wholly and without blemish." It has been thought that the Roman Catholic body must here be referred to; but it has been shown that King James, in a writ in 1622, designates the Anglican Church as "the Holy Church." Thus there were precedents for this application of the phrase. That any other communion is referred to in the declaration of the Assembly is highly improbable. The phrase, it may be observed, was taken from Magna Charta. In the penal code, blasphemy, sacrilege, sorcery, and idolatry were made capital crimes. An act was passed requiring the eating of fish on certain days. This was the adoption by the Roman Catholic legislature of a law which had been enacted by Protestants under a Protestant king, Edward VI., from other than religious motives. Baltimore became quite dissatisfied with the Jesuit missionaries, refused to concede the privileges that were demanded by them, which he characterized as "very extravagant," and at length took measures to prevent any more priests of that order from going out to the colony.

"Holy Church."

The war between King and Parliament in England produced very important effects in Maryland. Leonard Calvert, in 1643 or 1644, received letters of marque from Charles I., authorizing him to capture vessels belonging to the Parliament. On the other side, one Captain Ingle appeared in the

Revolution and counter-revolution.

Chesapeake, with a like commission from Parliament. Ingle was an ally of Clayborne. The Governor ordered his arrest. He escaped in some way, but in 1645 he returned from England, and made an attack on the Maryland government. Leonard Calvert fled to Virginia, where Berkeley protected him. Ingle and Clayborne landed at St. Mary's and took possession of the place, driving out the authorities. But Calvert returned, restored the former government, and, the next year, subdued the island of Kent. Ingle arrested the Jesuit fathers and carried them back to England. Baltimore desisted from all opposition to Parliament, and was at pains to conciliate what was now the dominant power in England. Virginia Non-conformists, expelled from that colony, were induced to settle on the Chesapeake Bay, near the site of Annapolis. *Non-conformists in Maryland.* The larger part of the Puritan exiles from Virginia before long planted themselves on the banks of the Severn. As early as 1643, Baltimore wrote to a Captain Gibbons, in Boston, proposing to give lands to such Massachusetts Puritans as might choose to emigrate to his colony. "But our captain," writes Winthrop in his diary, "had no mind to further his desire therein, nor had any of our people temptation that way." There was certainly a marked contrast between the treatment of Puritans in Virginia and their treatment in Maryland. In 1648, after the death of his brother, the proprietary gave a commission as Governor, to William Stone, a Protestant, whom he required to take an oath not to molest, on account of their religion, any persons who accepted the fundamental doctrines of Christianity. The oath specified the Roman Catholics in particular as to be protected against interference with their liberty of belief and of worship. This stipulation was deemed especially needful on account of the state of parties in England, and now that so large a majority of the people of the colony were Protestants. It was in these circumstances that, in April, 1649, the celebrated Act of Religious Freedom was passed, by which liberty of conscience in matters of religion was guaranteed to all Christians, with the exception of disbelievers in the doctrine of the Trinity. This was the first explicit guarantee of religious freedom that was promulgated in Maryland.

Act of Religious Freedom.

The course taken by Baltimore, in order to gain the favor of Parliament, was so offensive to Charles II., that, although an exile, he deposed the Proprietary, and appointed in his place Sir William Davenant as Royal Governor. The reason given was that Baltimore "did visibly adhere to the rebels in England, and admit all kinds of sectaries and schismatics and ill-affected persons into the plantation." Davenant collected a force of French to aid him, started on the voyage to take possession of the province, but was captured in the Channel. Baltimore afterwards appealed to this act of Charles in proof of his own fidelity to the government set up by Parliament.

In 1651, the Council of State, in pursuance of an act of Parliament, passed in the year previous, sent out four Commissioners, of whom Clayborne was one, who were instructed to reduce the plantations "within the Bay of Chesapeake" to obedience to "the Parliament and the Commonwealth of England." After finishing their work in Virginia, the Commissioners betook themselves to Maryland. This was in March, 1652. The Governor and Council refused to engage to issue all writs and proclamations in the name of "the Keepers of the Liberties of England," instead of in the name of the Proprietary. Stone was therefore removed from office, and the government of the colony was handed over to a Council of Six. After a few months, Stone yielded,

Overthrow of Baltimore's government.

and was reinstated in his place. The Virginians were now excited with the hope of incorporating Maryland in their colony, and applied to Parliament to enact this measure. While England, under the rule of Cromwell, was absorbed in the war with the Dutch, Baltimore thought the time favorable to recover his authority, and instructed Stone to exact an oath of allegiance to the Proprietary. In connection with this step, Cromwell was proclaimed Lord Protector. But the Puritans, who at the outset had declined to take the oath except in a qualified form, refused to comply with the new demand, and appealed to the Commissioners, Bennet and Clayborne. Stone (in July, 1654) issued a proclamation in which he denounced these Commissioners, together with the whole Puritan party, as the authors and fomenters of sedition. The advance of the Commissioners with an armed force against St. Mary's convinced Stone that resistance was useless. He was deposed, and the government was given into the hands of Captain Fuller and a Puritan Council. An Assembly was called, the right to vote for its members being withheld from Roman Catholics. The Assembly, thus composed, denied Baltimore's right to require any declaration of loyalty to himself, and passed an act which took away legal protection to Roman Catholics in the exercise of their religion. Instigated by the rebukes of Baltimore, Stone, in 1655, gathered forces and moved against Providence, the principal Puritan settlement. A battle ensued, in which the Puritans won a complete victory. Four of the prisoners were condemned to death by a court-martial, and were executed. Stone's life was spared. There was now a contest in England on the question to which of the contending parties Maryland should be committed. In September, 1656, the Commissioners of Trade made a report to Cromwell in favor

Puritan ascendency.

Baltimore's authority restored.

of Baltimore. He sent out his brother, Philip Calvert, as a member of the Council and Secretary of the Province. There were now two governments, one managed by the Puritans, and the other in St. Mary's County, under Josiah Fendall, whom the Proprietor had made Governor, but who proved himself to be an unscrupulous and unfaithful agent. In 1657, an agreement was made between the Proprietary and the Commissioners. Clayborne and his party found that they could not hope to procure the displacement of Baltimore. Their opponents were weary of the contest. The agreement, as it was finally adopted by Fendall and the Puritans, contained a pledge to maintain toleration, and a stipulation that, instead of imposing the oath of fidelity on the residents of the province, an engagement should be taken to submit to Lord Baltimore, and to withhold obedience from all who were opposed to him. The engagement to maintain toleration was prescribed by the Proprietary for the protection of the Roman Catholics. But his troubles were not at an end. After the death of Cromwell, Fendall himself proved faithless to the interests of Baltimore, and induced the House of Representatives to declare themselves free from any obligation to procure the Proprietary's assent to the laws which they should pass. Fendall went so far as to accept a commission as Governor from them. The movement was summarily put down by Baltimore, who now had the support of Charles II. Philip Calvert was made Governor. After the proclamation of Charles as King, Maryland continued tranquil until the English Revolution of 1688. The colony rapidly increased in population. The raising of tobacco was so profitable that efforts to promote the cultivation of cereals, and even to substitute coined money for that product as a medium of exchange,

Treachery of Fendall.

Philip Calvert Governor.

Slavery.

were futile. Negro slaves were early introduced into the colony, and their importation was encouraged by an act passed in 1671. But indentured servants continued to exist there and to increase in number. In 1659, a law was passed which provided that "any of the vagabonds or idle persons known by the name of Quakers, who should again enter the province, should be whipped from constable to constable out of it." But it is doubtful whether this act was ever actually enforced. Before many years the Quakers, in considerable numbers, established themselves in the colony.

The second Lord Baltimore died in 1675, and Charles Calvert succeeded to the title. He was obliged to enter into a controversy with William Penn respecting boundaries. Baltimore's southern boundary, as defined in his charter, was a line running east from Watkin's Point on the Chesapeake. His northern boundary was the fortieth parallel. Penn's boundary was declared in his charter to be the fortieth parallel, and a circle of twelve miles around New Castle. A wrong idea had been entertained as to the position of the fortieth degree. It had been supposed to be farther south. Baltimore insisted on the terms of his charter, and claimed, moreover, the portion of the Delaware peninsula which the Duke of York had granted to Penn. Penn demanded that the northern boundary should be run where the Lords of Trade had supposed it to be, and which gave him access to the head waters of the Delaware Bay. The decision of the Board of Trade in England, in 1685, gave to him what he claimed of the Delaware peninsula, but the other points in the controversy were not fully adjusted until long after. *Dispute with Penn.*

The Maryland charter, like all the other colonial charters, was obnoxious to James II. In 1687, an attack was begun upon it in the usual way, by a writ of *quo war-*

ranto. The Revolution of 1688 was the signal of a movement in the colony for the overthrow of the Proprietary rule. There was an unfortunate delay in proclaiming William and Mary, which, as far as Baltimore was concerned, was due to an accident. The insurgents were Protestants, largely of the Church of England, and were led by one John Coode. They formed themselves into an association. The State House and the records were surrendered to Coode and his followers. Baltimore's efforts in England to retain his province were ineffectual. Early in 1692, Sir Lionel Copley arrived in Maryland, bearing the royal commission as Governor. The Proprietary's authority was at an end, but he was suffered to retain the pecuniary benefits which he derived from the province.

<small>Overthrow of the Proprietary rule.</small>

The characteristics of society in Maryland in the seventeenth century were not materially diverse from those which prevailed in Virginia. The natural features—the soil and climate—were essentially the same. The Proprietary rule was the only important difference in the mode of government. The judicial system was better than that which existed in Virginia. There were competent and respected lawyers in Maryland earlier than was the case in the adjacent southern colony. Tobacco was the one chief product, and the fluctuations in its value caused the same troubles in one community as in the other. In both colonies, commerce was equally depressed. In both, the absence of towns produced a like effect on employments and manners. As was true of Virginia, the main part of the Maryland people were of English origin; but they were not, as there, of the same religious belief. Hence the alternations of toleration and coercion which run through its early history. The exclusiveness of the English Church, when it was in control, and the unworthy character of many of its clergy, increased the strength of

<small>Society in Maryland.</small>

the Dissenting sects, and was answerable to a considerable degree for the spread of religious indifference. The laws relating to slavery were harsh, but the treatment of slaves, as a rule, as in the more southern colony, was humane. Their condition for a long period was little removed from barbarism. The numerous imported convicts, when they were released from forced labor, became an idle and dangerous class of freedmen. The higher aristocracy were even less distinctively sundered from farmers immediately below them than in Virginia.

CHAPTER VI.

THE CAROLINAS UNTIL 1688

Grant of Carolina by Charles II.—The Two Settlements—"The Fundamental Constitutions"—North Carolina—Civil Disturbances — Sothel—Ludwell—South Carolina—Slavery—Scotch-Irish and Huguenot Immigrants—Civil Disturbances.

IT was on the shores of North Carolina that Raleigh's two colonies had been planted. In 1629, the territory comprised in both the Carolinas was granted by Charles I. to Sir Robert Heath, who afterwards transferred his patent to Lord Maltravers. Inasmuch as a "reasonable time" elapsed without any settlement being made, this patent was forfeited. Virginia assumed to make grants to trading companies, which had no permanent result. But in 1653, a small company of Dissenters from Virginia migrated to the Chowan River and began the Albemarle settlement. A considerable number of Quakers were included in it. About 1660, certain New Englanders bought land of the Indians on the Cape Fear River. They were not satisfied with the place, and abandoned it in disgust. In 1665, English colonists came over from Barbados to Cape Fear and planted the district subsequently known by the name of Clarendon. Two years before, in 1663, Charles II., who found it easy to gratify his favorites by the gift of extensive regions in the New World, granted to eight persons—including the Earl of Clarendon, General Monk, Duke of Albemarle, Lord Ashley Cooper, who

Grant of Carolina by Charles II.

was to become the Earl of Shaftesbury—all Carolina, from the thirty-sixth degree of north latitude. Sir William Berkeley, then Governor of Virginia, organized a government for the Chowan district, or Albemarle. William Drummond was appointed Governor. In the southern district, or Clarendon, John Yeamans, who had led the Barbados emigrants, received a commission as Governor. The Albemarle and the Clarendon settlements.

The Clarendon colony did not prosper, partly because there were more eligible places for settlement, especially the site of Charleston. The Proprietors, by the terms of the charter, were nearly absolute, as regards both Crown and Parliament; but "the advice, consent, and approbation" of the freemen were required to give validity to their laws. There was to be freedom in religion to all who did not disturb the peace. The Proprietors took pains to make liberal terms with New Englanders and with any who might be inclined to migrate to their province. In 1665, another charter was granted by the King, by which the boundaries of the province were made to be 36° 30' on the north and 29° on the south.

Seven years after the first charter was given, John Locke, who was an intimate friend of Shaftesbury, framed, in conjunction with him, what were called "The Fundamental Constitutions of Carolina," which were sanctioned and adopted by the Proprietors. This product of the genius of the most eminent statesman and the ablest philosopher of that day was an impracticable system of government. It was never carried out, and had no other effect than to embroil the Proprietors in disputes with the colonists. "To avoid erecting a numerous democracy" was one of the principal motives avowed in the preamble of this utopian scheme. The eldest of the Proprietors was to be a "Palatine," and the The "Constitutions" of Carolina.

country to be a county palatinate, like Durham. The other Proprietors were severally to hold seven other great offices—those of Admiral, Chancellor, High Steward, etc. The province was to be divided into seigniories, baronies, and precincts. To the different ranks of nobility, two-fifths of all the land was to belong, the other three-fifths being reserved for the people. There were to be eight supreme courts, one for each proprietor. There was to be a Grand Council. There was to be a Parliament, but nothing was to come before it which had not previously been proposed in the Council and approved by it. There was to be trial by jury, but only a majority was to be required for a verdict. No one was to be allowed to receive fee or reward for pleading in court for another. To avoid a multiplicity of laws, all laws were to become inoperative and void a hundred years from the date of their enactment. Seven persons might organize themselves into a Church. It was required that they should at least profess their belief in God and in the obligation to worship him, and set down in their creed a form of oath or affirmation to be used by witnesses in courts. No person above seventeen years of age who was not a church member was to hold any place of honor or profit, or enjoy the benefit or protection of law. Contrary to the wishes of Locke, there was inserted in the "Constitutions" a provision for the establishment of the Church of England, the building of churches, and the maintenance, through acts of the Parliament, of its ministry. No one was to be molested or coerced on account of his religious opinions. The statements under this head were in accord with Locke's well-known convictions in favor of religious liberty. "Landgraves" and "Cassiques" were included in the aristocracy to be established in the colony. Locke himself acquired the title of "Landgrave."

There were two colonies after the disappearance of the Clarendon settlement—Albemarle on the north, and the Ashley River colony on the south. Adopting later designations, we may style the one North, and the other South, Carolina. {North Carolina.} The settlers at Albemarle were reinforced by emigrants from New England. In 1667, Samuel Stephens became Governor, as the successor of Drummond. The form of government under which the people were living was one in which they had a share, and with which they were satisfied. There was considerable religious activity among the Quakers, who were visited a number of years later (in 1672) by George Fox. Before the death of Stephens, the attempt was made to enforce the new "Constitutions" and to displace the existing form of rule. This excited disaffection and resistance. {Civil disturbances.} One of the colonists, Thomas Miller, who went to England to represent their interests, returned to act against them and to carry out the measures of the Proprietors. The New Englanders refused to give up their trade with the West Indies or to obey the Navigation Laws, which he tried to enforce. The Quakers had their own grievances, and were in sympathy with the spirit of revolt. John Culpepper was the leader of the insurgents. Miller and the deputies of the Proprietors were displaced. Miller went to England, and was followed by Culpepper. The former was removed from office. Culpepper was tried for treason, but was acquitted. In 1683, Seth Sothel, who had bought Clarendon's proprietary right, took the office of Governor. {Sothel.} His rapacity—for his aim was to enrich himself—caused a rising of the people. He was banished by the Assembly for twelve months. This was in 1688. A large number of fugitives from Virginia, many of whom fled from there to escape the harsh punishments which followed Bacon's insurrection, had settled in Albemarle. The anarchical state of the colony was, in the main, the result of the indiscreet interference of the Proprietors. While Ludwell was Governor the people were delivered from oppression; but such was the disorder under his inefficient rule that the population was largely diminished. In 1693, he was made Governor of both colonies, and removed to Charleston.

<small>Ludwell.</small>

The Ashley River settlement was commenced in 1670, by a company of emigrants led by Joseph West, and by William Sayle, who was to take the office of Governor. They were sent out under the auspices of the Proprietors. The "Fundamental Constitutions," it was seen by them at once, could not be put in force. They established a mode of government in which the powers of the executive were limited, and delegates to the legislature were chosen by the people. In 1672, Charleston was fixed upon as the permanent site for the settlement. In 1671, there was an arrival of Dutch emigrants from New York. In the same year, negro slaves were imported. It was not long before they greatly outnumbered the whites. There were many additions to the colony from England. Among them was a company of Scotch-Irish, who came over in 1683. A small settlement of Presbyterian families from Scotland at Port Royal was swept away by a Spanish incursion. An event of great importance in relation to the future history of South Carolina was the coming of Huguenot emigrants, fugitives from the persecution which followed the revocation of the Edict of Nantes in 1685. They settled on the Cooper River. For a time they were not admitted to political rights, but after an interval these were granted to them.

<small>South Carolina.</small>

<small>The Huguenot settlers.</small>

Sayle died in 1671. In 1674, Joseph West took the office, which he administered for nine years with energy and prudence. Then for a long period there was much turbulence and a struggle of factions. A portion of the settlers consisted of worthless adventurers. The colonists resisted the prosecution for debts which had been elsewhere contracted. In this matter the Proprietors were at variance with them. There was contention with them, also, on account of the shelter and impunity granted at Charleston to piratical assailants of Spanish vessels. These doings threatened to bring on war between Spain and England. The party in favor of the King and the Church was formed by the Proprietors, although a majority of the settlers, and the soundest part of them, were Dissenters. Then attempts to enforce the Navigation Laws were sure to breed disturbance and excite resistance. A chronic source of trouble was the "Fundamental Constitutions," some of the peculiar features of which the Proprietors, from time to time, sought to introduce. The effort to enforce the adoption of them, which was begun by Governor Colleton in 1686, was withstood by the colonial parliament. In 1689, he declared martial law. Colleton was openly resisted, and was banished from the province.

Civil disturbances.

6

CHAPTER VII.

NEW ENGLAND TO THE PLANTING OF CONNECTICUT IN 1636

The Plymouth Company—The Popham Colony—John Smith in New England—The Council of New England—Puritanism in England—Religious Parties in Elizabeth's Reign—The Independents—The Scrooby Congregation—The Pilgrims in Holland—The Voyage of the Mayflower—The Settlement at Plymouth—The Government at Plymouth—Growth and Character of the Colony—Towns—Mason's Grant of New Hampshire—The New Puritan Emigration—Endicott at Salem—The Charter of the Massachusetts Company—The First Congregational Church—Alleged "Intolerance" of the Puritans—Transfer of the Massachusetts Company to New England—John Winthrop—The Great Emigration to Massachusetts—Sufferings of the Colony—Its Form of Government—Congregationalism—Roger Williams—Williams Founds Providence—Vane—Mrs. Ann Hutchinson—Winthrop again Chosen Governor—Heroic Spirit of the Colony—Council of New England Surrenders its Charter—Roger Williams and his Colony—Settlement of Rhode Island—The Settlements in New Hampshire—Gorges' Settlement in Maine.

The Plymouth Company.

THE Plymouth Company was almost eclipsed by the London branch of the Virginia Corporation. The London Company was rich and influential. All eyes were attracted to the body under whose auspices the Jamestown colony had been sent out. Yet the promoters of the Plymouth Company, especially Sir Ferdinando Gorges, from the outset a prime mover in the whole enterprise, were not inactive. On the return of Weymouth from his voyage, in 1606, several

Indians, whom he brought back with him, were trained, under the superintendence of Gorges, to serve as interpreters and intermediates between the English and the natives.

In 1607, a few months after the beginnings at Jamestown, two vessels were sent out by Gorges and his associates to establish a permanent colony. They carried one hundred and twenty persons, under Captain Raleigh Gilbert, with George Popham, a brother of the Chief Justice, as President. They reached Monhegan Island, a place of frequent resort for voyagers, situated off the Maine coast. They chose for the site of their settlement the near peninsula of Sabino on the main-land, where they erected a church, a storehouse, and other buildings. The ships carried back a glowing account of the new country. But the familiar record is once more to be repeated. The winter was very severe, Popham died, and the news of the death of the Chief Justice arrived. The disheartened colonists abandoned the settlement and returned to England. Thus ended the "Popham Colony." In 1614, Captain John Smith, the hero of the Virginia colony, again appears, this time on the coast of Maine. He explains the errand on which he came. He was to take whales or discover mines; or, failing in such endeavors, he was to obtain fish and furs. In these last attempts he was successful. But he did incidental work of far greater consequence. This tireless explorer moved along the coast in a boat from the Penobscot to Cape Cod. To a number of places he gave names, some of which, as recorded on his map, still remain. He gave to the region the name of New England. His "Description of New England," which he published on his return, is a somewhat picturesque, as well as generally accurate, account of what he saw. In this and in the sub-

The Popham Colony.

John Smith and New England.

sequent writings of Smith, there are not wanting a generous enthusiasm and more enlightened views relative to the ends and methods of colonization than were generally entertained. He continued to be employed by the Plymouth Company. He was anxious to combine with Gorges and the Plymouth leaders others who were possessed of larger means. "Much labour," he writes, "I had taken to bring the Londoners and them to joyne together, because the Londoners have much money, and the Westerne men are most proper for fishing; and it is neere as much trouble, but much more danger, to saile from London to Plimouth, than from Plimouth to New England." He was thwarted, however, by the ambition of both parties to be "lords of this fishing." He was bent on establishing a permanent colony on the coast which he had described and delineated. Twice he set sail to carry out his design, but was baffled each time by accidents. He would have set out a third time, but was kept back at Plymouth by head winds which prevailed for three months. Smith retained the well-earned title which he had received from the Plymouth Company, of Admiral of New England.

Gorges had expended large sums from his own private fortune in exploring and trading expeditions, and in unsuccessful exertions to plant settlements. These enterprises had been set on foot by him and his friends, acting in the name of the Plymouth Company. At length there was opened before them the prospect of large gains by a monopoly in the fisheries. It was just at the time when James was engaged in the experiment of ruling without a Parliament, and was dispensing monopolies with a lavish hand. Gorges was a supporter of the King's party, and was helped by influential noblemen. In 1620, he, and the "Gentlemen Adventurers" with him, obtained a patent, to take the place of

The Council of New England.

the charter of the Plymouth Company, granting to them, under the name of the Council of New England, the territory between the fortieth parallel—or about the latitude of Philadelphia—and the forty-eighth degree, which crosses the Bay of Chaleurs. The patentees were to have the right to plant and to govern settlements, and also to convey to individuals and companies subordinate grants, accompanied by powers similar to their own. The patent forbade any to visit the New England coasts without a license from the Council. This cut off the right to land and to dry fish, and created, practically, although not in direct terms, a complete monopoly in the benefit of the fisheries. As soon as the plan of Gorges and his associates for obtaining this charter became known, the managers of the London Company were up in arms. A determined, persevering protest was made against the bestowal of such a privilege. These managers were in disfavor, as being of the political opposition. But Sir Edward Coke and others were resolute in their hostility to the obnoxious measure. When Parliament met, the resistance was pressed. Although the patent was delivered to Gorges, the controversy went on for several years, the demand for "a free liberty of all the King's subjects for fishing" could not be withstood, and the Council was obliged to yield. With the loss of this coveted monopoly, the prospects of the organization were blighted, and it ceased to flourish. ^{Failure of Gorges.}

The permanent settlement of New England was to spring from a stronger sentiment than the love of gain, and from a nobler passion than the spirit of adventure. Its motive was found in religion. When King Henry VIII. broke off the connection of England with the Papacy, and made himself, in the room of the Pope, the head of the English Church, he did not change his theology. He did not himself intend ^{Progress of the Reformation in England.}

to forsake the Roman Catholic doctrines, nor did he mean to allow his subjects to adopt a different faith from his own. He was enabled to carry through the revolution which he effected, through that inbred dislike of foreign ecclesiastical rule, which had been of slow growth in England, but had come to be an established feeling. He was aided, likewise, by the doctrinal Protestantism, with which he had no personal sympathy, but which, under Lutheran influences, was getting a foothold among his people. But Protestants and adherents of the Pope the King treated with equal severity. He sent both classes of dissenters from his system to the stake or the scaffold. His iron will, aided by favoring circumstances, enabled him during his lifetime to maintain the middle position and to enforce an outward obedience. His youthful son,

Edward VI. Edward VI., was a Protestant by conviction, and when he succeeded to the throne, the growing, but hitherto repressed party which had espoused Protestant opinions, came to the front. The Anglican Protestant Church was brought into close fraternal relations with Protestant bodies on the Continent. Its constitution was framed. Its creed and Prayer-book were compiled by Cranmer and learned coadjutors. But the current of innovation was swifter than the majority of the nation approved. The reaction that followed under Mary

Mary. restored the Church of Rome to its old place of authority. But this renewed rule of a foreign ecclesiastic, the Queen's close relations with Spain, and the cruelties inflicted on the Reformers and their disciples, made the people ready for a Protestant successor in the person of Elizabeth. Not less than eight hundred exiles, embracing numerous able and learned ministers, who in the reign of Mary had fled from the fires of Smithfield, now came back. The sojourn of many of them with the Swiss Protestant leaders had brought them into full sympathy with the more radical type of Protestantism which had previously won favor among the divines who, in Edward's time, composed the formularies of the English Church. Thus there sprang up in full vigor, at Elizabeth's accession, the Puritan party, with which she herself, a Lutheran in her creed, and bent on maintaining her ecclesiastical prerogatives in the spirit of her father, had no personal sympathy. The growth of Puritanism.

Her policy in matters of ritual was that of compromise with the old religion. To the desire of the Puritans—who included in their ranks some of her own leading bishops—to exclude from the liturgy of the English Church peculiarities at variance with Policy of Elizabeth. the doctrine of Zwingli, and especially of Calvin, and to modify ecclesiastical arrangements, she interposed an inflexible resistance. Without entering into the theological controversies of that period, or approving the tyrannical temper and doings of the Tudor sovereigns who cast off the papal rule, we shall have to allow that probably one result of their conservative policy, and of the unbending will with which they pursued it, was the exemption of England from the intestine religious wars that desolated so large a portion of the Continent.

All through the reign of Elizabeth, the Roman Catholics were a very numerous portion of her subjects. A part of them hated her government, and were ready to co-operate in plots to dethrone and The religious parties. destroy her. But another portion coupled with an antagonistic faith feelings of patriotism and loyalty, that moved them to unite with their fellow-subjects in taking up arms to resist the attempts of Spain and the Catholic reaction on the Continent to subjugate England. Then there was, secondly, the Anglican Protestant party, which defended Episcopacy and approved of the Queen's ecclesiastical system in all its main features. But there was, in the third place, the Presbyterian party, which, like the Episcopalian, believed in a national church, but would have the government of it Presbyterian, instead of prelatical, and contended that, not the edicts of the Queen and of Parliament, but ecclesiastical assemblies should prescribe the creed, ritual, and discipline of the Church; their regulations, however, to be supported and enforced by the civil authority. The Presbyterians were in the national church; but they conformed to certain requirements in its polity and to certain prescriptions in the Prayer-book with reluctance, and under a protest, and in some cases refused to comply with them, and labored for a change, submitting, meantime, to the legal penalties of non-conformity. Puritans of every grade, it may be remarked, whether obeying the Act of Uniformity while chafing under its requirements, or passively declining to obey, were earnest to procure the abolition of pluralities and kindred abuses, and to substitute educated, devout ministers for the numerous illiterate and worldly pastors scattered through the parishes of England. But there was a fourth religious party, another branch or product of Puritanism, that demands attention.

Before the close of Elizabeth's reign, there sprang up the Independents, who sympathized in theology with the conforming and non-conforming Presbyterians. In truth, as regards dogmas, in distinction from polity, there was at this time little contention among English Protestants of whatever name. But the Independents did not believe in religious establishments. They were opposed altogether to national churches. A church, they held, was a local body of Christian believers, united in fellowship by a covenant, electing its own ministers and administering its own discipline by popular vote, with no interference, except in the way of fraternal counsel, from any other ecclesiastical body. Hence the name "Independents." As distinguished both from Episcopalians and Presbyterians, all of whom believed in an established church with a legally ordained creed, ritual, and discipline, they were designated as "Separatists." Before the close of Elizabeth's reign it was estimated by Raleigh that there were not less than twenty thousand Independents in England. The name of "Brownists" was often applied to them from one of their early leaders, Robert Browne, a preacher at Norwich, a man turbulent and unstable in his ways. Protected by his relative, Lord Burghley, he was able to escape from England and to serve for a time a congregation in Zealand. Thence he returned to accept a benefice in the English Church. He brought no credit either to the Separatists or to the communion in whose service he died. The appellation "Brownists" was never relished by the Independents, but was often affixed to them as a nickname. To reject the Church established by the law of the land, was construed by the Queen's government as sedition, and was punished by the penalties attached to that crime. In 1583, two of the Separatist ministers, named Copping and Thacker, both of them clergymen who had been ordained in the Established Church, were put to death for the crime of non-conformity, involving, as it was held, the denial of the Queen's supremacy. In 1593, three other godly ministers—Barrowe, Greenwood, and Penry, all of them graduates of Cambridge—were hanged for the same offence. *Persecution of the Independents.*

It was to a little Independent congregation at Scrooby, in Nottinghamshire, that the Pilgrims who settled at Plymouth originally belonged. It met for worship at the manor-house in Scrooby, occupied by William Brewster, who hospitably opened his doors to the persecuted flock whose faith he shared. Brewster had been a student at Cambridge, but left his studies to become the secretary of Davison, one of the Queen's Secretaries for Foreign Affairs, who was dismissed from office, heavily fined, and imprisoned, in consequence of Elizabeth's desire to shift upon him the responsibility of doing what she had required of him in connection with the warrant for the execution of Mary, Queen of Scots. By his friendly agency Brewster was made "post," or postmaster, of the place where he lived. Later he became a "ruling elder" of the religious society which held its meetings under his roof. Brewster was a man of sincere piety, and of a noble, generous spirit. The list of the books which he brought across the ocean, and left behind him at his death, indicates that he was well read in theology, and that his reading was not confined to this branch. The principal minister of the Scrooby church was John Robinson. He had been a Fellow at Cambridge. He was a man of uncommon ability and learning. In his theology he was a Calvinist, but he was of an unusually tolerant spirit. The Scrooby flock was made up of people of humble rank, mostly farmers and artisans. One of its members was young William Bradford, whose home was at Austerfield, a few miles from Scrooby. He lived to write the history of the Pilgrim emigration to America. His name belongs on the roll of honor by the side of that of Brewster.

The Scrooby congregation.

John Robinson.

When James I. assumed the Crown, it was soon evident that the severities of the last reign were not to be a whit diminished, but rather sharpened. Such were the annoyances and perils of Robinson's church that at length they resolved to leave home and country, and go over in a body to Holland. But when

The Pilgrims in Holland.

they tried to carry out their design, cruel hindrances were put in their way by the King's officers. At last, in 1608, they found themselves safely in Amsterdam. The two Independent congregations which had been planted there before, were engaged in disputes, in which the peace-loving Pilgrims desired to have no part. After a brief sojourn, although the change involved a loss in a temporal point of view, they departed to Leyden, where they were permanently established. They had to betake themselves to new occupations. Brewster became a printer. By patient industry they managed to earn a livelihood, and they won the respect of their Dutch neighbors. But they were Englishmen, and, glad though they were to escape persecution, they felt themselves to be strangers in a strange land. They could not be sure that their children, under the influences that surrounded them, would follow in their ways. They could not expect to do much in behalf of their peculiar religious ideas and practices. They arrived at the conclusion that it was best for them to cross the ocean and to found a community of their own, on territory subject to England. *Emigration to America.* To this end they entered into negotiations, which were prolonged and difficult, with the leaders of the London Company. At a time when it seemed doubtful whether anything would come from this effort, Robinson undertook to arrange with the Dutch to plant a colony, under their protection, near their American settlement. But this project was abandoned as soon as it was found practicable to make an agreement with certain London merchants to co-operate with them, and share in the cost of the voyage and first settlement. A patent was procured from the London Company. The King refused a charter to the projected colony. The Leyden brethren had sought to disarm apprehension on the part of the Virginia Company by sending over a document containing seven articles in which they set forth their position in reference to the civil power. In carefully chosen terms they went so far as to recognize the King's right to appoint bishops, among other officers of the realm, to govern dioceses and parishes " civilly according to the laws of the land." All that James would concede was a promise not to molest them as long as they behaved peaceably. There were no means of transporting at once more than a part of the Leyden church.

<small>The voyage to New England.</small> Only a part, therefore, could go. The rest were to follow when they could. As those who were left behind were the majority, they retained Robinson with them. Early in July 1620, their brethren bade them farewell at Delft Haven, and in the Speedwell, a small vessel which they had bought, sailed to Southampton. There delays and hindrances awaited them; and it was not until August 15th that the Speedwell, and its companion, the Mayflower, set out on their voyage. At the end of about a week both vessels put in at Dartmouth, because the Speedwell was declared to be leaky. Once more they started, and again the captain and crew of this vessel reported her—falsely, as it turned out—unseaworthy. Both ships turned back to Plymouth. Such as were weak or discouraged, parting sadly with their friends, were left behind, and, on September 16th, the Mayflower, now crowded with passengers, went forth on her solitary voyage.

Writers who have charged the Pilgrims with imprudence in braving the rigors of winter on the New England coast, forget the circumstances which, contrary to their intention, made this inevitable. On November 19th, they came in sight of the shores of Cape Cod. They found themselves—not, however, as some have supposed, through treachery on the part of their captain—outside of the limits of the Virginia Company. At first they resolved to seek a place near the Hudson; for although they knew that Northern Virginia was to be granted to a new company, the Council of New England, they did not know that the Hudson would fall within its boundaries. But after sailing for half a day, such were the difficulties of the attempt and the opposition of the captain and seamen, that they returned. It was not until December 21st—a part of the interval having been spent in exploring the cold and stormy coast by a party sent out for the purpose—that they landed on the shore of Plymouth, the spot which they selected for the site for their settlement. On November 21st, in the cabin *New Plymouth.* of the Mayflower, then in the harbor of Provincetown, in pursuance of an injunction of Robinson to frame a form of civil polity, and because there were signs of insubordination on the part of certain laborers, who were disposed to break loose from their contracts because they were not to disembark in Virginia, the Pilgrims united in a solemn compact, of which the following is a copy:

"In the name of God, amen. We, whose names are underwritten, the loyal subjects of our dread sovereign lord King James, by the grace of God of Great Britain, France, and Ireland, King, Defender of the Faith, etc., having undertaken *The Mayflower compact.* for the glory of God and the advancement of the Christian faith, and honor of our King and country, a voyage to plant the first colony in the northern parts of Virginia, do, by these presents solemnly and mutually, in the presence of God, and one of another, covenant and combine ourselves together into a civil body politic, for our better ordering and preservation and furtherance of the ends aforesaid; and by virtue hereof to enact, constitute, and frame such just and equal laws, ordinances, acts, constitutions, and offices, from time to time, as shall be thought most meet and convenient for the general good of the colony, unto which we promise all due submission and obedience. In witness whereof we have hereunder subscribed our names at Cape Cod, the 11th of November [O. S.], in the year of the reign of our sovereign lord King James, of England, France, and Ireland, the eighteenth, and of Scotland the fifty-fourth. Anno Dom., 1620."

Thus there began the first political community in America with a written constitution of its own making. There were forty-one subscribers to the compact. Seven of them were servants or hired laborers. The remaining thirty-four constituted "the colony proper." Of these eighteen were accompanied by their wives. Fourteen had minor children. Most of the thirty-four were from Leyden. Some had joined the Leyden men at Southampton. While some of the settlers were among them in consequence of the association of the enterprise with the merchants who were looking for pecuniary profit, the prevailing motive of the colony as a whole was that which had moved the Pilgrims to originate the plan. All hoped to reap advantage from fishing. King James had been somewhat propitiated when he was told that the Leyden applicants were to engage in this employment. This, he observed, was the occupation of the apostles. When the compact was drawn up, John Carver was chosen Governor. After his death, in the March following, William Bradford was made his successor.

By the terms of the partnership between the merchants and the Pilgrims, each emigrant was to have one share in the profits of the undertaking. One share was allotted for every ten pounds invested. Every youth above sixteen was to be counted as a shareholder. A fraction of a share was to be credited to each younger child. The colony was to be furnished with food and other necessaries from the common stock. At the end of seven years the accumulated earnings were to be divided among the shareholders. On November 21, 1621, a vessel arrived, bringing a patent (granted June 11) to the company from the Council of New England. There were no defined boundaries for the grant. Each emigrant might take up a hundred acres. Fifteen hundred acres were allowed for public buildings. The grantees were authorized to form a government and to make laws. Under this patent the colony lived for about eight years. Grant of a patent.

Grievous were the sufferings of the Plymouth settlers during the first winter, but not too great for their courage and patience. To range along the coast in the midst of sleet and snow, in quest of a suitable location, proved to have been only the beginning of trials. To build their log-houses amid all the exposures of midwinter was the next thing to be done. At one time all but six or seven were sick. Before spring came, one-half of their whole number were in their graves under the snow. Soon after landing they had heard a cry from savages that sounded hostile. A little military band was formed, with Miles Standish for a captain. Standish had attached himself to the Pilgrims, and came over with them, although not a member of the church. On March 26th, an Indian, named Samoset, who had picked up a little English from the crews of fishing-vessels, came to them, bidding them "Welcome." The visit was followed by the conclusion of a treaty with his chief, Massasoit, the head of the Wampanoags, whose hunting-grounds were on the southwest, near the Narraganset. A pestilence had prevailed in New England a few years before, and had thinned out the native population. In the patent granted to the Council of New England this event is referred to as a providential circumstance, fitted to encourage plans of emigration. It proved, indirectly, The first winter. The Indians.

the means of safety to the Plymouth settlers. Peace between the Pilgrims and the natives was imperilled by an undertaking of Thomas Weston. In 1622, under a patent which he had procured, he sent out sixty men, by whom a settlement was formed at Wessagusett (now Weymouth). Their disorderly practices excited the wrath of the Indians. Their lives, as well as the lives of the Plymouth colonists, were saved by the intervention of the latter. Several savages were killed in an encounter with Standish and two others. Robinson, when he heard of it, lamented that some could not have been converted before any were slain. Most of Weston's followers were aided in getting back to England. A few of them were received at Plymouth and joined the colony.

Thomas Weston.

In 1625, a Captain Wollaston attempted to form another settlement within the territory where the town of Quincy is situated. Wollaston gave up the attempt and went to Virginia. Thomas Morton, who had been a lawyer in England, got control of the people left behind by Wollaston. The riotous ways of Morton's company, who, in addition to other mischievous doings, sold fire-arms and ammunition to the natives, moved Plymouth to interfere. The "unruly nest" was broken up without bloodshed, Morton was sent to England, and his followers driven away. About April 15th, 1621, the Mayflower started on the return voyage to England. It carried back none of the settlers.

Wollaston.

With the Governor there was associated one assistant. In 1624, the number of assistants was raised to five. The Governor and assistants were elected by the body of freemen, who consisted at first of the original settlers, and, as population spread, of such as were admitted to the privileges of freemen in the several towns. In 1639, a system of representation was adopted, each town electing two representatives. The

Government at Plymouth.

magistrates and deputies sat in one assembly. For a time no law went into force without the express sanction of the body of freemen. The London merchants did not regard with favor the religious peculiarities of the colony. They considered them a hindrance to its growth. From time to time there were additions from abroad, a considerable proportion of which were from Leyden. Robinson died in 1625, not having been able to carry out his wish to join the portion of his people who were making for themselves a home beyond the sea. In 1624, the merchants sent over sixty persons, among whom was a minister, Lyford by name, who not only calumniated the colony in his letters, but set about an attempt to establish in it the Church of England. His treacherous character was brought to light, and he was compelled to leave. The colonists were under a contract of service and partnership with the mercantile "Adventurers." It was an improvement when an acre of land was given to each head of a family to cultivate for himself. There was a much more beneficial change when, in 1627, the resident adults—with the exception of a few who were not considered worthy of the privilege—became possessed, by purchase, of the stock and land. There could now be an equitable distribution of the common property among the settlers. In 1630, a patent from the Council of New England granted to Bradford and his associates the territory between defined boundaries—the Cohasset River on the north, and the domains of Pokanoket on the west. To give them increased means of trading and fishing, a tract of land fifteen miles wide, on each shore of the Kennebec River, was ceded to them. But there was a reservation which gave to the Council the right to establish such a government as they might wish to ordain. There was no certainty that Gorges might not conclude to institute a

Lyford.

Purchase of the stock and land.

government for all New England, of which he should be the head. There was still greater danger of legislative interference by the Crown. Against this the patent of the Plymouth settlers afforded no safeguard.

<small>Growth and character of the colony.</small> The colony gradually extended, mainly along the coast. In 1641, there had come to be eight towns, with a population of two thousand five hundred. In all but one of them there were educated ministers. A half century after the landing at Plymouth there were fifty towns and about eight thousand people. The Plymouth settlers established trade with the natives on the Kennebec and Penobscot, and to some extent in the valley of the Connecticut. With all their industry, so sterile was the soil that the colony remained poor. The consequence was that as the pulpits became vacant it became difficult to fill them with a learned ministry, and down to 1670 there appears to have been no provision for public education. The spirit of the colony in dealing with theological dissidents and fanatics was comparatively mild. In 1657, it was enacted that Quakers, who were the occasion of much disturbance, should be excluded from becoming freemen. Later, in 1671, it was provided that freemen should be sober and peaceable in their behavior, and orthodox in "the fundamentals of religion." But the "Old Colony," as it was called, through its entire history avoided harsh measures in dealing with theological malcontents, and not seldom served as an asylum for persons whose religious tenets or practices brought upon them discomfort in the neighboring community of Massachusetts Bay. Plymouth had obtained its lands by fair purchase of the Indians. Earnest efforts were put forth to convert them to Christianity. In 1675, about the time when King Philip's War broke out, it is estimated that within the limits of the colony there were not less than five or six

hundred "praying Indians." Brewster, the patriarch of the colony, died in 1644. He had had the care of the church, officiating as preacher as well as ruling elder, until 1629, when Ralph Smith, a regular minister was settled. An abridged catalogue of Brewster's library is extant. It speaks well for his intellectual character, for there is no doubt that the books were kept, not for show, but for use. It comprised four hundred volumes, of which forty-eight were folios and one hundred and seventy-seven were quartos. Besides numerous commentaries on the Bible, and other books of theology, we find on the list "The Prince" of Machiavelli, Bacon's "Advancement of Learning," Seneca's writings—these all in English. Among the non-ecclesiastical authors there is found one poet of merit, George Withers. Eleven of the books were printed by Brewster himself in Leyden.

Brewster.

It is a characteristic feature of New England from the beginning that its inhabitants dwelt together in towns. In this peculiarity, so fruitful in its consequences, political and social, there was a broad contrast with the Virginia settlements, where, as we have seen, the large landholders lived apart from one another on their estates. The character of the soil and of its products in New England was one main cause of this difference. Another reason was the interest of the people in religion, and their ecclesiastical system. The town was an organization for united worship, as well as for the conduct of secular affairs. The inhabitants fixed their abodes usually near the "meeting-house." Of the significance of the town in its political bearings, more will be said hereafter.

Towns.

A complete account of the doings of the Council of New England would contain the record of various grants of land, not seldom conflicting with one another, and of several attempts at settlement which had but small results. In such proceedings Gorges was actively concerned. In 1622, in connection with John Mason, he obtained the grant of the territory, which they named Laconia, between the Merrimac and the Kennebec, and extending to "the river of Canada." Two settlements were begun where are now Portsmouth and Dover, but for a long time were with difficulty kept in being. The Council undertook to divide its territory in New England among its individual members. To one of the twenty a portion about Cape Ann was allotted, but the patent for it was transferred by purchase to Plymouth. There a fishing-station was established by merchants in the west of England. The settlers there were suffered by Plymouth to remain. Conant, who had left Plymouth out of dislike for the religious system of the Pilgrims, became their head. Lyford and another delinquent, Oldham, both of whom had been expelled from Plymouth, joined them. In 1626, the Dorchester merchants dissolved their partnership and gave up their settlement. Only Conant and a few others remained there. These withdrew to Naumkeag, afterwards called Salem. The short-lived activity of this unincorporated Dorchester company was succeeded by another undertaking, which took its rise in the same place, but was quite different, both in its purposes and results.

Mason's grant of New Hampshire.

Conant at Salem.

The great Puritan emigration which gave rise to the settlements on Massachusetts Bay was undertaken, not by "Separatists," but by members of the Church of England who had never broken off their connection with it, or called in question the lawfulness of a national church. James I., when he was on the way from Scotland to London, was met by the "Millenary petition," in which upwards of eight hundred

The Puritan emigration.

ministers of the Established Church prayed for the abolition of pluralities and kindred abuses, and besought that certain practices, such as the sign of the cross in baptism, the interrogatories to infants, the use of the cap and surplice, might be discarded. At the subsequent conference at Hampton Court, the Puritan divines whom the King selected to be the spokesmen of their party, were treated with insult and derision. "If this be all that your party have to say," said the King, "I will make them conform, or I will harry them out of this land, or else worse." He took care to keep his word. He is not to be blamed for refusing on that occasion to incorporate in the creed of the Anglican Church new doctrinal articles, rigidly Calvinistic in their tenor, nor can he be blamed for not imposing the desired modifications in the liturgy on those of his subjects who might be in conscience averse to them. It is another question, however, whether he might not have granted a measure of liberty in matters of ritual without creating fresh contentions and divisions. There is no doubt that his spirit in dealing with so large a body of educated and earnest preachers, whose services it was most important to retain, was insolent and arbitrary. Thenceforward the Puritan clergy either conformed, unwillingly and under protest, to the particular ceremonies of which they disapproved, or abstained from doing so, preferring to endure the appointed penalties until a better day should come. Thus the Puritans were composed of a conforming and a non-conforming class. In their long struggle during the whole reign of James, and in the early years of his successor, in proportion as their hope of getting freedom for themselves and of making England what they thought it ought to be, waned, they would naturally revolve the question whether it might not be feasible to found a new community, to be modelled after their own ideas, beyond

Tyranny of James I.

the Atlantic. If their dissatisfaction with the Anglican ecclesiastical system was by degrees becoming more radical, it was a silent change, which had not grown to be a conscious, definite conviction.

The most influential of the early promoters of the movements which led to the settlement of Massachusetts was John White, rector in Dorchester. In his parish there were many who made voyages to America for fishing and trade. It was White who had put up the shipowners to begin the settlement at Cape Ann, his motive being a desire to promote the welfare of the mariners visiting that coast. He wrote to Conant to stay with the remnant of settlers at Naumkeag. Consultations were held in Lincolnshire and in London, as well as in the west country. In March, 1628, a grant of lands was made by the Council of New England to John Endicott and others. It included the territory from the Atlantic to the Western Ocean, and from a line three miles to the north of the Merrimac to a line three miles to the south of the Charles. Endicott himself, who was a strict Puritan, crossed the ocean with a small company, and took the place of Conant as head of the settlement at Naumkeag, which, as a memorial of the pacifying of the differences between Conant's people and the new-comers, received the name of Salem. Preparations were soon made for another settlement at Charlestown. Endicott visited Morton's company, or the remnant of it, at Merry-Mount, as they now called the place, caused their May-pole to be cut down, and "rebuked them for their profaneness." Later, as we have seen, this disorderly settlement was broken up by the Plymouth people. Early in 1629, the Dorchester Company was much enlarged, and procured a royal charter under the name of the "Governor and Company of Massachusetts Bay in New England." Besides

Endicott and the others with him, to whom the grant of land had been made, there appear in the list of patentees the names of Saltonstall, Theophilus Eaton, and others familiar afterwards in New England history. The company was authorized to elect from their own members a Governor, Deputy-Governor, and eighteen Assistants, and to frame laws and ordinances, not repugnant to the laws of England, for the regulation of their own doings, and for the government of the inhabitants of their territory. They were empowered to defend their colonies by force of arms against all invaders and disturbers. On the subject of religious liberty nothing was said. The corporation provided that there should be a local governor, and Endicott was continued in that office. With him were to be associated thirteen counsellors, a majority of them to be appointed by the Company. In their instructions to the settlers, they were told to remember that the propagation of the Gospel was to be the principal aim, to make fair bargains with the Indians for the land, to send home persons disaffected with their government.

Endicott was immediately reinforced by four hundred and thirty-two fresh emigrants, eighty of whom were women, and twenty-six were children. The vessels brought over tools, fire-arms, together with a large number of cattle and goats. *Endicott reinforced.* A part of the new-comers settled at Charlestown. Two of the four ministers who came over were Samuel Skelton and Francis Higginson, who remained at Salem. Higginson was a non-conformist divine who was held in high esteem. He had been a rector at Leicester, and when he was silenced by the government he became a "lecturer" to his former parishioners. He wrote home, expressing his pleasure at the appearance of the Salem colony. "But," he added, "that which is our greatest comfort and means of defence above all other is, that we have here the true religion and holy ordinances of Almighty God taught among us." There now occurred an event of great consequence in its relation to the subsequent history of New England. This was the formation of a church, and the election of Skelton and Higginson to be its ministers; the former as "pastor," and the latter as "teacher." "Every fit member" took part in the election. Skelton was then set apart for his office, Higginson and several of the "gravest" men laying their hands on his head, and prayer being offered. In the same way Higginson was inducted into office. The meeting was called by Endicott. Contrary to the common representation, it is clear from the letter of a witness who was on the ground, that the forming of the church, on the basis of a simple covenant, preceded the choice of the ministers. It is not true, therefore, that the community at large, or the prominent persons in it, acted in this matter as a parish, distinct from a church, might be conceived to act. At a later meeting the organization was completed by the choice of elders and deacons, the number of members being raised to thirty. It is not probable that on this occasion the ministers were ordained anew. The steps taken were in full accord with the method of "the Separatists," which had been deemed by the non-conforming Puritans reprehensible. Both the ministers, it should be remembered, were ordained clergymen in the Church of England. But the idea at the basis of these proceedings was that ordination and installation were equivalent, and that each signified the placing of a minister as an officer over a flock, by an appropriate religious rite. In the later system of Congregationalism, ordination to the ministry came to be regarded as distinct from installation, and took place once for all. It was not so at the beginning. Another remarkable circumstance

The first Congregational church.

is to be noticed. There came from the Plymouth church a delegation to recognize fraternally the new ecclesiastical organization at Salem. On the day appointed for the consummation of the act, when the covenant was renewed, Governor Bradford and his associates arrived in season to express their approbation and fellowship. *Fellowship with the Plymouth church.* Before the arrival of Skelton and Higginson, Endicott had found occasion to request the physician at Plymouth, Samuel Fuller, to come to Salem to minister to the sick. After Fuller's return, Endicott wrote to Bradford a cordial letter. Referring to Fuller, he says: "I rejoice much that I am by him satisfied touching your judgments of the outward forms of God's worship." "It is," Endicott adds, "far different from the common report that hath been spread of you touching that particular." The "Separatists" were not so far out of the way as he had thought them to be. Robinson's prediction was fulfilled, that his people would not find themselves at variance with their non-conformist Puritan brethren, as soon as both found themselves at a distance from the scenes of former controversy. Moreover, not only was a church, distinct from the christened members of the parish, formed at Salem, after the method of the Independents, but the Prayer-book was dropped. It is clear that the Salem colonists, when removed beyond the bounds of the Established Church and hierarchy of England, and free to think and to act for themselves, fell back on what they now considered to be the models of Scripture. In the matter of ecclesiastical changes they advanced at once to the goal which, imperceptibly to themselves, they had been really approaching. The non-conforming emigrants who came later followed in the same path.

But these proceedings at Salem were not pleasing to all. Two brothers, John and Samuel Browne, were members of the Council. They did not approve the disuse of the Book of Common Prayer, and, with some others who were inclined to join them, proposed to hold meetings by themselves. The ministers, they said, were Separatists, and would be Anabaptists. Finding "their speeches and practices tending to mutiny and faction," Endicott, on the return of the vessels the same year, sent them back to England. When the Brownes made complaint to the Company, alarm was felt lest the occurrence might give rise to difficulties with the Government. An official letter was written to Endicott expressing this apprehension and advising caution. What had been done, however, was consistent with the instructions of the Company. It was intended that there should be uniformity in worship in the settlement. There was no idea of establishing a colony where diverse forms of faith and modes of worship should subsist side by side. Whatever judgment may be passed upon the founders of Massachusetts in this matter, it is clear enough that a struggle for predominance between the rival sects, if such sects had been allowed, would have immediately ensued. The main purpose which the colonists had in view in crossing the ocean would have been frustrated. "A conventicle of a score of persons might be harmless; but how long would the conventicle be without its surpliced priest, and when he had come, how far in the distance would be a bishop armed with the powers of the High Commission?" These are the words of an American historian, Dr. Palfrey. "It may be," writes a candid English historian, Mr. Gardiner, "that the rulers of the little community were wise in their resolution. Their own religious liberty would have been in danger if a population had grown up around them ready to offer a helping hand to any repressive measures of the home

Government." Obviously the difficulty back of all such conflicts in those days, whether in England or America, was that, in the absence of a commonly accepted principle of religious liberty, each party, in case its opponent should get the power, had nothing to look for but subjugation. For one party to give ecclesiastical freedom to its adversary was to forge an instrument for its own destruction. Then it must be borne in mind that a colony is to be distinguished from a full-blown State. The colony is midway between the family and the State. The conditions of safety for a political community in its cradle are not the same as when it has outlived the days of weakness. Another English historian, Mr. Doyle, who has no predilection for the Puritans, justly remarks: "We must not condemn the banishment of the Brownes unless we are prepared to say that it would have been better for the world if the Puritan colony of Massachusetts had never existed." It is often said that elsewhere the experiment of different sects living side by side was successful. Rhode Island is adduced as an example. But Rhode Island for most of the seventeenth century was in a state bordering on anarchy, and might have been in a worse condition had it not been for the stable and well-ordered governments in the neighboring colonies. Maryland is also referred to as an example. But among the settlers of Maryland there was not that intense interest in religion which prevailed among the Massachusetts colonists, and was the mainspring in all of their doings. There were not the same materials for a conflict on this subject. We have seen, moreover, that the Proprietary in Maryland was, in fact, obliged to constrain, and even to exclude from the colony, certain overzealous religious propagandists. When religious discussion at length became sharp, toleration gave way. As for Pennsylvania, not to dwell here on other differences, it was settled a half century later than Massachusetts, at a time when the fervor of religious controversy was beginning to abate, and when the impolicy of coercion in these matters was more widely discerned. Endicott sailed to Massachusetts fifteen years before Penn was born. Pennsylvania was founded only seven years before William of Orange came to the throne. By that time experience had done a great deal to evince the inutility of coercion in matters of conscience. The New England Puritans in some cases erred on the side of harshness, even in carrying out their own principles, aside from the character of the principles themselves. But whatever may be set down, fairly or unfairly, to their discredit, on the score of intolerance, it is undeniable that they founded great and enlightened commonwealths. That a better result would have ensued had they—the circumstances being what they were—pursued a system more consonant with modern ideas, is a speculative opinion, which, of course, it is impossible to bring to any practical test.

Endicott's colony was only the forerunner of Puritan emigration on a larger scale. The aspect of public affairs in England soon became more threatening than ever. In March, 1629, Charles I. dismissed his third Parliament, and entered on the experiment, which was continued for eleven years, of governing England without a Parliament. All signs portended either the ruin of civil liberty or the outbreaking of civil war. In 1628, William Laud was appointed Bishop of London, and was rising to the rank of the King's principal adviser in ecclesiastical matters. He was introducing that system of tyranny which eventually brought him, like his royal master, to the block. His policy, as petty as it was inquisitorial and arbitrary, was put into action to extinguish Puritan opinions, and to

Tyranny of Charles I.

Laud.

punish with imprisonment and death all deviations from the established ceremonies. A large number of men of birth and fortune, residing in different places, after consultation with one another, decided that it was expedient to lay the foundations of a new England across the sea, where the principles which they cherished might take root and flourish, beyond the reach of regal and prelatical despotism. In 1630, the Company of Massachusetts Bay took the bold step of transferring itself and its charter, and thus the whole government of its colonists, to its American settlement. Transfer of the Massachusetts Company to New England. There was no legal obstacle in the way of such a transfer. One of the men who had promised to emigrate in case this movement should be agreed upon was John Winthrop, a native of Groton, in Suffolk. He belonged to an ancient family and was possessed John Winthrop. of a good estate. In his youth he had strong inclinations to the ministry, but he concluded to take up legal studies. A man of profound religious convictions, he was in full sympathy with the Puritan cause, and ready to undergo any sacrifice for the promotion of it. At this time, Winthrop was forty years of age. His name is inseparably associated with the history of Massachusetts. He blended a resolute will with a calm and magnanimous spirit. Allowing for the unavoidable difference between a Puritan gentleman of that day, and a Virginia gentleman upwards of a century later, we may discern points of likeness between Winthrop and Washington. Both are marked by a certain grave self-control and dignity of character.

The Massachusetts Company chose Winthrop for its Governor for one year. Among his associates were other persons scarcely inferior in social standing. Such were the Deputy-Governor, Humphrey, and Isaac Johnson, sons-in-law of the Earl of Lincoln, and also the steward of his household, Thomas Dudley. Dudley had fought on the Protestant side in France. He was a man more austere in his character than Winthrop. The bulk of the emigrants then, as afterwards, belonged to the middle class of Englishmen who had experienced the uplifting influence of an earnest religious faith. It may be observed here that a large majority of the original settlers of New England were from the eastern counties of the mother country. The expedition departed in eleven ships, carrying about seven hundred emigrants. These were followed in the course of the year by about three hundred others. From the ship in which Winthrop was about to sail, he and some of his associates sent an address to their "brethren in and of the Church of England." "We esteem it," they said, 'an honor to call the Church of England, from whence we rise, our dear mother, and cannot part from our native country, where she specially resideth, without much sadness of heart and many tears in our eyes." These words were utterances of the heart, but they were not intended to refer to the prelatical government or the legal forms of worship of the religious community from which the authors of the address were parting. In their minds the Church was far more than these, and separable from them. They had no thought of being considered a body of schismatics. It is often forgotten at the present day that the form which Protestant Christianity would finally take in England was yet to be determined. The ferment was not over; the crystallization was still in the future. Within less than a score of years from the departure of Winthrop, Puritanism was for the time completely in the ascendant in Church and State. The most of Winthrop's company, it must be supposed, as far as ecclesiastical arrangements are concerned, were in a state of mind in which the progress to Independency would cost no struggle. Not otherwise can we account

The great emigration to Massachusetts.

for their adoption of that system as soon as they reached their new abode.

On June 22d (N. S.), the Arbella, with Winthrop on board, arrived at Salem. He found the colony there in a distressed condition. Many had died, many were sick, and provisions were scanty. One of the ships was sent back to England to bring new supplies of food. Charlestown was selected as the place of settlement. The new-comers, however, found it expedient to divide. Watertown, Roxbury, and some other places were settled by different sections of them. At Charlestown a church was organized. The proceeding was similiar to that which had taken place at Salem. John Wilson, a graduate of Cambridge, who had been a clergyman at Sudbury, in Suffolk, was chosen to be the minister. He was set apart by the imposition of hands, without renouncing the ordination which he had received in the Church of England. *The new settlement.*

The distribution of land was after the plan which had been pursued by the Virginia Company. To the shareholders were given two hundred acres for every fifty pounds subscribed, together with a due portion of the expected profits from trade. If an emigrant, the shareholder was to have fifty additional acres, and the same number for each member of his family. Fifty acres were to belong to each emigrant who was not a shareholder. Discretionary power was given to the Governor and Council to add to the last appropriation, in particular cases. *Allotment of land.*

The colony, notwithstanding its strength and ample preparations, had to pass through an experience of privation and misery like that which befell previous settlements. Winter arrived before the people were at all prepared to encounter its rigor. Even before the beginning of December, not less than two *Sufferings of the colony.*

hundred died. Among them was Lady Arbella Johnson, the wife of one of the leading settlers. Her bereaved husband soon followed her. About a hundred disheartened sufferers returned to England. Through all the trials of that period, Winthrop was serene and steadfast. As far as the duties of his office allowed, he labored with his own hands, inspiriting all around him by his example. Early in February, a welcome supply of food arrived. The Governor found it expedient, in connection with many others, to remove to the other side of the river, to a site which received the name of Boston. The English town of that name was familiar to a portion of the settlers. There the Assistants met and the public business of the colony was transacted.

At first the Governor and Assistants were chosen by the body of freemen. These met four times in the year, and by them the laws were enacted. But it was found inconvenient to hold these meetings, and in October, 1630, it was left to the Assistants to elect the Governor and Deputy-Governor, and to frame the laws. But this arrangement, which put so much power in the hands of the Assistants, gave rise to disaffection. In 1631, the inhabitants of Watertown refused to pay a tax which the Assistants had levied. The result was that a representative body was established. Two delegates were to be chosen by each town, and the body of delegates was to determine questions of taxation. Soon another change was made. The legislative authority, which had been vested in the freemen, was handed over to the General Court, which consisted of the delegates from the towns, with the Governor and Council. A democratic tendency developed itself. With this tendency, Winthrop, although he did not covet power for himself, and aimed at nothing but the public good, did not sympathize. Later, when the people of Connecticut were forming a government, he wrote to them: "The best part of a community is always the least, and of that least part the wiser are still less." In the impartial administration of his office he could not avoid giving offence to some. For a while his popularity declined. In 1634, he was not chosen Governor. A proposition from leading Puritans in England to join the colony, provided it would establish distinctions of rank, received no favor. In 1644, the deputies began to sit as a distinct body. The form of government was now assimilated to the English model. There was one feature in the political arrangements of marked importance. As early as May, 1631, it was determined that none should be admitted to the exercise of political privileges except members of churches. The motive assigned was that "the body of the commons may be possessed of good and honest men." It was a kind of theocratic system of rule. The founders adopted a test which they deemed to be most likely to secure the blessing of good government, and "to shut out from their counsels the emissaries of Wentworth and Laud"—the minister and the prelate who were working together for the civil and ecclesiastical enslavement of England.

The deputies a distinct body.

The "theocracy."

The Congregational system gave to each local church the complete power of self-government, at the same time it was held that all the churches were bound to stand in fraternal relations one with another, and to exercise a mutual "watch and care," analogous to the care of each church over its individual members. But the settlers of Massachusetts, in common with Calvinists generally, while they denied to the State the power to control the Church within its own province, nevertheless ascribed to the civil authority the right and obligation to promote the unity and well-being of the

Congregationalism.

churches, repress ecclesiastical disorder, and protect orthodox doctrine against heretical assaults. Thus the autonomy of the several churches was qualified by the superintendence of the General Court. The undefined extent of this jurisdiction of the civil power left room for contentions to arise between the central and the local authority.

If Winthrop and his associates cherished the hope of religious unity in the wilderness to which they had withdrawn, their hope was speedily disappointed. The first serious difficulty was connected with Roger Williams. Less than a year after their arrival he made his appearance among them. Williams was of Welsh extraction, was educated at Cambridge, and was befriended in his youth by Sir Edward Coke. He was a man of uncommon talents, of sincere piety, and of a kindly spirit. He was also of a restless temperament, with a certain antagonistic element in his nature which made him a born polemic and propagandist. He was an enthusiast, lacking that ingredient of hatred which turns the enthusiast into the fanatic. Williams was an extreme "Separatist," standing about where Robinson stood in the early stage of his mental progress before he attained a more catholic outlook. Williams maintained that it was a sin to recognize any of the parish churches in England as true churches. It was a sin, he contended, even to hear their pastors preach. He refused to minister in the church at Boston, because it had not publicly renounced its fellowship with the churches as well as the Church of England. He wrote a paper to disprove the right of the King to grant the patent, which was the constitution of the colony. He took no steps to diffuse this doctrine, but the broaching of it in a written dissertation naturally created alarm. It opened the prospect of a collision with the English authorities, who would be ready enough to take notice of proofs of disloyalty in the Puritan colony. Next, Williams, at Salem, where he became the assistant of Skelton, persuaded Endicott to cut the cross out of the royal ensign, an act involving more peril than the dangerous theory about the unlawfulness of the patent. Along with all this hazardous teaching, he likewise affirmed that the magistrates had no right to administer to those who were not freemen an oath of loyalty to the colony, since he deemed it in every case a sin to administer an oath to the unconverted. This was at a time when the administration of this oath was deemed essential to the safety of the colony. Such were the sincerity and eloquence of the young Welshman that he won influence, especially in the Salem church. In connection with various notions which even now would be generally characterized as whimseys, Williams promulgated an opinion which was novel at that time, but one that has obtained so wide an acceptance as to confer on him lasting distinction. He asserted that there ought to be no interference by the State in matters of religious belief and worship, except so far as is necessary for the maintenance of civil order. This doctrine of "soul-liberty" was not one of the main grounds of his expulsion from the colony, and is not made prominent in his own account of it. But it ripened in his mind into an immovable conviction, and was the corner-stone of the political community which he founded. The General Court, by a not very large majority, passed a vote to banish him. To avoid being sent back to England, in January, 1636, he left Salem, accompanied by a few friends, leaving his family behind him, and "after being sorely tossed for fourteen weeks, not knowing what bread or bed did mean," he reached the shores of the Narraganset. He had been the sole minister at Salem since 1634, and might have remained there until spring

Williams founds Providence.

had he not refused to desist from preaching in his own house. He had been advised by Winthrop to betake himself to the country of the Narragansets. There he planted the city of Providence, on lands which he purchased from the Indians. In his dealings with the Indians he was invariably just and humane. More than any other Englishman he was trusted by them. He never felt any malice towards the Puritans of Massachusetts. He spared no effort, and shrank from no danger, in order to prevent Indian attacks upon them. For Winthrop he had a special attachment. When hard questions are to be solved, or troubles spring up in his own settlement, it is to Winthrop that he turns for counsel.

During the period of the troubles respecting Roger Williams, the colony was strengthened by large reinforce *Increased emigration.* ments from England. Laud was promoted to the Archbishopric of Canterbury. Thenceforward there was no security for high or low who ventured to deviate in any particular from the ceremonial laws. In that year not less than seven hundred Englishmen came over to Massachusetts, among whom were men of remarkable talents and of high repute at home. In one of the parties were John Haynes, a rich landholder from Essex, and three eminent ministers—Stone, Hooker, and *Hooker and Stone.* Cotton. Of these Hooker and Cotton were the most distinguished. All three were educated at Emmanuel College, Cambridge, a great nursery of Puritan preachers. It is a proof of the esteem in which Thomas Hooker had been held in England, that a petition to Laud to revoke the decree that silenced him, was signed by forty-seven conforming ministers. He escaped to Rotterdam, where he became a colleague of Dr. Ames, a famous Independent preacher, whose influence on his opinions, and on Cotton and other English ministers, helps to explain the modification of their ecclesiastical views.

Hooker returned to England and contrived to elude the agents of Laud by going on shipboard in disguise. John Cotton had ministered for many years with eminent success in the great church of St. Botolph, in Boston, a large town, a few miles from the sea-coast of Lincolnshire. The high esteem of the Bishop of the diocese did not avail to shield him from the persecution of Laud. After being concealed in London, he succeeded in going on board a ship in the Downs, and made a safe passage across the ocean. He was chosen to be the colleague of Wilson in the Boston church. Stone and Hooker settled at Newtown. In the autumn of 1635, Henry Vane, then only twenty-three years of age, arrived in Massachusetts. His religious feelings and his zealous sympathy with Puritanism had moved him to join the colony. The distinction of his family, the high station of his father, who was a Privy Counsellor, and his own attractive qualities made him at once a leader—a position which he was quite prompt to assume. At that moment there was no little dissension among the principal men. Winthrop was thought by Dudley and others to have been too lenient in his administration. In a free conference explanations were made and good feeling was restored. In the spring of 1636, Vane was chosen Governor, as the successor of Haynes, who had followed Dudley, and Winthrop was chosen Deputy-Governor. There was a conservative party, which had the support of Cotton, that was averse to making changes in civil officers; but the popular feeling ran the other way. *Arrival of Vane.* *Vane chosen Governor.*

A more serious difficulty than the trouble caused by the proceedings of Roger Williams and his novel opinions, was occasioned by the arrival in Boston, in 1634, of Mrs. Ann Hutchinson. Among the sects which arose in the wake of the Reformation, those denominated Familists, Antinomians, and Anabaptists, were in *Mrs. Ann Hutchinson.*

the highest degree obnoxious to the Protestant leaders. They were held in abhorrence by the Puritan settlers, not only because their opinions were considered heretical, but, also, because their tenets and practices were believed to be subversive both of morality and of civil order. A sweeping condemnation of all the sectaries who bore these names is far from being sustained by an impartial study of the facts. Nevertheless, there was enough in the records of the past to account for the intense feeling of antipathy and dread which prevailed respecting them. Mrs. Hutchinson was a clever woman, absorbed in religious thoughts and speculations, and eager to diffuse her ideas. When her house in Boston began to be thronged twice in the week by women, for whose edification she reviewed, in a critical way, the sermons of the previous Sunday; when it was noised abroad that she was unsparing in her judgments of the clergy, all of whom, with the exception of Mr. Cotton and her brother-in-law, Mr. Wheelwright, were declared to be in darkness in regard to fundamental points of Christian truth, to be under a "covenant of works," and not under a "covenant of grace;" and when her own teaching appeared to be of a piece with the mystical and Antinomian teaching of the Familists, a wide-spread anxiety and strenuous opposition were awakened. It was one of her peculiar doctrines that the Holy Spirit is personally united with the soul of every true believer.

Her opinions.

Another of her opinions was that a salvable condition is not proved by sanctification or a good life, but by an immediate, inward revelation to the soul. The resurrection, she taught, is spiritual, and takes place at conversion. Her theories were looked upon by the clergy as pernicious in their practical tendencies, and capable of being turned into a warrant for looseness of life. But her own life was pure, and there were many who were drawn into sympathy with her ideas. This was the case with young Vane. The greater part of the Boston church were of the same mind. Even Cotton, whom in England she had admired as a preacher, for a while did not oppose her, and was counted by her friends, and even by some of her clerical opponents, as one of her adherents. Wheelwright was an ardent supporter of her opinions. On a fast-day, appointed partly to allay "dissensions" in the churches, he preached an exciting sermon. It was considered by the magistrates to be seditious in its spirit, and even to hint at the use of force; although this last accusation does not appear to be warranted by a candid construction of its meaning. An ecclesiastical synod sat at Newtown for three weeks. Eighty-two opinions having, it was alleged, more or less currency, were pronounced erroneous.

Wheel-wright's sermon.

The preponderance of numbers was decidedly with the adversaries of the new views. The Boston church had to give way. Cotton joined with his colleague, Wilson, in condemning the offensive tenets, respecting the character and bearing of which he professed to have been misinformed. Mrs. Hutchinson was publicly examined by the ministers, was at last excommunicated by the church, and obliged to leave the colony. Wheelwright was banished. Six years afterwards, he wrote letters asking pardon for the vehement and censorious spirit which he had shown. He had failed, he confesses, to set his opinions in a clear light, in distinction from hurtful errors advocated by others. The sentence of banishment against him was recalled. His writings show him to have been a trained theologian and a writer of uncommon force. An order of the court was passed to the effect that none should be received "to inhabite" within their jurisdiction "but such as should be allowed by some of the Magistrates." Winthrop published a "Defence" of this decree, in which he writes, in reference to the case of Wheelwright: "If we conceive and find by sadd experience that his opinions are such, as by his own profession, cannot stand with externall peace, may we not provide for our peace, by keeping off such as would strengthen him, and infect others with such dangerous tenets?" The victory of the Conservatives was complete. In 1637, Vane was superseded by Winthrop. The election was warmly contested. It was felt by many that the fate of the community depended on the result. Judge Sewall says, in a letter to Calamy: "My father has told me many a time, that he and others went on foot from Newbury to Cambridge, fourty miles, on purpose to be made freemen and help to strengthen Govr. Winthrop's Party." Perhaps the theological trouble might have had a peaceful solution had not Vane's leadership been involved in it. He soon returned to England to take part in larger contests. Even Cotton's popularity was shaken for a time. He had thoughts of removing to New Haven; "the true ground whereof," he says, "was an inward loathnesse to be troublesome to godly mindes and a feare of the unprofitableness of my Ministry there [in Massachusetts], where my way was suspected to be doubtfull, and dangerous." In the course taken by the authorities in the whole matter, zeal for orthodoxy was mingled with a sense of the political dangers involved. It deserves to be mentioned that in the midst of the conflict Wheelwright attempted to appeal to the King. The appeal was, of course, disallowed.

Winthrop chosen Governor.

Simultaneously with the troubles within the colony which have been narrated, its freedom was threatened from the side of the English Government. The Massachusetts settlers were aware of the importance of doing nothing to provoke the jealousy or

Danger from England.

excite the hostility of the authorities in England. Their policy was to keep in the shade as far as practicable, until the polity of the new community which they were planting should take firm root. But this coveted quiet they found it impossible to preserve. At the outset, it was natural for Charles I. and his counsellors to think that their scheme of despotic rule in England would be furthered by the voluntary exile of the Puritan emigrants, who were inflexibly hostile to it. But with the rapid increase of emigration which took place as their conspiracy against liberty was carried into effect, another apprehension arose. They began to fear that a new power, involving peril to their designs at home, might be growing up on the other side of the Atlantic. Moreover, disaffected persons who returned to England, whether of their own accord or by compulsion, brought forward their accusations and complaints. Laud and his party took alarm at the representations that were made concerning the spirit and doings of the transatlantic colony. One Ratcliffe, who had been severely punished for what Winthrop styles "most foul, scandalous invectives against our churches and government," was voluble in his charges of disloyalty against the settlers. Another enemy in England was Morton. He was the same who had been seized by Standish, and sent home. The next year he came back to Mount Wollaston, but for ill-treatment of the Indians and various "misdemeanors" he was again shipped to England by the magistrates of Massachusetts. One Gardiner was a third, who for like offences was expelled from the colony, having been previously punished with severity. In 1634, an order in Council detained "divers ships now in the river of Thames ready to sail to" New England. The reason assigned was the frequent departure thither of so many ill-affected persons, "discontented not only with civil but ecclesiastical government." Early in 1635, news came to Boston of an intention to send out a General Governor for New England, and of the creation of a special commission, with Laud at its head, for the unrestricted management of all the American colonies, and for the annulling of their charters. An order of the Council required the transmission of the charter of Massachusetts. The crisis put to the test the prudence and the courage of the colonists. Everything that was prized by them, and for the sake of which they had made such sacrifices—many of them casting away ease and affluence and prospective honor in their native land—was now in jeopardy. The men of Massachusetts were equal to the occasion. It was resolved to erect fortifications on Castle Island, and to drill "unskilful men" in military exercises. Dudley, Winthrop, and others were appointed to direct and command in any war that "might befall for the space of a year next ensuing." This was in September, 1634. In January of the next year the advice of the ministers was invited. "They all agreed," says Winthrop, "that, if a General Governor were sent, we ought not to accept him, but to defend our lawful possessions (if we were able); otherwise to avoid or to protract." In March, further preparations for armed resistance were made. The cannon were to be mounted at the fort, and beacons were made ready to be kindled on the discovery of danger. In order to procure a sufficient supply of bullets, they were made a legal tender of the value of a farthing apiece. This was the only answer rendered by Massachusetts to the demand for the transmission of her charter.

Commission for ruling the colonies.

Heroic spirit of the colony.

In April, 1635, the Council of New England, despairing of success in its undertakings, surrendered its charter to the King, on condition that its territory, a great part of which had been given away in patents, should be apportioned among its several members. The project which had been formed for destroying the rights and privileges of Massachusetts fell to the ground when it was on the verge of an attempted realization. Mason, who was one of its principal authors, died. Gorges, another leading instigator of it, who was to be the General Governor, was now old and took no steps to carry out the plan. More than all things else, it was the situation of public affairs in England that saved the colony from the threatened attack on its liberties. The contest provoked by Laud's attempt to force Episcopacy on Scotland, and by the struggle respecting ship-money, diverted attention from the affairs of a remote settlement. The Massachusetts patent was for the time safe. *Council of New England surrenders its charter.*

When Roger Williams left Salem, he spent the winter among the Pokanoket Indians. The natives were always friendly to him. Had he been able to carry out his ardent wish, he would have spent his life alone among them as a missionary. He had no difficulty in obtaining from the chiefs of the Narragansetts a grant of land at the head of the Bay. There he planted the settlement to which he gave the name of Providence. As soon as he had received enough from the sales of land to settlers to make good what he had paid out, he gave farms to new-comers without charge. With twelve other "masters of families," he formed a republican government. They were to admit whomsoever a majority of them should approve, to a share in their privileges. Constraint was to be allowed in civil affairs only. In 1638, Williams was immersed by an Anabaptist named Holyman, and then he himself immersed Holyman and ten others. There was thus constituted the first Baptist church in America. But the restless spirit of Williams did not permit him long to remain content in this new ecclesiastical connection. He had doubts about *Roger Williams and his colony.*

a rite which had come down through the channel of the national and hierarchical churches. He was consistent at least in his undying antipathy to these organizations. He continued a Baptist about three months. Thenceforward he stood aloof from all church fellowship, and became, like Vane and others, one of the "Seekers," who waited for a revived apostolate, and looked for a new heavens and a new earth. However erratic he might be in his opinions, and pugnacious in the assertion of them, he was never weary in well doing.

A number of those who were on the side of Mrs. Hutchinson, including William Coddington, John Clarke, Mr. Hutchinson and the members of his family, were persuaded by Roger Williams, instead of going to Delaware Bay or Long Island, as they at first designed, to settle on the beautiful island of Aquetnet, which lay beyond the limits embraced in the Plymouth patent. These nineteen persons united in a body politic, entering into a covenant with one another to obey the laws of God. They bought the island—which was afterwards called the Isle of Rhodes, or Rhode Island—for "forty fathom of white beads." But dissensions soon arose in the little company, in which "individualism" was so potent a force. Coddington and his adherents removed to the southern end of the island, and named their place of settlement *Newport*. Those who were left behind called their town *Portsmouth*. Before long the two plantations were politically united. Coddington was chosen Governor.

<small>Settlement of Rhode Island.</small>

Wheelwright, on his expulsion from Massachusetts, moved northward and planted on a branch of the Piscataqua River a settlement that received the name of *Exeter*. Other adherents of Mrs. Hutchinson's party migrated to Cocheco, or *Dover*, which had been first settled as early as 1623. In 1637, one George Burdet, who had been employed for a

<small>The settlements in New Hampshire.</small>

year or two as a preacher at Salem, was accepted at Dover as a minister. He was extremely hostile to the Massachusetts Puritans, if he had not been their secret enemy from the beginning. He acted as a spy of Laud. Knollys, an Anabaptist of the Antinomian type, collected a church after Burdet left. He was equally inimical to the Massachusetts colony. Captain John Underhill was elected Governor at Dover. He was a zealous Antinomian in the Hutchinson controversy, was disfranchised, and subsequently was banished from Massachusetts. He had made at Boston a public confession of gross immorality, as well as of slanderous utterances against the magistrates, but no faith was put in the sincerity of his professed penitence.

The ambition of Gorges to fill the post of Governor-General was frustrated by the course of events. When the Council of New England, in 1635, was dissolved, a large district fell to him as his share of the territory. In 1638, he procured a charter from the King, making him the Lord Proprietary of this extensive region, lying between the Piscataqua and Kennebec Rivers, and reaching northward a hundred and twenty miles from the sea. He was made the supreme ruler in Church and State, although it was provided that there should be a representative body of freeholders. He made his son Deputy-Governor, with six Counsellors at his side, who were severally to bear the titles of Chancellor, Field-Marshal, Master of Ordnance, etc. One of the two principal settlements was Agamenticus, or York. The other was Saco. The municipal officers of York comprised the majority of adult males. For about ten years all this titular grandeur was exhibited by a handful of settlers in the forests of Maine.

Gorges' settlements in Maine.

CHAPTER VIII.

NEW ENGLAND FROM THE PLANTING OF CONNECTICUT IN 1636 TO 1688

The Early Settlers in Connecticut—The Migration to Hartford—The Government of the Three Towns—The Founding of New Haven—Its Government—The Fiction of the "Blue Laws"—Settlement at Saybrook—Saybrook Joined to Connecticut—The Pequot War—The New England Confederacy—Commission for the Management of the Colonies—Samuel Gorton—War of the Narragansetts and the Mohegans—Acts of the Confederacy—The Cambridge Synod—John Clarke—Maine and Massachusetts—The Quakers in Massachusetts—The Navigation Law—The Charter of Connecticut—Union of New Haven and Connecticut Colonies—The Royal Commission—King Philip's War—Annulling of the Massachusetts Charter—Royal Government in New England—Andros—Revolution in Massachusetts—Society in New England.

IN the colonization of New England, next in importance to the planting of Massachusetts was the settlement of Connecticut, or of different centres in the territory which now bears this name. There were claims of the Dutch on this region. A Dutch captain, as we have seen, had coasted along the southern shore, discovered the Housatonic River, and explored the Connecticut. The Dutch built a rude fort at Hartford. But the Plymouth people, with their usual promptness in profiting by new openings for trade, had sent up the river a vessel, which fearlessly passed by the guns of this fort, and, in 1633, established a trading station near the mouth of Farmington River, on the site of Windsor.

Early settlers in Connecticut.

John Oldham, with three companions, travelled by land from Dorchester to the Connecticut. After he came back, in a number of Massachusetts towns the project was discussed of emigrating to that region. While this subject was talked over, a party from Dorchester made their way, in 1635, to the neighborhood of the Plymouth factory. A party from Watertown also began a settlement at Wethersfield. A few months later, a company of sixty followed, some of whom, on account of the severity of the winter and their consequent sufferings, returned. The great migration to Connecticut was led by Thomas Hooker, the pastor of the church at Newtown (now Cambridge). From the time of his arrival in Massachusetts, his character and talents had commanded the highest respect. Every effort was made to induce him, and those who proposed to accompany him, to continue in the colony. John Haynes was the leading layman of the party. But their minds were fully made up, partly, perhaps, on grounds that were not avowed. The principal reason assigned for departing was Hooker's opinion that the towns were too near one another. It is not improbable that the Massachusetts political system, with its close union of Church and State, was becoming distasteful to him. Certain it is that in the new community, of which he was to be the principal founder, that system was not adhered to. More than the leaders in Massachusetts he believed in popular rights and the diffusion of political power. In the spring of 1636, Hooker and Stone, with their congregation, comprising the women and children as well as the men, one hundred in all, set out on their pilgrimage through the woods, driving their cattle before them. Their prudent arrangements made their journey, in the beautiful season which they chose for it, comparatively easy. At the end of a fortnight they reached Hartford. People from

The great migration to Hartford.

Dorchester and Watertown followed in the course of the summer. Emigrants from Roxbury, led by William Pynchon, selected as the site for their settlement the place afterwards known as Springfield. In the first year the government of the settlements was in the hands of a Commission appointed by the Massachusetts authorities. The rights of the Plymouth people, founded on prior occupation, were not duly regarded by the men of Dorchester. At the end of a year no further attempt was made by Massachusetts to exercise jurisdiction over the lower towns on the river, and when the Indian hostilities, into which they were soon plunged, were over, they framed their permanent government. In this act Windsor, Hartford, and Wethersfield united. It is an error, however, to suppose that the towns, prior to this act, considered themselves to be independent communities. Haynes was chosen Governor. In the organic law that was adopted there was no mention made of any exterior authority, either in America or in England. In distinction from Massachusetts, there was no ecclesiastical test for the admission of freemen. The towns might admit to a participation in political rights whomsoever they chose. The Governor was to be elected by the freemen, and Deputies were to be chosen twice in the year. While in Massachusetts non-freemen might propose measures in town-meeting, but were excluded altogether from the suffrage, in Connecticut they were given the right to vote in the choice of Deputies. These, together with the Governor, and at least four magistrates, were to constitute the General Court. At a later time the legislative body was divided into two houses. "The rule of the Word of God," in the absence of special enactments, was to be recognized. There were no oaths of allegiance required except to "the jurisdiction." The new State was independent. Provision was soon made for the incorporation of new towns, on the model of the towns in Massachusetts.

In the founding of the colony of New Haven, John Davenport was the clerical leader. Davenport was the son of a Mayor of Coventry. As minister of St. Stephen's Church, Coleman Street, London, he had provoked by his Puritan ways the displeasure of Laud, and being driven abroad, had served for some time as the minister of an English congregation in Amsterdam. He came over to America in 1637, bringing with him Theophilus Eaton, an opulent London merchant, who had been one of his parishioners at St. Stephen's. They declined to comply with the solicitation to remain in Massachusetts, and, in the spring of 1638, they planted the place called Quinnipiac, which the next year was named New Haven. On the first Sunday after their landing, Davenport preached in the open air under an oak. After a few days the settlers formed a compact of civil order. They agreed to proceed, in the affairs both of Church and State, according to the rules of the Bible. After taking a year for reflection on the best form of permanent organization, "the free planters," meeting in a spacious barn, determined that seven men should be selected, to settle the form of government. As in Massachusetts, it was determined that the free burgesses, as well as the magistrates, should be composed exclusively of church members. Davenport disavowed the theory that to the Church in all cases belongs, to the exclusion of all others, the right to exercise the powers of government. In his little treatise on the subject, he distinguishes between "a commonwealth yet to be settled" and one "already settled." He defended the peculiar provision of the New Haven Constitution on grounds of expediency. Church membership, he contended, was in this case as good a test as could be found of competence to make a right use of political privileges. At the outset, the laws of Moses, "being neither typical nor ceremonial, nor having any reference to Canaan," were provisionally adopted as the civil code, "till they be branched into particulars." One consequence was that English laws of entail and primogeniture were avoided. Another result was that the number of capital offences, which at that time in England was thirty-one, was reduced to twelve. Much that has been written about the severity of penal legislation in the Connecticut settlements is mythical.

Fiction of the "Blue Laws." The legend of the "Blue Laws" is the invention of Samuel Peters, a mendacious refugee, who, in 1781, published in England a "History of Connecticut." Included in this odd medley of fact and fiction are these grotesque enactments, which never existed except in the imagination of the author of this book. Like the colony having its centre at Hartford, the New Haven colony, as far as its Constitution could make it so, was an independent republic. The settlement of Davenport and Eaton was rapidly strengthened by new-comers. In 1639, Milford was settled, and, about the same time, Guilford.

Towns planted near New Haven.

At first each of the settlements in its government was independent of the others, as was not the case in Connecticut. After certain preparatory steps, the three towns, in 1643, were united in one political community. Eaton was chosen Governor.

The population of the town of New Haven at this time was not far from four hundred. In this estimate are included a large number of servants. The New Haven "planters" were possessed of larger means than the settlers in the other colonies. They had expected to busy themselves mainly in trade and commerce. But the circumstances were such that they were led to devote themselves principally to agriculture.

In 1631, the Earl of Warwick, the President of the Council of New England, made to Lord Say and Sele, Lord Brooke, and certain associates, a grant of territory in New England extending from Narragansett River westward one hundred and twenty miles along the coast of Long Island Sound, and thence to the Pacific. Warwick's authority to bestow this patent has by some been questioned. The patentees, in 1635, gave a commission to the younger John Winthrop to take the rank of Governor, and directing him to build a fort at the mouth of the Connecticut River. Winthrop was educated partly at Trinity College, Dublin, and had travelled on the Continent. Not equal to his father in talents, he was still an accomplished man, of remarkably pleasing manners. He had followed his father to Massachusetts, but on the death of his wife had returned to England. He had now come back, and proceeded to do the work committed to him. He sent a party to the mouth of the river, where with the aid of two cannon which they had mounted, they prevented a Dutch trading vessel from sailing up the stream. A small fort was erected by Lion Gardiner, an engineer whom Winthrop brought over from England. In 1639, George Fenwick, a barrister by profession, established himself there with his family, giving to the place the name of Saybrook. In 1644, for a compensation, he made over the fort, as he was probably authorized to do by the Proprietors, to the government of Connecticut. That colony had lost Springfield, which fell under the jurisdiction of Massachusetts. This loss was partly made up by the acquisition of Saybrook, which had kept the Dutch from acquiring power on the river, and partly, also, by the accession of Southampton on Long Island, a place which had been planted, as an independent settlement, by about forty families from Lynn, in Massachusetts.

Settlement at Saybrook.

Saybrook joined to Connecticut.

When the company led by Hooker and Stone threaded their path through the woods, the pleasure which they found in the songs of the birds and in the spring flowers was not mingled with the dread of hostile Indians. It was the peaceable state of the natives that rendered such a journey safe. But trouble with them was soon to arise. The scattered clans of savages on the west of the Connecticut were tributary to the Mohawks, of whom they stood in fear. East of the Connecticut were the Mohegans, and east of the Mohegans, extending from the River Thames to the western border of Rhode Island, was the territory of the powerful tribe of the Pequots. The terror inspired by this tribe had made the Indians on the Connecticut desirous that the English should settle among them as a means of protection. The Narragansetts, on the east of the Pequots, had with difficulty preserved their independence of them. The Pequots were sly in their proceedings, but their enmity to the whites became constantly more manifest. Murders were committed for which no redress, but only smooth professions and promises, could be obtained. The cruel murder of John Oldham, near Block Island, roused the Massachusetts government to send thither an expedition under Endicott to inflict punishment. But the harsh doings of Endicott at Block Island, and afterward, when he landed among the Pequots, only served to exasperate the savages, without lessening their power. The Pequots endeavored to form an alliance with the Narragansetts, by whom they were disliked but feared. This union, that would have been so dangerous to the whites, was prevented by the magnanimous and courageous interposition of Roger Williams, who, at the risk of his life, spent several days and nights in the settlements of that tribe at the time when the Pequot deputies were with them for

The Pequot War.

The service of Roger Williams.

the purpose of inducing them to form the league. Meantime the cruelties of the Pequots continued. Massachusetts and Plymouth responded to the application of Connecticut for aid. Since the danger was imminent, without waiting for the promised help, Captain John Mason, at the head of ninety men, with an auxiliary force of Mohegans, and of Narragansetts whom he persuaded to join him, succeeded, at the dawn of day, on May 26 (O. S.), 1637, in surprising a large village of the Pequots. A fierce contest ensued, the wigwams were fired, and most of their inmates, as they sought to fly, as well as most of the warriors who were in the combat, were slain. It was a bloody victory. The Indian forces with Mason, such was their terror of the Pequots, afforded no efficient aid. The achievement was the work of the little band of whites. The safety of Connecticut was assured. The remnant of the hostile tribe resolved to join the Mohawks on the Hudson. By them Sassacus, the Pequot chief, a warrior who had reigned over twenty-six subordinate sachems, was killed. The fierce tribe over which he had ruled, was annihilated. By the destruction of the Pequots the eastern colonies were brought into easier communication with Connecticut.

<small>Mason's successful attack.</small>

The next event of capital importance after the Pequot War was the organization of the New England Confederacy, between the four colonies of Plymouth, Massachusetts, Connecticut, and New Haven. American history is the record of a continuous process of union. Distant settlements were brought together under larger colonial jurisdictions. From time to time colonies joined one another in leagues. At last the thirteen colonies combined under a single independent government. An epoch in the history of this progress was the formation of the confederacy of the four New England communities. It had been discussed for

<small>The New England Confederacy.</small>

several years before the contracting parties could agree on the terms of union. The difficulty lay partly in effecting an adjustment by which the preponderance of Massachusetts in population and property should be adequately recognized. In 1643, the hindrances were removed and the Articles of Confederation were signed. The motives of the measure are set down in the preamble. Mention is made of the distance between the colonies, and of the people of several nations and strange languages by which they were encompassed. They felt the need of combining not only for self-protection against the savages, but also for common defence against attacks from the Dutch on the Hudson, which might not improbably occur, as well as against inroads of the French, whose settlements lay on the north and east of the English colonies. The Swedes had begun a plantation on the Delaware, but these were not strong enough to be formidable. Kieft, the Dutch Governor, had already protested against the alleged encroachments of the New Haven people, had driven off a party of English settlers from the western end of Long Island, and had broken up a factory established by New Haven people on the Delaware. Another reason for union was the "sad distractions in England." The issue of the great civil contest there could not be foreseen. It was thought advisable to be in readiness for unknown contingencies. The Puritan colonies might be required to look to themselves alone for counsel and security. Fenwick, who was perhaps arranging to sell the Saybrook fort to Connecticut, participated in the counsels of the framers of the Confederacy. The Articles of Union established "a firm and perpetual" offensive and defensive league between the several communities. Each colony was to retain its independence. No two were to be resolved into one without the consent of the rest. Levies

The terms of Union.

of men, money, and of supplies for war, were to be made on the colonies respectively, according to a defined ratio. In case any colony was invaded, the others were to send relief, the contributions of men and money being proportionately fixed. The business of the Confederacy was to be managed by a Board of Commissioners, two from each colony, all of whom were to be church members. The agreement of six Commissioners was to be required for the adoption of any measure. In the absence of such an agreement, the concurrence of the General Courts of all the colonies was to be binding. The Commissioners were to choose an officer to preside over them, but to have no other prerogatives. The Commissioners were to endeavor to secure peace and concert among the Confederate colonies, and to pursue a firm and just course toward the Indians. Fugitives from justice and runaway servants were to be returned. The Maine settlement of Gorges, between which and the Puritan colonies there was no sympathy, was not embraced in the Confederacy. "They ran," says Winthrop, "a different course from us, both in their ministry and civil administration." The disorderly condition of the Narragansett settlements furnished an additional reason for not including them. Some who had left Massachusetts for Aquetnet returned. Mrs. Hutchinson and her family, dissatisfied with the system adopted there, migrated to a place within the Dutch territory. She, with her whole family, except one daughter, who was taken captive, were massacred by the Indians.

The fall of the royal power in England placed the colonies under the immediate control of Parliament. A few months after the Confederacy was formed, a new Commission was created, of which Warwick was the head, and of which Say and Sele, Vane, Pym, and Cromwell were among the members, for the management of all the English plantations in America. To this commission was given the authority which had been exercised by the Privy Council and by the commission of Laud. Early in 1643, Roger Williams sailed from New Amsterdam for England, in order to procure a charter for Providence and the adjacent settlements on the south. The party then in the ascendant were in sympathy with his ideas concerning liberty of conscience. When in England, he published his "Key to the Indian Languages," and two controversial papers on his favorite theme of "soul-liberty" in reply to Cotton. Williams was aided by his friend Vane, and in March, 1644, a charter was granted him. The three towns of Providence, Portsmouth, and Newport were incorporated as a body politic, under the name of "Providence Plantations," with authority to establish such a form of civil government as a majority of the inhabitants should approve. To the Commissioners there was reserved the power "to dispose the general government" of the community, in respect to its relation to the other colonies, as they might from time to time see fit to determine. After Williams returned with his charter, it was a good while before order emerged out of confusion.

Commission for the management of the Colonies.

Charter to Roger Williams.

No interference with the New England colonies was attempted by the newly created Commission. Nothing beyond advice and persuasion was resorted to by such of the Puritan leaders in England as favored the views of Williams, to mollify the policy of Massachusetts; and this kind of intervention was without effect. It was on Massachusetts that the burdens of the new Confederacy principally fell. This may serve to explain, if it does not excuse, a certain domineering spirit, and an occasional stretch of authority on the part of that colony.

Treatment of the New England Colonies.

At the first meeting of the Commissioners of the Confederacy, in September, 1643, Winthrop was elected president. The right of Connecticut to plant settlements on Long Island, which was denied by the Dutch, was recognized. Indian troubles formed one of the principal subjects of attention. There existed a hostile feeling between Miantonomo and the Narragansetts, of whom he was the chief, on the one part, and the Mohegans, who were ruled by Uncas, on the other. The Mohegans were the friends and allies of the Connecticut settlers. Indications that evil designs against the English were harbored by the Narragansetts had led the Massachusetts authorities to summon their chief to Boston, and to require of him explanations. He had lately sold land to Samuel Gorton and his party, whom the Massachusetts authorities regarded as lawless fanatics and as enemies. Gorton was a clothier from London, an enthusiast who had been expelled from Plymouth for behaving himself "mutinously and seditiously," toward "both magistrates and ministers." He went to the northern settlement on Rhode Island, where he received corporal punishment for abusing the magistrates and decrying their authority. Thence he removed to the north of the river Pawtuxet, near Providence. Roger Williams wrote of him : "Master Gorton, having foully abused high and low at Aquidneck, is now bewitching and bemadding poor Providence, both with his unclean and foul censures of all the ministers of this country (for which myself have in Christ's name withstood him), and also denying all visible and external ordinances in depth of Familism," etc. It was a part of Gorton's theology that the ministry and sacraments have no rightful place among Christian disciples. The previous settlers who lived in his neighborhood applied to the Massachusetts government for protection, and

The Narragansetts.

Samuel Gorton.

placed themselves under its jurisdiction. Then followed communications between the magistrates at Boston and Gorton's people, in which the latter poured out abundant abuse and menaces. Moving over to the south of the river, they purchased land of Miantonomo. The sachems in the vicinity, however, who denied that they owed any allegiance to that chief, refused to sanction the purchase, and they, too, made an application at Boston for protection against the intruders. Then followed a visit of the Narragansett chief himself to Boston, where the dispute with the sachems was decided against him. Possibly anger, provoked by these circumstances, excited in him the determination to carry out at once his thoughts of vengeance. At the head of about a thousand warriors he marched against Uncas; but in a battle fought near the present town of Norwich he was defeated and captured. Uncas was left by the Commissioners, whom he consulted, to decide upon the fate of his prisoner, who had "treacherously plotted and practised" against his life. Apart from other misdeeds with which the Narragansett chief was chargeable, "it was now clearly discovered to us," writes Winthrop, "that there was a general conspiracy among the Indians to cut off all the English, and that Miantonomo was the head and contriver of it." He was put to death by Uncas.

Defeat of the Narragansetts by the Mohegans.

A summons to the Gortonians at Shawomet, the name of their settlement, to appear in Boston and respond to the charges of the neighboring sachems, was answered with railing and contempt. A force of men was then sent which broke up the settlement and brought nine of the company as prisoners to Boston. Among them was Gorton himself. Only a majority vote of the deputies saved him from capital punishment, one of the charges being "enmity to all civil

Capture of Gorton and his party.

authority." The sentence passed was a severe one, but in the course of four or five months the men were released. They were forbidden to remain in Massachusetts, or to go to Providence or Shawomet. They took up their abode on Rhode Island.

The Commissioners of the Confederacy sent to the Swedes on the Delaware a remonstrance against their proceedings in driving out a company of emigrants from New Haven. To this complaint a satisfactory answer was rendered. The Dutch being disposed to attack Connecticut, they were informed that the Confederacy would stand by its members. Massachusetts displeased the Board of Commissioners by allowing a Frenchman, La Tour, who professed to be a Protestant, and was contending with D'Aulnay for the governorship of Acadia, to enlist men in Boston. The Commissioners passed a law forbidding any State to allow troops to go forth "against any people" without the consent of the Confederacy. *Acts of the Confederacy.*

Parliament, when it was victorious in the contest with Charles I., naturally regarded New England with special favor. In 1642, New England was exempted from the payment of import and export duties, which were exacted of the other colonies. Two years later, Massachusetts passed a law making it a penal offence to attempt to create a party in favor of the King. The magistrates ceased to take the oath of allegiance to him. But liberty and self-government, which the people were always resolute in maintaining, had still to be guarded. Massachusetts, not without doubt and misgiving, allowed a commissioned vessel of Parliament to capture a ship in Boston harbor; but later the magistrates refused permission to a ship, not provided with a commission, to seize on a prize in the harbor, and would have sunk the offending vessel if the *Liberty guarded.*

captain had not desisted from his attempt. The political and ecclesiastical revolution in England might afford a plausible pretext to disaffected persons of various sorts to set on foot schemes for subverting the form of government established in Massachusetts. Such people cunningly laid hold of whatever causes of discontent might exist, one of which was the limitation of suffrage to church members.

Among the Puritans in England, the Presbyterians were in the ascendant. The need of union with Scotland in the warfare against the Royalists raised them to power. The Westminster Assembly, which was convoked by Parliament in 1642, adopted their system. In New England the attachment to Independency, or Congregationalism, as it was beginning to be called, was not to be shaken. There was a determination on the part of the clerical leaders, and among the people, not to allow it to be superseded by the Presbyterian any more than by the Episcopal polity. But there arose in Massachu-

Vassall and his party. setts a faction, of which one William Vassall was the head, that really aimed at nothing less than the overthrow of the charter government and the introduction of a Governor-General to be appointed in England. To bring in Presbyterianism was one feature of their revolutionary scheme. A petition with seven signers was presented by them to the Court, calling for reforms and a redress of grievances. An appeal to the authorities in England was threatened in case their wishes were not complied with. Such menaces were always considered treasonable. They involved an attack on the independence of the colony. The magistrates met the exigency with their accustomed spirit. The plotters were arrested and fined. When some of them urged their cause before the Commissioners for the Colonies in England, and when Gorton was also bringing forward his list of accusations, the Legislature of Massachusetts addressed to Parliament a dignified, impressive, and, as it proved, an effectual remonstrance against an interference with their "chartered liberties" and with their "well-being" in "the remote part of the world" to which they had resorted. "Let not succeeding generations have cause to lament"—such was their earnest and pathetic plea—that "these liberties were lost in the season when England itself recovered its own." "We rode out the dangers of the sea," they said, "shall we perish in port?" *Address of Massachusetts to Parliament.*

In 1648, a synod, representing the four Confederate colonies, was assembled at Cambridge, which set forth the Congregational system in explicit terms, provision being made for giving effect to the principle of mutual fellowship among the churches —the element in which the New England church polity differed from bare Independency. Some of the churches hesitated about assembling in a synod at the call of the civil magistrates, lest the act might carry in it an unsafe concession to the civil power. But objections of this character were waived, and the system that was framed still left the magistracy at liberty to interfere by coercive measures in the case of a church that should be deaf to fraternal counsels and obstinately irregular or heretical. *The Cambridge Synod.*

Massachusetts acted uniformly in an independent spirit, both with reference to the government in England and in relation to her colleagues in the Confederation. She declined to receive a new charter from Parliament, in exchange for the old charter, not wishing to concede to any branch of the English Government such a right as a measure of this sort would imply. She continued, without authorization from abroad, to coin money, and thus exercised a prerogative peculiar to sovereignty. She declined two pro- *Massachusetts in relation to England.*

posals of Cromwell, one of which was that her people should emigrate to Ireland, and another that they should be transported to Jamaica. In the Confederacy she refused to accede to the requirement of Connecticut, even when it was sanctioned by the vote of the Commissioners, that the Springfield people, in order to maintain the fort at Saybrook, should pay a duty on exports sent down the river. Her determination not to submit to the control of the Confederacy—even in cases where the law was on its side—in opposition to what she thought right and expedient, was manifest in her dealings with the Dutch. The Connecticut and New Haven colonies were incensed when a Dutch smuggling vessel was seized in New Haven harbor by order of Stuyvesant, the Dutch governor at New Amsterdam. The quarrel, thus engendered, dragged on for several years. War broke out between England and Holland. The western colonies believed that the Dutch were conspiring with the Indians to attack the New England colonies, and they wished to declare war against them. But Massachusetts stood out against the vote cast by her three colleagues. Connecticut and New Haven, unable to induce Massachusetts to recede from her position, applied to Cromwell for help. He sent over a fleet with a land force on board. Massachusetts would go no further than to permit five hundred volunteers to be raised within her bounds. But the defeat of the Dutch in the English Channel, and the conclusion of the war between the two nations, rendered a resort to force on this side of the water needless and impossible. These were not the only cases in which Massachusetts refused to be bound by the acts of the Confederacy, on grounds which, however plausible and conscientiously urged, failed to convince her three allies that she was not violating the agreement which she had made when she entered into the Union.

In relation to the Confederacy.

The elevation of Cromwell and the growing influence of the Independents in England protected Massachusetts against the efforts of the mutinous signers of Vassall's petition, and put an end to the project for bringing in Presbyterianism. But the same changes opened a more encouraging prospect to enthusiasts and fanatics who were the foes of the ecclesiastical system and policy of the confederated colonies. Gorton was enabled to regain his lands. He changed the name of Shawomet to Warwick, in honor of the nobleman who had lent him assistance. There was a strong motive for the Narragansett settlements to unite under the patent of Williams, for they were endangered by territorial claims of both Plymouth and Massachusetts. Yet three years passed before the union was secured, and it continued only for a like period. Coddington applied in vain for the admission of Rhode Island to the Confederacy. In 1651, Coddington returned from England with a commission, derived from the Council of State, to establish a government over the islands of Rhode Island and Canonicut. This measure encountered a strong opposition from a portion of the settlers. The leader was John Clarke, who had fled from Massachusetts at the time of the Antinomian controversy. At Newport he was the principal member and the minister of an Anabaptist church—to use the name then current—which after a few years was gathered there. The spread of this sect had led the Massachusetts people, in 1644, to promulgate a law making banishment the penalty of the wilful and continued propagating of its tenets. This law was not enforced on those who deported themselves quietly. The President of Harvard College at the time when the law was framed was an avowed disbeliever in infant baptism. After keeping away from Massachusetts

Gorton.

The Narragansett settlements.

The Baptists in Massachusetts. John Clarke.

for fourteen years, Clarke, with two companions, prominent in his sect, came to Lynn to visit a blind man, a Baptist like themselves. On Sunday, as the matter is related in Clarke's own account of it, not being ready to manifest fellowship with the Puritan worshippers by uniting with them in divine service, and not feeling inwardly called to enter their church for the purpose of publicly testifying against them, he discoursed in the house where he was staying, to his companions and three or four others, who came in, he says, unexpectedly. He was interrupted by the appearance of two constables. The Rhode Islanders were arrested; but their fines were paid either by themselves or by others, with the exception of one of the party who received corporal punishment. What ulterior object, if any, Clarke had in paying this visit, and holding his meeting in defiance of the law, it is, perhaps, unsafe to say. But any candid reader of "Ill Newes from New England," the publication that he put forth in England, in which the circumstances are recounted, will not fail to see that the opportunity to bear witness to his opinions in the heart of the enemy's country was highly prized, and that his failure to get up a debate with the ministers was a source of disappointment to him. His rival, Coddington, succeeded in setting up his government. But Clarke was a man of talents and energy. He went to England, and with the aid of Roger Williams, who was also there, he procured, in September, 1652, the revocation of Coddington's commission. But dissension and contention continued to prevail in the Narragansett towns. "How is it," wrote Vane, in 1654, "that there are such divisions amongst you—such headiness, tumults, disorders, injustice? . . . Are there no wise men amongst you?" etc. "They had brought on themselves," Williams told them, the reputation of being "a licentious and conten-

<small>Affairs in Rhode Island.</small>

tious people." This unhappy state of things is partly accounted for by the circumstance that Rhode Island served as an asylum for eccentric spirits who were denied an abode, or found themselves uncomfortable, in the adjacent colonies. At length, in 1654, Roger Williams, who was a peace-maker, as well as a gladiator, persuaded them all to unite under the charter which he had brought to them in 1644. He was himself chosen President.

In 1646, John Winthrop, the younger, began a plantation on the Pequot River. His settlement was only thirty miles from the house of Roger Williams, who had moved into the Narragansett country, to a place near the site of North Kingston. At one time Williams thought it would be well to prevail on Winthrop to become the Governor of Rhode Island. The latter planted his settlement under the auspices of Massachusetts, but the Commissioners decided that it belonged under the jurisdiction of Connecticut. In New Haven colony, Branford was founded, and, in the Connecticut colony, Fairfield and Stratford. For a considerable time government was administered in both colonies with nothing more than the rudiments of a written code. The town of Plymouth gradually declined in strength, but the colony prospered, and continued to be distinguished by its upright and liberal spirit. *Connecticut and New Haven.* *Plymouth.*

Threatening movements of the Narragansetts were renewed in 1645, and were kept up for several years. They were anxious to wreak vengeance on Uncas and his tribe, and it was thought that they had in mind a deeper and more extensive plot. Finally, in 1650, Captain Atherton was sent from Massachusetts with a squad of men to bring their chief to terms. Atherton seized him in his own wigwam, and compelled him to fulfil his stipulations. *The Narragansetts.*

Winthrop, "the father of Massachusetts," died in 1649.
For a few years after this date there was continued prosperity in the colony. The leading figure in
public affairs was John Endicott, who grew
wiser as he grew older, and was an efficient and useful
magistrate. Between the years 1652 and 1658, Massachusetts brought under its jurisdiction the towns
of Maine. That colony had never been united
by its proprietor, and was mostly left to care
for itself. Moreover, a portion of the land, including forty
miles on the coast, was claimed, under what was alleged
to be a prior patent, by a member of the Long Parliament,
Alexander Rigby. Massachusetts asserted that the grant
to Gorges was abrogated by the surrender of the Plymouth Company's charter to the King, and, also, that her
own boundary included the most northerly waters of the
Merrimac, and gave her the whole region as far as Casco
Bay. By the annexation of the Maine settlements the
dominion of Massachusetts embraced the whole intervening territory north of Plymouth. The inhabitants of
Maine consisted of the servants and agents of the landowners.

The intrusion of the Quakers, and the tragic events
growing out of the struggle to keep them out, form an
unpleasant chapter in Massachusetts history.
The early disciples of George Fox were often
of a totally different spirit from the quiet and
kindly Society of Friends with which we are familiar.
If they abjured war and practised non-resistance as far
as the use of carnal weapons is concerned, they made
up for it by a belligerent use of the tongue. They comprised many fanatics, on fire with religious zeal, conceiv-
ing themselves called of God to pronounce anathemas
upon established civil and ecclesiastical systems, and to
travel from place to place for the purpose of "bearing

witness" against office-bearers in Church and State. Their incursion into New England was dreaded like the approach of a pestilence. If the sect of Mormons had existed in those days, the approach of a swarm of missionaries of that sect would have been regarded with less dismay, for not so much danger would have been anticipated from their influence. In the prospect of a visitation from the Quakers, the General Court of Massachusetts, in 1656, passed a law for the punishment of any of them who should come into the colony, and for the sending of them "out of the land." When they actually arrived, their disorderly conduct was such as would have subjected them, even in our days, to police restraint and legal penalties. When expelled, they persisted in coming back the second and the third time, and, it is lamentable to relate, in pursuance of a law passed by the General Court by a slender majority, but in agreement with the advice of the Federal Commissioners, several of them were hanged. When experience made it evident that harsh penalties were ineffectual, and when capital punishment ceased to be inflicted, the wild doings of these unwelcome visitors did not cease. Some of them still continued to walk stark naked along the streets, and into the congregations met for worship. In Virginia and other colonies there were extremely severe enactments against the Quakers, but there was no infliction of capital punishment.

While the extravagances of the Quakers had the effect to sharpen the weapons used against them, it must here, as always, be kept in mind that, with the Puritans, to prevent the propagation of what they considered hurtful religious errors was held to be an obligation of civil society. "I look upon toleration," said President Oakes, of Harvard College, in an election sermon, in 1673, "as the first-born of all

The theory of intolerance.

abominations." "It was toleration," Cotton said, "that made the world anti-christian." Nathaniel Ward, of Ipswich, in that quaint specimen of Puritan humor, "The Simple Cobbler of Aggawam," writes: "He that is willing to tolerate any unsound opinion that his own may be tolerated, though never so sound, will for a need hang God's Bible at the devil's girdle." When coercion was used against the Puritans themselves, the sin according to their view did not lie in the use of force, but in using it, not against pernicious errors, but against the true Gospel. In the pocket of Thomas Dudley, when he died, was found a verse from his own pen, in which toleration was called the egg that would hatch a cockatrice,

"To poison all with heresy and vice."

It is needless to reiterate that this idea of the obligations of civil society almost universally prevailed.

In the Congregational churches, especially in the colonies of Massachusetts and Connecticut, there were movements tending to lessen the strictness of the requisites for church membership. Of this character was the adoption by many churches of what was called "the Half-way Covenant." This measure obtained the approval of a synod which met at Boston in 1657. Adults who had been baptized in infancy, but were not considered by themselves or others to be regenerated persons, were allowed, on condition of assenting to the church covenant and agreeing to submit to the discipline of the church, to bring their children to baptism. The common idea that the motive of the change was to open the door to a wider extension of political rights, appears to be not well founded. Such a consequence did not follow, as the class of persons referred to did not vote, even in church af-

The Half-way Covenant.

fairs. Moreover, the proposal that led to the change was first made in Connecticut, where the suffrage had never been confined to church members. Another innovation was to some extent introduced. The practice sprung up of inviting to the Lord's Supper, as "a means of grace," persons not morally unworthy, who, nevertheless, had not been received as converts into communion with the church.

As the period of the Commonwealth in England drew toward its close, several of the New England worthies passed away. Hooker had died in 1647. The death of Brewster, foremost among the first settlers at Plymouth, had occurred four years earlier. In 1657, Bradford, who had been from the beginning a main pillar of the Plymouth colony, died. In 1655, Edward Winslow, his associate, who had rendered great services to both the Eastern colonies, had gone before him. Standish, the military leader at Plymouth, died in 1656. In 1652, John Cotton, the famous minister of Boston, was buried; Haynes, the companion of Hooker in founding Connecticut, died in 1654, and Eaton, the New Haven Governor, in 1658.

Death of the founders.

On the restoration of the Stuarts, in the person of Charles II., the New England colonies knew not what to expect. In none of them had Oliver Cromwell or Richard ever been proclaimed. In the first year of the new reign, a Council of Foreign Plantations was established, with powers like those which had rested in the Parliamentary Commission, previously in charge of colonial affairs. In the new reign one of the early measures repugnant to the wishes of the colonies was the sharpening of the provisions of the Navigation Act. A loyal address from Massachusetts was graciously answered. At the same time, however, there came an order for the apprehension of Whalley and Goffe, who

Charles II.: The Navigation Law.

had been members of the High Court of Justice that condemned Charles I. The New England magistrates, especially those of New Haven, where shelter and protection had been afforded them by Davenport and others, showed no zeal in carrying out this mandate. On the contrary, they aided the regicides to escape. These found a safe and permanent asylum with Russell, the minister of Hadley. John Dixwell, another of the signers of the death-warrant of Charles, spent the closing years of his life at New Haven, under an assumed name. He died just before the news was received of the accession of William and Mary.

The regicides.

Connecticut had made scarcely any delay in acknowledging the new King, and won some advantage, in comparison with her sister colonies, by this promptitude. Winthrop was sent on a mission to England to see if he could procure a charter. His culture, his moderate temper, his influential friends, and his attractive manners, made his mission fully successful. The charter that he obtained was extremely liberal in its provisions. In its assignment of boundaries, the New Haven colony was included within Connecticut. Winthrop had engaged that New Haven should not be deprived of her freedom of choice in this matter, in which her very being as a community was involved. He did not disregard his pledge. But the desire of extension on the part of Connecticut was too strong to be overcome by any remonstrance, or by the earnest and prolonged resistance of New Haven, backed by the judgment of the Commissioners of the Confederacy. The authorities in England were probably desirous of blotting out that member of the Union whose polity accorded with that of Massachusetts. The incorporation of New Haven in Connecticut was consummated in 1665. To John Davenport the blow was a severe one.

Charter to Connecticut.

Union of New Haven and Connecticut colonies.

He accepted a call to be the successor of Wilson in the First Church in Boston, where he died in 1670.

In 1663, John Clarke obtained a new charter for Rhode Island of unprecedented liberality. In it was a provision securing absolute freedom "in matters of religious concernments." Clarke's hostility to Massachusetts ways contributed to his success at Court.

New charter of Rhode Island.

On the accession of Charles, complaints were at once made to him by the Quakers of the treatment which they had received in Massachusetts. To the answer of the magistrates the King replied in courteous and gentle terms, but directed that offenders of that sect should be sent to England for trial. This order the magistrates did not regard, since a compliance with it would have been to part with their own judicial authority in all cases. They preferred to set the Quakers free. But the Massachusetts government took steps adapted to secure favor at Court, one of which was the suppression of a book by John Eliot, containing obnoxious theories of a political nature—a book which he was quite ready to recall. Two representatives, Bradstreet and Norton, were sent to England to meet accusations against the colony, and to convey a loyal address to the King. About the time of their departure the General Court passed an act for a fresh coinage of silver money; a not very timely proceeding, considering the strained relations with the English Government. The answer which the representatives brought back, in the autumn of 1662, was liberal in its promises in relation to the preservation of their patent and charter; but it required that all freeholders of competent estates, of orthodox opinions, and not vicious in conduct should have the privilege of voting; that worship in the use of the Prayer Book should be allowed; that the oath of allegiance should be taken

Complaints against Massachusetts.

by the colonists, and that justice should be administered in the King's name. This last requirement was complied with, but the other demands were neither refused nor accepted. Two years later, a Royal Commission, consisting of four persons, was appointed to visit New England. The principal member of the Commission was Nicolls, a man of talents and experience. One of his associates was Maverick, a signer of the Presbyterian petition. The expectation of the coming of the Commissioners, and a sense of the peril involved in it, was one of the motives that moved New Haven to relinquish its opposition to the union with Connecticut. In Massachusetts, a measure was adopted for securing the safe custody of the charter, and military preparations were made to meet any contingency that might arise. One errand of the Commissioners had reference to warfare against the Dutch. In this part of their business they were aided by the General Court. The Court likewise altered the law relating to suffrage, so that freeholders rated at ten shillings, and having certificates of character from the ministers, might vote. Charles had given New Amsterdam to his brother, the Duke of York, the boundaries of the ceded territory being declared to be the Connecticut and the Delaware. On the surrender of New Amsterdam to the Commissioners, it was agreed by them that Connecticut should retain its territory on the mainland, but that Long Island should be attached to the Duke of York's province. The Commissioners had no opposition to encounter in Connecticut or in the other colonies. It was in Massachusetts that the conflict had to be sustained. They journeyed to Maine, and organized the towns there which paid allegiance to Massachusetts, under a government to be managed by themselves. They had brought over two sets of instructions, one of which was private. They would only communicate their demands, one by one, to the magistrates in Boston. One part of the errand was to feel the pulse of the people and ascertain how the appointment of a royal governor would be received. When the Commissioners proposed to sit as judges, and to hear an appeal from the Governor and Company, they were not permitted to carry out their purpose. Baffled and beaten, they retired in wrath. Circumstances prevented them for a considerable time from presenting their report and complaints. Massachusetts, with a politic generosity, sent a present of masts to the King for the royal navy, a gift which proved to be of signal service.

Eight years passed after the victory over the Royal Commissioners; the liberty of the New England colonies was still in peril, when they suffered a new and terrible calamity in the great Indian War, *King Philip's War.* which afflicted them all, but fell with crushing severity on Plymouth and Massachusetts. For forty years, since the struggle with the Pequots, peace had been maintained with the native tribes. The Indians had obtained the use of fire arms, and were keen marksmen. On the whole, they had been treated with substantial justice. The lands possessed by the whites had been purchased at a fair price. For hunting and fishing, the chief occupations of the natives, there was ample room along the streams and in the forests. There might be harsh and cruel conduct in occasional instances on the part of individuals among the whites, but the colonists, as a rule, were strict to mark such iniquities and to inflict condign punishment. There were nearly sixty thousand English in New England, and perhaps an equal number of Indians. The whites dwelt in unprotected towns and hamlets, mostly scattered along the coast. West of the Plymouth territory, on the eastern shore of Narragansett

Bay, were the Pokanokets or Wampanoags. West of the same bay was the home of the Narragansetts. These were the two still formidable tribes in Southern New England.

The Pokanokets begin the war. It was the Pokanokets who commenced the war against the whites, which spread far and wide. Massasoit, their former chief, had been the lifelong friend and ally of the English. At his death he left his power to his two sons, who took the English names of Alexander and Philip. They did not manifest the pacific spirit of their father. Their disaffection and the jealousy and hostility of their young warriors did not spring so much from any specific grievances of which they could make complaint, as from a more or less conscious impatience of that condition of dependence and constraint in which, owing to inevitable circumstances, they found themselves placed. The fetters that rested on their sense of freedom did not chafe the less for being accepted by them in treaties into which they had voluntarily entered. Their territory became more and more curtailed by grants which they could not well avoid making. For any infraction of their agreements they were called to account and restitution was punctually exacted. Of their motives and plans the colonists became more and more suspicious, and, in most cases, probably on good grounds. The penalty which was demanded of them was the surrender of their guns, which their leaders were more ready to promise than they were disposed, or even able, to perform. Shortly after Alexander had been conducted to Plymouth, to give account of himself, he fell sick and died. It seems likely that Philip imagined that his brother had been poisoned. He began the war, not as the result of a deep-laid conspiracy, in which various tribes were parties with him, but out of anger and revenge. The murder, by his instigation, of an informer, who had betrayed his purpose, and the execution by the

English of the murderers, or of the Indians who were supposed to be guilty of the crime, was the signal for the commencement of the sanguinary struggle. It opened, in 1675, in two attacks on the town of Swanzey, in the Plymouth colony. The houses were burned and the inhabitants slaughtered. For two years, during which the war lasted, the dwellers in towns and villages were exposed to the sudden, merciless assaults of their savage enemies. Nowhere could the laborer till the ground with any feeling of security. Mother and child went to bed at night in dread of being awakened by the terrible cry of pitiless barbarians. To anticipate the combination of the Narragansetts with Philip, it was necessary to attack that tribe. A brave and determined assault was made on their fort or camp, where South Kingston now stands, by the troops of Plymouth, Massachusetts, and Connecticut. After desperate fighting, and with a heavy loss of life, they defeated the Indians and burned their wigwams. The example of Philip and his followers was contagious. Other tribes joined in the war against the English. The towns in Western Massachusetts were visited with fire and slaughter. One of the most frightful instances of massacre was the destruction of Lothrop, with nearly all his men, ninety in number, "the flower of Essex," at "Bloody Brook," in Deerfield. The capture of their fort broke the power of the Narragansetts. Canonchet, their sachem, was taken by a band of Connecticut volunteers, and, for breaking treaties, was delivered up to Indian allies of the whites to be put to death. At length Philip was driven to his lair, at Mount Hope, on the Narragansett. Beset in this place of retreat by the troops under Captain Church, he attempted to escape through the forces that enclosed him, but was shot by one of the Indian auxiliaries of

Horrors of the war.

The Narragansetts worsted.

Death of Philip.

Church. The conception of Philip as having by his genius organized an extensive league, as a man of princely virtues and of heroic courage, is the mythical creation of later writers. It is nearer the truth to say that having begun with robbing the Plymouth people of their cattle, he gradually gave the reins to his ferocity, and by the massacre of defenceless villagers drifted into a war which spread of itself from tribe to tribe.

In Washington Irving's attractive but misleading essay, Philip is depicted as a chivalrous "king." "He went down," it is said, "like a lonely bark, foundering amid darkness and tempest, without a pitying eye to weep his fall, or a friendly hand to record his struggle." There is a suggestion of a very different estimate of the Indian warrior in a sentence of the Puritan captain, Church, who says of the fallen savage: " They drew him thro' the Mud into the Upland, and a doleful great naked beast he look'd like." After the death of Philip a year elapsed before the war was fully ended. Besides the terrible loss of life which filled all the settlements with lamentation, there were left heavy burdens of debt on the Eastern colonies, and a universal feeling of weakness and depression.

When Philip's war began, " the praying Indians " numbered not far from four thousand. Some of them, mostly of the Nipmuck tribe, proved treacherous and aided the enemy. The effect was a distrust of the whole body, and a panic which demanded that the most rigid precautions should be taken to keep them from doing harm. The benevolent missionary, Eliot, and another noble friend of the Indians, Daniel Gookin, did their utmost to dispel the prevalent fear and to protect the objects of it. But they could not quiet the prevailing alarm. The Christian Indians of Natick and some other places were transferred to Deer Island, in Boston harbor. They demonstrated their fidelity to the English,

The Christian Indians.

and many of them, formed into companies, lent effective military assistance.

But while confidence in the Christian Indians as a body was by degrees restored, the result of the war was to infuse into the minds of the English an intense horror and detestation of the Indians generally. <small>Hatred of the Indians.</small> They were regarded as an execrable race, with the worst qualities of wild beasts, but with an amount of intelligence added that rendered them far more hateful and dangerous. It is the feeling that commonly springs up at the present day among frontiersmen in relation to neighboring Indian tribes. It finds expression in some of the sermons of Puritan ministers, not usually lacking in humane feeling. The perpetual dread and heart-rending cruelties from which the colonies suffered explain such measures as the offering by the legislatures of New York and New England of large bounties for Indian scalps. Rewards were paid for the destruction of the savages as for the killing of wolves.

The circumstances were propitious for the undertaking of Charles II. and his advisers to deprive the New England colonies of their liberty. They were making a general attack upon charters in England, <small>Attack on the New England charters.</small> and charters which it was unrighteous to meddle with might be included with such as deserved to be annulled. From the date of the absorption of New Haven into the colony of Connecticut, the vitality of the Confederacy was extinct. There was little chance for concerted action in the way of resistance to well-laid plans of subjugation. In 1676, Edward Randolph, <small>Randolph.</small> an emissary of the English ministry, a man who proved to be a persevering enemy of New England, arrived in Boston. He was a relative of John Mason, and part of his errand was to take care of Mason's claim to New Hampshire. He brought complaints of the neglect of the Navigation Act by the Massachusetts government. As required by the King, two messengers, Stoughton and Bulkeley, were sent to England, but with powers carefully defined and limited. To avoid trouble respecting Maine, Massachusetts, much to the disgust of the King, purchased the claim of Gorges, which covered the district between the Piscataqua and the Kennebec. The land between the Kennebec and the Penobscot was held by the Duke of York. Maine was now governed as a separate province by Massachusetts. In 1679, against the wishes of the New Hampshire towns, they were separated from Massachusetts, and organized as a royal province. In 1682, Edward Cranfield was made Governor—a greedy adventurer, who was clothed with almost absolute power, and whose misgovernment, running through several years, became at last unbearable. In 1685, to avoid deposition by the English Government, he fled to the West Indies. But his departure did not end the period of tyranny and anarchy in New Hampshire, which lasted until the union was renewed with Massachusetts. The merchants and manufacturers in England clamored for the enforcement of the Navigation Act in this colony. In 1678, the crown lawyers gave the opinion that the charter of Massachusetts had been rendered void by the offences which had been committed by the administration under it. Nothing was left undone by the colony, through the usual means of procrastination, petition, and remonstrance, to ward off the catastrophe. The Court refused to allow its agents, Joseph Dudley and John Richards, to leave it to the King to act his pleasure, in the faint hope that his final decision might be favorable. In October, 1683, the agents returned. Soon after, the charter was declared to be null and void. Massachusetts, robbed of the Constitution under which it had been planted, and which had subsisted for more than fifty years, was left without any guaranty of political rights.

In the contest for the preservation of the charter, Randolph had behaved as an implacable enemy, and Dudley as a time-serving politician. But there was no power of resistance. There was no longer, as at a former day, a strong body of Puritans in England whose co-operation could be relied on. Above all, there was no longer in Massachusetts the unanimity which had existed when previous aggressions were attempted. There was a middle party, a party not indisposed to compromise and to yield. The Puritan theocracy, the ideal on which the hearts of the preceding generation had rested, had begun to crumble away, through the growth of population and the alteration of sentiment. The inhabitants no longer consisted almost exclusively of farmers, resolute in their principles, and ready to shed their blood to keep off foreign control. There existed, especially in Boston, a large class who were possessed of wealth, many of whom were engaged in commerce, and whose tone of feeling was affected by their mercantile and social connections with the mother country. Randolph had not labored in vain to diffuse in this class a spirit of compliance. {A middle party in Massachusetts.}

The accession of James II., an avowed Roman Catholic, increased, if that were possible, the feeling of despondency among the people of Massachusetts. As far as their religious system was concerned, they had nothing to expect from him but antipathy. {Royal government in New England.} One thing was certain; no favor would be shown to the cause of popular freedom. On May 14, 1686, Randolph, the untiring enemy of the Massachusetts people, arrived with the order from England to set up a provisional government, to consist of a President, Deputy-President, and sixteen Councillors, of whom Randolph was to be one.

The limited powers lodged in the new government were to be exercised without any popular assembly. Its authority was to be extended over Massachusetts, Maine, New Hampshire, and the "King's Province," or New York. Joseph Dudley, who was to be President, was the son of Thomas Dudley, the unbending Puritan magistrate of a former day. But the son had turned his back on the example and precepts of the father, and was ready to break down the liberties which the elder Dudley had done so much to build up. Once in office, however, the new President was inclined to conciliate the patriots, and the people who followed their lead, so that Randolph wrote letters to England complaining of him. Care was immediately taken by the Council in England for the introduction of Episcopal worship. Ratcliffe, a clergyman of the Established Church, was sent to Boston, and when the use of one of the Puritan meeting-houses was refused, the Episcopal services began to be held in the Town Hall. At the instigation of Randolph, proceedings were begun in England for the abrogation of the charters of Rhode Island and Connecticut, and he at once set about to put an end to government under these instruments. But while the contests provoked by this proceeding were in progress, Sir Edmund Andros arrived in Boston, under an appointment from the crown, as Governor of New England. When the charter of Massachusetts was annulled, the colony was left absolutely subject to the King. Its inhabitants were not only stripped of political rights; it was even held that all the land was the property of the Crown, and its possessors were soon given to understand that they must bargain for the ownership of it by paying quit-rents. Andros assumed the government on December 20, 1686. Plymouth and the portion of Maine called the County of Cornwall, which

had belonged to the Duke of York before his succession
to the crown, were included under the jurisdiction of
the new Governor. The only limit on his power of making
laws was the necessity for the concurrence of a Council
whose members he had the authority to displace, and
the requirement of the royal sanction. The Governor
could impose taxes with the Council's consent. The severe
punishments which followed upon instances of refusal
to submit to this arbitrary prerogative showed that
resistance was useless. Andros could institute courts of
justice, and no appeal could be taken from their decisions
except to the King. Dudley was appointed censor of
the press. Without his leave nothing could be printed.
The Governor demanded the keys of the Old South
Church in order that the Episcopal services might be held in it. The demand was refused, *Episcopal worship.*
but he carried out his determination to hold these services
within its walls on Sundays and holidays, at times
when the congregation to whom the edifice belonged
were not using it. This high-handed proceeding was
the object of an unceasing protest on the part of those
who were wronged by it, until in April, 1688, Andros set
out to erect a house for Episcopal worship. The new
building was not finished in time for the Governor to
attend service in it. It was opened for this purpose for
the first time on June 8, 1689. The antipathy of the
Massachusetts Puritans to the Episcopal forms of worship
was naturally considered by Andros and his supporters
as a narrow, fanatical prejudice. But whatever
of sectarian narrowness was involved in the opposition to
these forms, their introduction was part and parcel of
the system of tyranny which the Stuarts were striving to
force upon the people. So far as they had this character,
the resistance had a justifiable motive.

The levying of taxes by the fiat of the Governor, the

enforced renewal of land-titles, and the exaction of excessive fees, filled the minds of a liberty-loving people with indignation. The same measures were carried out in Maine, and, to some extent, in New Hampshire. In December, 1686, Rhode Island was joined, without any resistance on her part, to the dominion of Andros. At the same time he entered on the task, which it took nearly a year to accomplish, of annexing Connecticut to his dominion. In October, he visited Hartford. There is a tradition that while the discussion was proceeding with the magistrates, in the presence of a numerous company, the lights were suddenly extinguished, and the charter taken from the table and hidden in the hollow trunk of an oak tree, which was known in later times as the "Charter Oak." Some occurrence of interest at the time, perhaps the hiding of a duplicate copy of the charter, is the ground of this legend. The restriction of the number of meetings which the towns were allowed to hold, and the reduction of the powers of the towns, was one of the obnoxious acts that ensued upon the Governor's return to Massachusetts. In June, 1687, New York and the Jerseys were added to the territories subject to him. While Boston was to be the capital of the extensive "Dominion," which was to have the name New England, a Deputy-Governor was to reside in New York. A military expedition, which Andros led into Maine against the Indians, brought great sufferings upon those who took part in it. This increased the unpopularity of the Governor, who was unjustly suspected of sinister designs in connection with the enterprise—with nothing less than a secret purpose to destroy the Massachusetts troops. He had previously captured Castine from the French.

Andros at Hartford.

The dominion of Andros.

Public affairs in England now took a turn favorable to the interests of the colony. James II. was bent on two objects. He was determined to rule in a despotic way, and he was earnest to promote the interests of the Church of Rome. He began his reign with a persecution of the Puritans. The Covenanters in Scotland, and the Nonconformists in England, were pursued with unrelenting cruelty. *[Altered policy of James II.]* The blood-thirsty Jeffreys was a judge after the King's own heart. Divines like Richard Baxter, respected by all good men, were loaded with insult and cast into prison. The purpose of James was to divide power and offices between the Church of England and the Church of Rome, of which he was a member. Finding that he could not build up the Roman Catholic cause by the aid of Episcopalians, he turned to the Dissenters, and, by an unconstitutional exercise of power, suspended the execution of penal laws against them. He professed to be a believer in liberty of conscience. This new policy culminated in the Declaration of Indulgence. This naturally gave pleasure to such Nonconformists as looked only at the immediate gain, without penetrating the King's design, or considering that an act which brought to them relief enslaved the nation, converting, as it did, the monarch into a czar. The disaffection in Massachusetts prompted the sending of a messenger to implore redress at the English Court. Increase Mather, the most eminent minister in the colony, and quite competent for such an errand, was selected for the purpose. *[Increase Mather in England.]* Randolph tried to detain him by a vexatious prosecution for libel, but Mather contrived to elude the attempt. He was graciously received by the King, whom he propitiated by presenting from certain ministers and churches addresses of thanks for the Declaration of Indulgence, the true intent of which their authors had failed to comprehend. But Mather made no real progress with his suit. Meantime the English people were fast getting ready to drive James from the throne. Mather arrived in England on May 25, 1688. The first information of the landing of William of Orange at Torbay reached Boston on April 4, 1689. There was no longer any barrier to stay the current of popular indignation. On April 18th, at nine o'clock in the morning, troops were moving in different parts of the town. They escorted a number of the old magistrates to the Council Chamber. Randolph and many other coadjutors of Andros were arrested and put in jail. Troops poured in from the country places until they reached the number of fifteen hundred or two thousand. The Governor himself was taken, and was ultimately lodged in the Fort. There was considerable difficulty in shielding Dudley from popular violence. A provisional government was created. The Governor and magistrates who had been chosen at the last popular election before the annulling of the charter were associated with a newly chosen body of deputies, and with them constituted the General Court. On May 29th, William and Mary were proclaimed in Boston with all possible expressions of public joy. In Plymouth, the old government was likewise reinstated. The same thing was done in Connecticut. In Rhode Island, the old officers were restored, but the Governor declined to serve. When James fell from power, the machinery of tyrannical government which he had erected in New England fell with him. Andros, its agent, was hated in New England, but he had simply carried out the will of the government of which he was the agent. As regards his personal character, apart from his sympathy and official connection with an odious system, there is no ground for serious reproach.

We have now to glance at some of the peculiar features of society in New England.

John Adams records in his diary that he gave to a Virginian "a receipt for making a New England in Virginia." The secret lay in the adoption of town-meetings, training-days, town-schools, and ministers. "The meeting-house and the school-house," he said, are "the scenes where New England men are formed." The four chief things were, "towns, militia, schools, and churches."

<small>Society in New England.</small>

It should be remembered at the outset that the inhabitants of the New England colonies were homogeneous in race and in spirit. They were of pure English stock. Those of a different descent were an insignificant minority. The twenty thousand settlers who came over prior to 1641, when immigration practically ceased, were mostly from the East Anglian counties. A portion of them were from Devon and Cornwall, and some came from London. The speech of the people was good English of that day. What have been considered peculiarities acquired in their new home were mostly brought over from the localities whence the colonists came, where, in some instances, however, they long ago ceased to be in vogue. The habit of prefixing the aspirate *h* where it does not belong, and of dropping it where it does belong, could not have prevailed in the old country as it has since spread there, since it never existed in New England. The tendency to a "nasal utterance" must have sprung up on this side of the ocean, owing to some quality of the atmosphere, or, perhaps, in a certain degree, from a Puritan habit of prolonging the vowel sounds.

<small>The people homogeneous.</small>

Legislation and the administration of justice took their form from the English system, modified by the influence of the Mosaic civil code and by a natural sense of equity. Trial by jury was early established in Massachusetts and in the other colonies, except New Haven. In Massachusetts there were town

<small>Government and laws.</small>

courts and county courts, and above them the Court of Assistants, with the General Court, the supreme tribunal to which appeals in important causes might be carried. Sixteen years after the landing of the Pilgrims, the first code of laws was framed at Plymouth. Its provisions followed no model, but were determined by the peculiar circumstances and needs of the colony. In Massachusetts the adjudication of causes was left for a long time to the discretion of the magistrates, as there was no recognition of the binding force of the common law of England. The people became more and more earnest in calling for a written code, especially after deputies were elected by the towns. But delays were interposed and considerable time elapsed before the popular demand was satisfied. Experiments were made in the composition of a body of laws, but the schemes proposed were not acceptable. Cotton offered to the Court "a copy of Moses his Judicials," which he had compiled, but no action was taken upon it. At length, in 1641, there were adopted one hundred fundamental laws, which were called "The Body of Liberties." They were drawn up by Nathaniel Ward, the minister of Ipswich, who had been bred to the law in his youth, before he became a minister, and was quite competent for his task. Under this code there were twelve capital crimes, to which a thirteenth, rape, was added the next year. At that time, in England, the number of capital offences was thirty. The spirit of the Massachusetts code is disclosed in the opening paragraph : "No man's life shall be taken away ; no man's honor or good name shall be stained ; no man's person shall be arrested, restrained, banished, dismembered, nor anyways punished ; no man shall be deprived of his wife or children ; no man's goods or estate shall be taken away, nor any way endangered, under color of law, or countenance of authority; unless it be by virtue or

In Massachusetts.

equity of some express law of the country warranting the same, established by the General Court and sufficiently published, or, in case of defect of the law in any particular case, by the Word of God;—and in capital cases, or in cases concerning dismembering or banishment, according to that word to be judged by the General Court." In 1642, Connecticut adopted the provisions of the Massachusetts code as regards capital offences. *In Connecticut.* Before that time it had no written collection of laws. As we have seen, a selection of the Mosaic civil laws was at first the only statute-book of New Haven colony; and this continued to be the fact until 1656.

The organization of the towns was closely connected with the central place of the church in the social system, and with the attractions of the "meeting-house." To the meeting-house all the people, except *Town organization.* such as were kept at home by some necessity, were compelled by law to repair twice on Sunday. The abodes of the inhabitants were commonly in the immediate neighborhood. In addition to the ownership of farms in severalty, there were pastures and woodland which were for the benefit of all in common. The town was a political society, having its own defined prerogatives, officers peculiar to itself, chosen by popular vote, and its own deliberative assemblies where public measures of local interest were discussed and determined. In these village parliaments the democratic idea in its original form was realized.

There was no standing army, but the people were all soldiers. Only those were exempted from military drill whose occupations naturally excluded them, as was the case with ministers and with fishermen, *The militia.* who were obliged most of the time to be absent from their homes. Military offices were posts of honor. The regular training days were occasions of importance in which the whole community took an interest.

In a community where religion was an absorbing concern, the clergy could not fail to hold a prominent place.

The clergy. On account of their sacred office, but, also, by reason of their ability and learning, in the absence of any other liberally educated class to divide power with them, the ministers were, from the beginning, the recognized leaders of society. Since government, in some of the colonies entirely, in all of them mainly, was in the hands of the distinctively religious class, the ministers were consulted in civil affairs, and great weight was attached to their opinions, especially in all cases where moral questions were distinctly involved. But they were, also, honored counsellors in their parishes in matters of private concern. Their medical knowledge was not inconsiderable, and when trained physicians were very few, it was employed in the service of the people. The presence of lawyers in the colonies was discouraged, from the conviction that controversies should be settled without resort to legal technicalities, and because of the purpose to keep clear of obnoxious parts of the English system of jurisprudence. When the legal profession came to be allowed, it was with restrictions as to the number of advocates, and in other particulars. Ministers were actively concerned in the framing of laws and in the adjustment of disputes. It naturally devolved on them to exercise a large measure of control in organizing and managing schools of every grade. In short, especially in Massachusetts and the western colonies, the clergy were the principal guides of the community. Yet the deference paid to them was not of a slavish kind. Laymen understood their rights, and their constant participation in the proceedings of towns and churches accustomed them to the exercise of an independent judgment.

The intellectual activity of the New England people was a prime characteristic. Most of them were English yeomen. With them came over substantial country gentlemen, and some merchants of large means. But it was true of all that their minds had been deeply stirred by the theological controversies of the age. If it was true of the bulk of them that they read few books, the Bible, in the whole range of its literature, was an ever-present, stimulating companion. Morning and night, and on the Lord's day, they hung over its pages with eager and absorbed, as well as reverent, attention. Whatever has to do with man as a spiritual being had in their eyes a transcendent importance. Hence a marked distinction of the principal New England communities is the interest that was felt from the beginning in the education of the people, and the heavy burdens that were cheerfully assumed to effect the object. Schools were soon set up in all considerable towns, save in Plymouth colony, where the poverty of the people explains the exception. In 1647, the law of Massachusetts required that a school should be supported in every town having fifty householders, and that a grammar-school should be established, where boys could be fitted for college, in every place where the householders numbered a hundred. The pecuniary sacrifices cheerfully undertaken for the foundation of Harvard College and for its continued support, indicate the importance that was attached to learning and culture, and the natural fear on the part of the educated class that in these "ends of the earth" there would come a degeneracy in these particulars. It was only six years after the arrival of Winthrop, when the General Court appropriated for the foundation of the college a sum "equivalent to the colony tax for a year." Seven magistrates and six ministers were appointed a committee "to take order for it." Two years

Intellectual activity.

Education.

October 28, 1636.

later, John Harvard died at Charlestown, bequeathing his library and half of his estate (or about £700), to carry out the plan. In 1657, the New Haven colony required every plantation not having a school to provide one. There the plan of a college was early favored. It was prevented from being realized until 1700, owing to the sparseness of population and to the conviction that the want was met by the institution previously planted at Cambridge. Besides the instruction imparted in school and college, we must not omit to notice the stimulus and training of an intellectual, as well as spiritual nature, which were received by the whole people from the pulpit. In common with Puritan preachers generally, the New England ministers were teachers of doctrine. They addressed the understanding of their hearers. They discoursed from Sunday to Sunday on the most profound themes of theology, as well as on the plain practical precepts of Christianity. Their sermons were the subject of conversation in their parishes, not only on the Lord's day, but, more or less, through the week, in the field and at the fireside. A number of the systems of theology which have been composed by New England divines in the colonial period, as well as later—as late as the early decades of the nineteenth century—consisted of sermons that were delivered before country congregations, composed mainly of farmers. The habits of attention, of discrimination, and of reasoning which were thus nurtured, must be taken into account if one would comprehend the mental life of New England.

The tendencies of society in New England were in the direction of social equality. There were very few large landed estates. There was no law of entail.

Social distinctions. There was freedom in the disposition of property by will, except that in the allotment of intestate estates the older son received a double portion. Yet it would be a mistake to conclude that there were no distinctions of rank, openly or tacitly recognized. The high position accorded to the clergy has already been adverted to. The magistrates, who were generally selected from the families most respected, and on account of their own intellectual and moral worth, were held in special honor. The idea entertained of the divine origin of government and of the sanctions of law secured to the rulers, although chosen by the people, popular reverence. The social superiority of certain families was publicly recognized. It was the custom to allot seats to the congregation in the houses of worship according to the dignity of its several members, which was carefully and formally determined. The ordinary designation of man and woman was "goodman" and "goodwife," "Mr." and "Mrs." (Mistress) being titles confined to the men and the dames and daughters of the superior class. In the catalogue of the colleges, far into the eighteenth century, the same respect to rank was paid. Those who were first in the alphabetical order were seldom first in the list of students. Negro slavery existed in the New England colonies, but the slaves were domestic servants, laboring in the house and on the farm. Their proportionate number was never large, and they were kindly treated. Yet slavery was not condemned. Samuel Sewall published in 1700 the first attack upon the system as immoral.

The strong hold which the Puritan faith, in its radical type, had upon the convictions of the community, is the key to the explanation of the most striking peculiarities of New England society. It was about the "meeting-house" that the town clustered. There—except in Rhode Island—all the people, who were not kept away by some necessity, were compelled to be present at two extended services on the

Religion in New England.

Lord's Day. This requirement, it should be observed, was not peculiar to New England. There was the same law in Virginia and other colonies, as well as in England. The Puritans—and of the New England Puritans it may be said with most emphasis—set up the Bible as the one guide of life, to the exclusion of ecclesiastical authority and precedents, no matter how long established and how venerated they might be. They required a warrant from Holy Writ for all ecclesiastical usages. Consistently with their theory on this subject, they discarded the observance of Easter and of Christmas, and of all other feasts and fasts which in their judgment had no revealed sanction. They substituted for them a day of fasting in the spring and a day of thanksgiving in the autumn, when the harvest had been gathered in. These observances corresponded to Jewish sacred days; but even fast and thanksgiving must be appointed by the magistrates, and appointed annually. Sunday, or "the Sabbath," as it was styled, was considered an observance enjoined by the decalogue upon the human race for all time, and the mode of keeping it was regulated by the Old Testament sabbatical statutes. It was a day of rigid abstention from labor and from recreation of all sorts. There was some doubt whether it should begin on the morning of Sunday, or, following the Jewish manner of reckoning, on Saturday, at sundown. In Massachusetts, the former custom came to prevail; in Connecticut, the latter. Forms of prayer were discarded in public worship, being considered to be destitute of a Biblical warrant. The Scriptures were not even read in public worship, unless the reading was accompanied by exposition. The sermon was of an hour in length, and in the earlier days was delivered without the aid of notes. Instrumental music in churches was not allowed. No singing was allowed in worship, except from a metrical version of the Psalms.

The presence and aid of a priest had for ages been deemed essential in the marriage ceremony and in the burial of the dead. As a part of the radical protest against the right of a priesthood to exist in the church, marriages were for a long time celebrated exclusively by the civil magistrates. The Pilgrims from the beginning followed in this particular what they had observed to be the Protestant custom in the Low Countries. Burial-places were commonly not adjacent to the meeting-houses, and the dead were buried in silence, without any religious services. The religious ideas and institutions of the Puritans, carried into the family, as into every department of life, a tone of conscientious strictness. There was deep affection, but there was often reserve in the expression of it. The natural gayety of the young was kept within bounds by the punctual enforcement of restraints. The prevalent moral code, pure in its spirit and lofty in its aims, took on a shade of austerity.

Sumptuary laws were a branch of the paternal theory of government which prevailed in New England, as elsewhere, in the seventeenth century. Especially was extravagance in dress, and an undue display of finery, on the part of people of inferior social rank, the object of legal prohibition. *Sumptuary laws.* A law of Massachusetts in 1634 forbade "immoderate great sleeves" and "slashed apparel," and the use of gold or silver belts or hat-bands by any who were not already possessed of them. In 1651, the wearing of gold or silver lace, or great boots, was made unlawful for any except magistrates and their families, or persons having two hundred pounds a year. In Connecticut, in 1676, it was ordained that persons wearing gold or silver buttons, any but a specified kind of lace, or silk scarfs, should be taxed for one hundred and fifty pounds. In 1636, in Massachusetts, a law was enacted that buyers of wines, liquors, or tobacco, should pay one-sixth of their value into the public treasury. In one year the law was enforced which imposed the same tax on purchasers of fruit, spice, or sugar. The inroads of fashion, as the century drew to its close, were looked upon with stern disfavor. The first introduction of wigs is recorded by Judge Sewall in his diary with feelings of sorrow and anger. If laws were thought necessary to keep down show and expense in matters of dress and domestic economy, much more was their aid employed to prevent and to punish dicing, card-playing, and also the drinking of healths, which was regarded as an offensive custom. In the early days, dancing was prohibited as frivolous and as leading to impurity. Later, the strictness of the law on this subject was relaxed in Massachusetts.

It was the glory of the Puritans that they insisted on the law of righteousness, and required that conduct should be conformed to it. The health of the soul and the approbation of God were the objects of supreme regard. But into the Puritanism of New England the leaven of the Renaissance did not enter. It is true that education was prized. The study of the Latin and Greek classics was fostered by the clergy. But that element which it is now the fashion to call Hellenism—that play of the mind which appears in the higher forms of imaginative literature and in art—was absent. An intense moral and religious earnestness had the effect for the time to exclude this form of intellectual life.

Whatever tinge of asceticism belonged to the Puritan ideal of family and social life, it did not reach to the matter of provisions for the table or the exercise of hospital-

Thanksgiving festival. ity. It is an interesting fact that the first Thanksgiving festival was at Plymouth in the autumn of 1621, when Massasoit and ninety of his people were feasted for three days on wild-fowl and venison. Thanksgiving-day was always the occasion of joyful family gatherings by the blazing hearthstone and at the dinner of turkey and plum-pudding. There were other times of relaxation and pleasure, which were of regular recurrence. Election-day, when the magistrates assumed their office, was one of these occasions. Training-days, of which there were several annually, when the military companies went through their drills in full panoply, were holidays, when the young regaled themselves with the spectacle and engaged in sports on the green. Wrestling-matches and shooting-matches were favorite games. There were neighborhood gatherings which combined work with pleasure, such as quilting-parties of women in-doors, husking-parties, and assemblies of men for the "raising" of the timber frames of houses. At such gatherings refreshments would not fail to be provided. The old English relish for good cheer and for manly out-of-door games was not extinguished by Puritan sobriety and the necessity of constant toil.

The inhabitants of New England were industrious. Farming was the principal occupation. But while in places, as, for example, in the valley of the Connecticut, the soil was fertile, it was more commonly sterile, and subsistence was wrung from it by hard labor. Knitting and spinning were occupations by women in the household. Within ten years from the landing of Winthrop, the weaving of cotton and woollen fabrics was begun by a few emigrants from Yorkshire. Labor was rapidly diversified. The important mechanical trades were soon plied in the larger villages. The chief source of profit was from the fisheries. Ship-building, which began at once, was zealously prosecuted. Commerce sprang up and flourished. The export of fish to the West Indies and to Europe brought back supplies of foreign products which added greatly to the comforts

Employments.

of living. As time went on, the style of building was constantly improving. The square meeting-houses, with their pyramidal roofs, beneath which the earlier settlers met, bringing with them their muskets to repel attacks of the Indians, gave place to rectangular buildings, sometimes of large dimensions. The dwelling-houses, with long roofs descending in the rear, which took the place of the first low log-houses, were superseded, in the case of families of larger means, by houses quite commodious and even stately.

CHAPTER IX.

NEW YORK TO 1688

Hudson's Discovery—Block's Exploring Voyage—The "New Netherland" Company—West India Company Chartered—The Dutch at Manhattan and Albany—Purchase of Manhattan Island—The Patroons—Van Twiller Succeeds Minuit—The Swedish Settlement—Trouble with the Indians—Peter Stuyvesant—Treaty with Connecticut—Attack on the Swedes—Delaware Purchased—Religious Contests—Demand for Popular Franchise—Relations to Connecticut—Holland and England—Conquest of New Netherland by the English—The New Government—War between England and France—Lovelace—New Netherland Retaken by the Dutch—Restored to the English—New York Described by Andros—Dongan—Charter of Liberties—New York a Royal Province—The Revolt of Leisler.

NEW YORK, or New Netherland, as it was first called, after a period passed out of the possession of the Dutch, its original settlers. Had it been retained in their hands it would have severed the chain of English colonies along the Atlantic coast, and have established a barrier in the way of their eventual union in one political system. At the opening of the seventeenth century, the Confederated States of the Netherlands were emerging victoriously from their long and heroic contest for liberty against the power of Spain. In 1609, there was concluded a truce for twelve years, which contained an acknowledgment by Philip II. of their sovereignty and independence. Just at the time when this memorable peace was signed, Henry Hudson sailed from Amsterdam in the Half-Moon, to search for a passage to India by the northeast

Hudson's discovery.

or the northwest. Hudson was an English mariner who had made two voyages from England already in quest of India by way of the northern seas. Not disheartened by repeated failures, he now made a third attempt under the auspices of the Amsterdam directors of the Dutch East India Company, a corporation in which had been vested the most ample powers of colonization and government in the East, and which brought the largest pecuniary rewards to the enterprise of its projectors. After doubling the Cape of Norway, Hudson, finding in the ice and in the discontent of his men insuperable obstacles to a further progress, turned his prow toward America. Having reached the coast of Newfoundland, he sailed southward until he entered Delaware Bay. Then, reversing his course, he came in sight of the hills of Navesink, went in past Sandy Hook, and anchored in the lower bay of the future site of New York. He explored the neighborhood, and had converse with the Indians, which was generally of a friendly character. Still in quest of a route by water to India, in the month of September he sailed up the great river which was one day to bear his name, as far as the site of Albany. His appreciation of the charms of the scenery was enhanced by the delight natural to the discoverer whose eyes first beheld the noble stream and its adjacent shores, with their steep heights and verdant forests. He found the natives generally hospitable, although once he had to repel an attack. The reports of Hudson on his return—in particular, the prospect that was opened for a very lucrative trade with the Indians in furs—caused other vessels to be sent out by Amsterdam merchants on the same path. In 1614, Hendrick Christiaensen built a trading-house—"Fort Nassau"— on the west of the Hudson, a little below the site of Albany. It was designed partly as a warehouse and partly for defence. A few men were also left on the south end of Manhattan Island as the nucleus of a settlement. In the same year another sea-captain, Adrian Block, having lost his ship, embarked in a small vessel which he had built on that island, and coasted along the shores of New England. He went up the Connecticut River, entered Narragansett Bay, and sailed past Cape Cod as far as Boston Harbor. The Dutch captain gave his name to a large island which he visited. Under his supervision a "Figurative Map" was drawn, and was submitted by the deputies of a company of merchants to the States-General at the Hague. A charter was granted to the "New Netherland" Company to trade in that region for three years, from 1615. After that date it was renewed, year by year, until 1621. "New Netherland," as delineated on Block's map, embraced the whole of New England. In the same summer in which he made his exploring trip, John Smith was likewise examining the eastern coast of the same territory, to the northern part of which he attached the name of New England. In 1620, merchants of Holland were willing to send out to the shores of the Hudson, John Robinson and his Pilgrim followers; but Robinson and his people demanded a guaranty of protection which the States were not disposed to grant, and the Pilgrims themselves felt reluctant to break off all connection with their native land. For several years prior to this date, the States had been engrossed in theological and political contests of the gravest character. Barneveldt, the republican statesman, perished on the scaffold, and Grotius owed his life to the ingenuity and heroism of his wife, who planned his escape from prison. Hindrances to the organization of another great commercial corporation were at length removed, and, in 1621, a charter was given to the Dutch West India Company. Included in its powers

Block's exploring voyage.

The "New Netherland" Company.

West India Company chartered.

was the exclusive liberty to plant colonies on the American coast. The privileges of the Company in regard to planting settlements and governing them, and acquiring provinces, were almost unlimited. They were similar to those which had been conferred on the great Dutch corporation which managed the commerce and trade of the East. The Company was to be governed by a board of nineteen, a majority of whom belonged to the Amsterdam branch. One of the members of the board was to be appointed by the States.

The new Company was established, not mainly to found colonies, but for purposes of trade. But before it was fully organized, complaint was made by the representives of the Plymouth Company to the Privy Council. Sir Dudley Carleton, the British ambassador at the Hague, demanded of the States-General that they should prohibit any further prosecution of the enterprise. The whole country north of Virginia, Carleton asserted, had been granted by patent to the subjects of the King of England, to whom it belonged "by right of first occupation." No definite answer was obtained to this protest. In the spring of 1623, the first real attempts to colonize New Netherland began. A company of Walloons—Protestant emigrants from the Belgian provinces—was sent over. Eight men were left at Manhattan to take possession of the island for the West India Company. A part of the colonists sailed up the river and built Fort Orange, on the site of Albany. In 1624, civil government began under the rule of Cornelius Jacobsen May, as the first director. Under his administration, which lasted for a year, another Fort Nassau was completed on the South River—the Delaware. In 1625, two large ships loaded with cattle and horses, swine and sheep, arrived at Manhattan. Emigration continued, and when William Verhulst, in that year, succeeded May, the

The Dutch at Manhattan and Albany.

colony numbered more than two hundred. There was an alliance between Charles I. and the Dutch, and all the circumstances were favorable for the growth of the settlement. Peter Minuit, who came over as director early in 1626, bought the island of Manhattan of the natives for about twenty-four dollars.* There was correspondence with Bradford at Plymouth, and an embassy to him; but although there were mutual arrangements for trade, Bradford signified to the authorities at New Amsterdam that they had no clear title to their lands. *[margin: Purchase of Manhattan Island.]*

In 1628, Michaelius, a minister of the Reformed Church, came over and organized a church with fifty communicants. Before that, two "Consolers of the Sick," as they were styled, had read to the people on Sundays texts of the Bible and the creeds. These persons were of a class of recognized officers in the Church of Holland. The exports of the colony for several years were far less profitable to the West India Company than were the exploits of their sailors, by whom Spanish vessels, laden with silver, were intercepted and captured. The company organized its colonists by the establishment among them of distinct subordinate colonies, or independent lordships. The lord of the manor, the "patroon," as he was styled, had to be a member of the Company. By planting a colony of fifty adults anywhere, except on the island of Manhattan—which was to be under the direct control of the Amsterdam chamber—he became a feudal prince, with very extensive prerogatives and privileges, ruling over a broad extent of territory, of which he was the absolute owner. The colonists were to be subject to the patroon, whose service they might not leave *[margin: The patroons.]*

---

* It is a small sum, but had it been placed at compound interest, at the rate of six per cent., it would have amounted, at the end of two hundred and sixty-five years, to $122,472,860.

without his permission. His lands might extend for sixteen miles in length, or eight miles on either side of a navigable river if both banks were occupied. They might extend as far into the interior as "the situation of the occupiers" would permit. Special enticements were held out to colonists to emigrate under patroons. They were to be exempt for ten years from taxation. But all colonists, whether independent or subject to patroons, were forbidden to manufacture woollen, linen, or cotton cloth. The interests of the weavers at home were rigidly guarded. All settlers beyond the limits of Manhattan Island were required to purchase their land of the Indians, but the Company agreed to supply as many negroes "as they conveniently could," to be their slaves. The domains of the patroons became very extensive. The landed possessions of Van Rensselaer grew until they included a district extending twenty-four miles on the Hudson below Albany, and stretching in width for a distance of forty-eight miles. Another director was lord of what is now Staten Island, Hoboken, and Jersey City. In 1629, two directors of the Amsterdam chamber bought of the Indians the land between Cape Henlopen and the mouth of the Delaware River. By their control over the places most convenient for trade, the patroons held to a great extent a monopoly of commerce, deprived poor emigrants of this means of profit, and gave occasion to frequent contentions with the central government. In 1631, an expedition under Pieter Heyes established a small colony near the present town of Lewiston, in Delaware, and by this act of occupancy acquired a title to what was one day to be a State. Crossing to the Jersey shore, Heyes purchased from ten Indian chiefs a tract of land on the shore of the bay, north of Cape May, twelve miles in length, and extending inward for the same distance. A record of his purchase was attested by Minuit and his

The domains of the patroons.

council. The settlers at Lewiston incurred the hostility of the Indians, in consequence of which they were all slain, and the house which they had erected was burned.

The quarrels of the patroons with the agents of the West India Company, growing out of differences connected with the fur trade, were such as Minuit could not adjust. He was recalled, and, in 1633, an unworthy and incompetent successor, Wouter van Twiller, arrived to take his place. He accomplished nothing in his controversy with the settlers of Connecticut. The Dutch could justly allege that their fort at Hartford was built before the coming of any English occupants of the soil. But this was not allowed by the Connecticut people as sufficient to nullify the English title derived from the grant of King James. The Connecticut settlers, moreover, planted a portion of Long Island. On the south, as well as the east, the possessions claimed by the Dutch were threatened. In 1638, a colony of Swedes and Finns, sent out by a company which owed its existence to Gustavus Adolphus and his great chancellor, Oxenstiern, made a settlement within the limits of the present State of Delaware, near the mouth of Christiana Creek. The fort which they erected they named Fort Christiana. Kieft, who was now the director at New Amsterdam, sent home an account of the arrival of the Swedish emigrants, and made a protest to Minuit, who, being at this time in the service of Sweden, was their leader. But it was not deemed expedient to resort to force to expel the newcomers, who were protected by the flag of Sweden. Fresh emigrants arrived, and in 1643, Printz, the Swedish Governor, took up his abode and built a fort on the island of Tinicum, a few miles below the site of Philadelphia. Thus a New Sweden was growing up in the neighborhood of the Delaware Bay and River.

Van Twiller succeeds Minuit.

The Swedish settlement.

The rashness and wilfulness of Kieft were responsible for serious troubles with the Indians. Quarrels sprung up between the natives and the traders. The Algonkins would have welcomed peace for the sake of being protected against the Mohawks, who regarded them as tributaries, and sent a force of warriors to enforce their claim. But Kieft availed himself of the occasion to make a murderous attack on the Algonkins, which they, with the aid of allies far and near, avenged. Ann Hutchinson and her family perished at their hands. At last, in 1645, a delegate from the Mohawks appeared, and with his assent, the Algonkin sachems and the authorities of New Netherland concluded a treaty.

Trouble with the Indians.

On May 27, 1647, Peter Stuyvesant began his government, Kieft having been superseded. "The island of New York was then chiefly divided among farmers; the large forests which covered the Park and the adjacent region, long remained a common pasture, where, for yet a quarter of a century, tanners could obtain bark and boys chestnuts; and the soil was so little valued that Stuyvesant thought it no wrong to his employers to purchase of them, at a small price, an extensive bowery just beyond the coppices, among which browsed the goats and the kine of the village." Under the freedom of trade—export duties being, however, required—the colony, had it been well governed, might have rapidly advanced in prosperity. But Stuyvesant, although energetic and honest, was a choleric and tyrannical ruler. He sternly resisted the demands of the people for municipal government. The example of New England increased their natural desire to have some part in political management. At length he consented that the people should nominate eighteen Councillors, from whom he was to appoint nine. But the arrangement for filling the vacancies was such that the people had no further agency in

Peter Stuyvesant.

the matter. The disaffected Councillors at length succeeded in making their petitions heard by delegates, who obtained in Holland from the States-General good measures; but the Company did not adopt them, and Stuyvesant did not alter his course.

The spread of the New England settlers westward moved the Dutch Governor, in 1650, to repair in person to Hartford. A treaty was made—which was never ratified by England—that made Oyster Bay, on Long Island, the western boundary of the New Englanders, and Greenwich as their limit on the mainland. The Governor was more successful against the Swedes. An attack by the Swedish Governor, Rysingh, on a Dutch fort near Christiana, was followed, in 1655, by an expedition of Stuyvesant to the Delaware River. The Swedish forts were taken, and the jurisdiction of the Dutch over the territory was acknowledged. *Treaty with Connecticut.* *Attack on the Swedes.*

In 1656, Delaware became by purchase subject to the city of Amsterdam as proprietary. The monopoly in trade which that city established prevented their settlements from prospering or increasing in numbers. While Stuyvesant was conquering New Sweden, ravages were committed by the Indians near New Amsterdam. *Delaware purchased.*

During the administration of Stuyvesant, there occurred, under his countenance and aid, a lamentable outbreaking of intolerance against the Lutherans. The Established Church of Holland exercised authority over the colonies of the West India Company in relation to religious and ecclesiastical affairs. The ministers were commissioned and sent out by the classis of Amsterdam, a body answering to a presbytery. The clergy were strict Calvinists. In 1656, there were four Dutch clergymen in New Netherland. They were active *Religious contests.*

in their religious duties, and some attempts were even made to teach the Gospel to Indians. But nothing of any account was done for popular education. There were no schools, except at Manhattan and one or two other places. Ecclesiastical animosity was kindled against the Baptists and the Lutherans. Lutherans were fined and imprisoned. But the Governor was rebuked by the West India Company for his acts of persecution. A little later, in 1657, a proclamation, somewhat similar to enactments of Massachusetts, was issued against the Quakers. During a series of years, without the approval of the Company, forcible measures were taken against them. They were fined, whipped, imprisoned, and banished. Persecution ceased in New Netherland, when, in 1663, the Company, in their despatches to Stuyvesant, condemned "rigorous proceedings" against "sectarians," as long as they should be modest and moderate in their behavior, and not disobedient to the government.

In 1652, in consequence of persistent, earnest complaints and petitions, a court of justice was constituted for New Amsterdam; but in the selection of its members the people were to have no part. In 1653, the villages of their own section sent, each of them, two delegates to a convention, which set forth in a remonstrance and petition their demand for a popular franchise. Stuyvesant, who was supported by the Company, rejected their requests with an abundant display of arrogance, and dissolved the convention. As time went on, the troubles, both of the Governor and of the colony, multiplied. The claims of Lord Baltimore to the territory between New Castle and Cape Henlopen were denied, and the Dutch jurisdiction there was maintained. But the endeavors to withstand the encroachments of Connecticut were ineffectual, although Stuyve-

Demand for popular franchise.

sant made a journey to Boston, in 1653, and laid his grievances before the Confederate colonies.

The charter which the younger Winthrop had obtained from Charles II., gave to Connecticut the northern half of New Netherland and the whole of Long Island. In addition to all other perils, the Dutch were at war with the Esopus Indians. Their treasury, moreover, was exhausted. Stuyvesant, instigated by the municipal government of New Amsterdam, was ready to appeal to the people. An assembly of delegates from the villages sent a spirited remonstrance to the Amsterdam Chamber, in which these calamities were attributed to the neglect and mismanagement of the authorities in Holland. The men of Connecticut made no delay in their efforts to extend the actual jurisdiction of their colony over the towns on Long Island. To add to the complications, John Scott, who had been placed by Connecticut as a magistrate there, announced in the English villages that the island had been granted by the King to his brother, the Duke of York. Scott was made "President" of a number of towns which were not ready to be annexed to Connecticut. He set about bringing the Dutch villages under his sway. The details of the conflict of Stuyvesant with him, of the Governor's controversy with the Connecticut authorities, and of their proceedings against Scott, need not here be given. These contests were terminated by the arrival of an English fleet, carrying a body of troops, for the purpose of conquering New Netherland. They were sent by the Duke of York, Lord High Admiral, to whom his brother, Charles II., had made a grant of the territory lying between the Connecticut and the Delaware Rivers, and comprehending Long Island. The English seizure of New Netherland was due, in the main, to commercial rivalry. It was a product of the contest of England and Holland for the

Relations to Connecticut.

Holland and England.

dominion of the seas and the profits of commerce. It was against Holland that the Navigation Act of 1660 was chiefly directed, an Act which was passed under the Commonwealth, and was energetially carried out under Charles II. Cromwell had proposed to take possession of New Netherland, but he gained such advantages by the treaty of 1654 that he desisted from the plan, and recognized the Dutch title. Under the rule of the trading corporation to which it belonged, New Netherland did not thrive. Its population was not above seven thousand, when in the New England colonies there were more than a hundred thousand inhabitants. The New Netherlanders were conscious of the disadvantages under which they labored in comparison with their more prosperous English neighbors. In England it was well understood that Virginia and Maryland would not be withheld by legal enactments from trading with the Dutch. If the Navigation Act was to be carried out, and an immense loss to English merchants thereby prevented, the law must be put in force along the entire coast. In 1663, the farmers of customs complained that there was a loss to the kingdom of ten thousand pounds a year. When the States-General called upon Clarendon, the Lord Chancellor, for a settlement of boundaries between the Dutch and the English territory in America, it was resolved, despite Cromwell's concession in 1654, to proceed in a summary way and to take possession of New Netherland. Clarendon, at the same time, was determined to bring the territory to be acquired, as well as the colonies already subject to England, under the control of the King, and to prevent any further growth of local independence. The territory which had been conveyed, in 1635, to Lord Stirling, comprising a district in Maine, and Long Island, was purchased from him. A force of four hundred and fifty regular troops, in four ships, which carried also

the Commissioners for the regulation of the English colonies, was sent over, under the command of Colonels Nicolls, Carr, and Cartwright. Stuyvesant made all the exertions that a spirited soldier would naturally make, to prepare for resistance. *Conquest of New Netherland by the English.*
But resistance was hopeless. When the city authorities of Manhattan, the clergymen, and the officers of the burgher guard, united in begging the imperious Governor no longer to oppose the inevitable, he yielded up the place. The surrender of Fort Orange and of the places on the Delaware soon occurred. The royal province, and New Amsterdam as well, which then contained fifteen hundred inhabitants, now received the name of New York. Fort Orange was named after the Duke's second title, Albany. The municipal officers of New Amsterdam continued in power. The property, the civil rights, and the religion of the citizens were guaranteed in the capitulation. The neglect with which they had *The new government.*
been treated by the home government made it easier to break the tie of loyalty to Holland. Nicolls, as the deputy of the Duke of York, acted as Governor. To him and his Council public authority was entrusted. There was to be no election of magistrates by the people. The courts were constituted after the English models. The significant features of the code of laws, called the Duke's Laws, were "trial by jury, equal taxation, tenure of lands from the Duke of York, no religious establishment, but requirement of some church form, freedom of religion to all professing Christianity, obligatory service in each parish on Sunday, a recognition of negro slavery under certain restrictions, and general liability to military duty." By a friendly arrangement, divine service, according to the forms of the English Church, was held in the Dutch house of worship at New Amsterdam, when the service of the Reformed Church was over. The city

government was altered to conform to the customs of England. Nicolls was an able and faithful ruler. But he was painfully disturbed by the news that, from motives of friendship, the Duke of York had inconsiderately made a grant of the territory of Nova Cæsarea, or New Jersey, to Sir George Carteret and Lord Berkeley. The right of jurisdiction, although not expressly conveyed, was claimed by them.

The refusal of Clarendon to accept the terms proposed by Louis XIV., for peace between England and Holland, led to a declaration of war by France, and to a counter-declaration by England, in January, 1666. An order was sent out to the American colonies to conquer New France. But it was found to be impracticable to engage in hostilities in that direction. The French, not satisfied with the relations in which they stood with the Five Nations, made war upon them, and succeeded in forcing them to recognize Louis as their protector and sovereign. The peace of Breda, which ended the European war, confirmed the English in their possession of New Netherland. Nicolls was permitted to return to England. He was succeeded by Lovelace, who was prudent, and of a moderate temper. Fisheries and trade with the other colonies were encouraged. The triple alliance of 1668, in which Great Britain was joined with Holland and Sweden, tended to cement the union of the Dutch and English inhabitants of New York. There was occasional trouble about taxes, especially on Long Island, and there were contests respecting boundaries with Connecticut and with Massachusetts.

In 1673, in the war against Holland, in which the English and French were allied, New York surrendered to a Dutch squadron, and the rule of the Hollanders was extended over the province, to the joy of many of the old Dutch inhabitants. The Prince of Orange was sagacious enough to see that New York would be a precarious possession, and in the treaty of 1674 it was restored to the English. <small>Returned to Sir Edmund Andros received the government the English.</small> from the hands of Colve, the Dutch ruler in this interval. Andros was a firm, and, on the whole, a wise Governor. He abstained from the use of force to bring Western Connecticut under his authority. He cultivated the friendship of the Mohawk Indians, and formed an alliance with the Iroquois, an act of the utmost importance in relation to the great conflict with the French that was sure to come. The new patent that was issued to the Duke of York in 1674, enlarged his authority. He enforced the Navigation Act, and by promoting intercourse with England did much to make New York "the most English in sentiment of the American colonies." In a description of New York, from the pen of Andros, in 1678, he <small>New York speaks of it as containing twenty-four towns or described by villages, enumerates its products and exports, Andros.</small> and says that the men capable of bearing arms are two thousand in number. He adds: " Religions of all sorts— one Church of England, several Presbyterians and Independents, Quakers, and Anabaptists of several sects, some Jews, but Presbyterians and Independents most numerous and substantial." Under the direction of the Governor, a classis of the Reformed Church was established in New York for the purpose of ordaining ministers. In reference to New Jersey, Andros contended for the jurisdiction of the Duke there, arrested Carteret, and refused to liberate him after a jury had acquitted him. The disputes in regard to New Jersey, in connection <small>Dongan.</small> with complaints against him on some other matters, led to his recall to England, where he was fully exonerated from blame. In 1683, Thomas Dongan, an

Irish officer, was made Governor. He brought with him instructions to issue writs for an Assembly to share with the Governor and Council in the work of legislation. No tax was to be levied without its sanction. But no act was to be valid without the assent of the Duke. The As-

Charter of liberties.
sembly passed a "charter of liberties and privileges," among which was included a guaranty of "freedom of conscience and religion" to those "who profess faith in God by Jesus Christ." The act was approved by the Duke, but not until October, 1684. Dongan was himself a Roman Catholic. As far as the relations of New York to the Indians and the French were concerned, he did everything that he could to promote its interests. He made friends with the natives, and baffled the designs of the French.

The Duke of York, on his accession to the throne, as James II., in 1685, abolished the popular Assembly.

New York a royal province.
New York became a royal province instead of a nominal duchy. The treacherous treatment of the Iroquois by the French fortified their alliance with the English. In 1688, Andros arrived on his mission to consolidate the northern colonies under a vice-regal government. On August 11th, he began the exercise of his authority in New York. He went to Albany and renewed the covenant with the Iroquois. He notified the Governor of Canada that the Five Nations would be protected as the subjects of the King of England. The feeling of the Protestant inhabitants of New York was the same as that of Protestants in the other colonies and in England. There was a distrust of James and a belief that his policy of religious toleration was a part of a scheme by which he hoped more effectually to build up the Roman Catholic cause in England, and to advance the dominion of the papacy. When the news of the Revolution of 1688 arrived, the people rose under the

leadership of a German named Leisler, who seized the fort. The government was placed in his hands. Nicholson, the Deputy Governor, sailed for England. Leisler was arbitrary and violent in his proceedings. In opposition to him, another government was set up at Albany. As we shall see, it was not until 1692 that the conflicts and dissensions which ensued upon the Revolution passed by, and the province again found itself under a stable government.

<small>The revolt of Leisler.</small>

CHAPTER X.

NEW JERSEY TO 1688

Grant to Berkeley and Carteret—Settlement at Elizabeth—Settlement at Newark—East Jersey—West Jersey Acquired by Penn and His Associates—Sale to Penn of Carteret's Rights—Scottish Emigration to East Jersey—Effect of the Revolution of 1688.

THE immediate gift of the territory of New Jersey by the Duke of York to two courtiers, Lord John Berkeley and Sir George Carteret, proved a fruitful source of contention and injustice. It was called "Nova Cæsarea" in honor of Carteret's brave defence of the island of Jersey, which he held for Charles II.; but the corresponding English name soon supplanted the Latin. The deed of transfer gave to the two proprietors all the powers which belonged to the Duke, "in as full and ample a manner as they had been possessed by him." For the reason that powers of government were not explicitly mentioned, there was afterward much dispute on the question whether they were included in the Duke's grant. In February, 1665, the proprietors prepared an instrument comprising "concessions and agreements," for all present and prospective settlers. This document served as a constitution for the community under their charge. The government was to be lodged in a Governor, Council, and an Assembly of representatives. The Governor and Council were to appoint and remove all officers. They could levy no tax without the consent of

<small>The Constitution.</small>

the Assembly. The Assembly was to frame the laws, which, in order to be valid, must be approved by the Governor, and at the end of a year sanctioned by the Lords Proprietors. Tracts of land were offered to emigrants, male and female, including servants as well as freemen. After 1670, annual quit-rents were to be paid by landholders. Oaths of fealty to the King and fidelity to the Lords were required of all freemen. Liberty of conscience was guaranteed. Land was given to parishes for the support of ministers. Philip Carteret, a relative of Sir George, was made Governor. He brought over with him a small company of settlers, by whom the town of Elizabeth was founded.

On arriving at New York in the summer of 1666, Carteret was informed that Nicolls, the Deputy Governor, ignorant of the deed granted by the Duke, had confirmed certain parties in the possession of a tract of land on the New Jersey shore, west of the strait between Staten Island and the mainland, and also of a tract near Sandy Hook. Middletown and Shrewsbury (in what is now Monmouth County) grew up on the tracts thus bestowed. Carteret and his company found that at the place now called Elizabeth some settlers had already taken up their abode. The publication of the "concessions" drew additional emigrants from the eastern colonies. In 1666, on a part of the Elizabethtown tract some of these emigrants planted Newark. They adopted the rule of the New Haven colony, from which they came, that only church members should vote. The New Jersey settlers were at peace with the Indians about them, since these were subordinate to the confederacy of the Five Nations. The first Assembly was convened at Elizabethtown in 1668. Two sessions were held in that year. But during the next seven years no meetings of the Assembly took place. This was probably ow- *Philip Carteret, Governor.*

The first Assembly.

ing to the dissatisfaction of the settlements, which had received their lands from Nicolls's grant, and were not disposed to come into subjection to the rule of the Proprietors. In 1670, the other towns objected to paying quit-rents. An Assembly was held in 1672, composed of deputies of Elizabethtown and of the places in sympathy with this settlement, but this body was not recognized by the Governor and Council. It proceeded to appoint a "President," to act in the room of a Governor, and James Carteret, a son of Sir George, who was passing through New Jersey, so far disregarded the rights of his father as to accept the place. Governor Philip Carteret repaired to England to make known the situation and to procure a remedy. Messages came from Charles II. and the Duke of York to Deputy-Governor Berry confirming him in his authority, and commanding the settlers to yield obedience. The effect was the restoration of quiet and union. The Dutch reconquest of New York, in 1673, brought in no essential changes and caused no commotion in New Jersey. When New York was restored by treaty to the English, the Duke of York confirmed his previous grant to Carteret of his moiety of the territory in East Jersey. In 1676, the line between East and West Jersey was defined to run from the "east side of Little Egg Harbor, straight north through the country, to the utmost branch of the Delaware River," in 41° 40' north latitude.

In 1674, Berkeley had disposed of his portion of the undivided province to John Fenwicke, in trust for Edward Byllinge, both of them Quakers. By other acts of sale and transference, West Jersey became the possession of William Penn and four of his Quaker brethren. In 1677, and in the following year, there was a large emigration of Friends to West Jersey. The Constitution which was prepared for the colony by

<small>West Jersey sold to Penn and others.</small>

Penn contained an emphatic assertion of the doctrine of religious freedom. The right of trial by jury was guaranteed. Executive authority was lodged in a body of commissioners. The power to enact laws was conferred on an Assembly to be chosen by popular vote and to meet yearly.

Philip Carteret came back, in 1674, as Governor of East Jersey. Andros, the Duke's Governor in New York, bent on carrying out the provisions of the Navigation Act, claimed the exclusive right to collect customs in East Jersey and to interfere with direct trade there. His negotiations with Carteret produced no result. Hence the arrest of the latter, his trial and imprisonment in New York, even after he was acquitted. The decision of the Duke of York was in favor of Carteret, the East Jersey proprietor. The Duke claimed only the reserved rent. The death of Sir George Carteret led to the sale of his rights in East Jersey, which now became the property of William Penn and twenty-three other proprietors. *East Jersey purchased by Penn and others.* Among them were Royalists, Dissenters, and Quakers. This was in March, 1682. Robert Barclay, an eminent author and leader among the Friends, was appointed Governor, but he remained in England, his Deputy being a lawyer, Thomas Rudyard. Rudyard's successor, Lawrie, a London merchant, brought out with him a body of laws, supplementary to the "Concessions." Lawrie wrote to the English Proprietors: "There is not a poor body in all the province, nor [one] that wants." A publication, in 1685, by the Proprietors, setting forth the advantages offered to settlers, led to the emigration of two hundred in one vessel, the Henry and Francis. A visit to Governor Dongan, at New York, established amicable relations between him and Lawrie. In 1684, a "Board of Proprietors," resident in the colony, was put in charge of certain details of business which had before been referred to the Proprietors in England. By them the town of Perth—Perth-Amboy—was built up. In West Jersey, in 1680 and 1681, Edward Byllinge was made Governor, and Samuel Jenings his deputy. The Assembly made the attempt to elect Jenings as Governor, but this claim to choose the Governor was not allowed in England.

There was a large influx of emigrants into East Jersey from Scotland. Lord Neill Campbell, a brother of the Earl of Argyle, was made the successor of Lawrie. He was followed, in 1687, in the same office, by Andrew Hamilton, who had been a merchant in London. When the purpose of James II., to unite the northern colonies under one government was discovered, both East Jersey and West Jersey thought it wise to make no resistance. Both provinces were annexed to New York. By the Revolution of 1688, and the overthrow of the government of Andros, the provinces were left under no other control than that of the county and town officers. The Proprietors abstained from resuming their authority. Hamilton at first maintained a kind of neutrality, and soon sailed for England to consult with the Proprietors there. When he reached England he resigned his office as Deputy Governor.

The Jerseys annexed to New York.

CHAPTER XI.

PENNSYLVANIA TO 1688

Early Life of Penn—Grant to Him by James II.—Penn's Charter—His Constitution—The Body of Laws—Penn's Treatment of the Indians—Emigration to Pennsylvania—Religion in the Colony—Penn in England—Disorder in the Colony—Pennsylvania Described.

No one of the founders of the English colonies in America who themselves crossed the ocean was in his own time so famous as William Penn. He is associated with George Fox as the second principal leader of the Society of Friends, to whom he was endeared by great services and great sufferings in behalf of their cause. His birth and social position gave him access to people of rank in England, including Charles II. and James II., both of whom, especially the latter, were disposed, from friendship for his father, to further his plans. The father, Admiral Sir William Penn, on the deposition of Richard Cromwell had declared for Charles. He distinguished himself by wresting Jamaica from the Spanish in 1655, and, ten years later, in battle against the Dutch. While at Oxford the younger Penn, who in childhood had at times been the subject of strong religious emotions, was much influenced by the preaching of Thomas Loe, a Quaker, and after a two years' residence was expelled from the University, partly on account of his refusal to attend its regular worship. This brought on him the wrath of his father, who turned him out of doors. He was sent by the Admiral, who was by no means implacable, to Paris, to be cured of his folly, as it was deemed, by means of social gayeties. The remedy appears to have been for the time effectual. He mingled in the pleasures of the French court, and during his stay on the Continent visited Italy. Yet, while he was in France, he was taught for a while by Amyraut, a liberal-minded Calvinistic theologian of high repute. Abroad, as well as in his varied experiences at home, he gained an acquaintance with different sorts and conditions of men which proved of essential service to him. After his return, he once more met Loe, in Ireland; his religious feelings were awakened anew, and he espoused, heart and soul, the religious ideas of the Quakers, to whom, through good report and evil report—almost exclusively through evil report—he forever adhered. Penn united a considerable measure of natural shrewdness with an unaffected devoutness. The numerous writings that sprung from his prolific pen display, in connection with the mystical vein to be looked for in a believer in "the inner light," an uncommon vitality of thought and style. Like so many of his sect in its early days, while an enemy of war, he was an ardent polemic in the field of debate. He shows a relish for "the joy of strife"—the *gaudium certaminis*—when the war is one of words. He is most spirited on his favorite theme, freedom in the concerns of religion.

<small>Penn's character.</small>

Penn's connection with New Jersey naturally suggested to him schemes of colonization on a larger scale. In these he found a special incentive in a desire to provide a refuge for his persecuted brethren. After the death of Charles I., a debt of £16,000, which the crown owed to Admiral Penn, was discharged by a grant of territory to his son. The charter, which was signed on March 4 (O. S.), 1681, fixed the boundaries of Pennsylvania, a

<small>Grant to Penn.</small>

name which Charles II., desiring to honor the Admiral, insisted on attaching to the region defined in the grant. It included three degrees of latitude and five degrees of longitude on the west of the Delaware, with the exception of a district about Newcastle, which was limited by an impossible boundary. As we have already stated, a mistake as to the geographical place of the fortieth parallel was made in the stipulation. Penn claimed—what was finally adjudged to be his—the lands on the Delaware which had been settled by the Dutch and the Swedes. He wanted the waters and shores of the river and bay of Delaware to the ocean, and this concession he obtained, in 1682, from the Duke of York by deeds of enfeoffment. The three counties of Delaware, or "the territories," as Delaware, in distinction from the Pennsylvania grant, was called, were thus annexed to his dominion, but held by a different tenure.

By the charter, Penn, as Proprietary, was made Governor. He was empowered to make laws with "the advice, assent, and approbation of the Freemen of the said countrey, or the greater parte of them, or of their Delegates or Deputies." A transcript of all the laws was to be submitted to the Crown for approval within five years after their enactment. If within six months they should be declared inconsistent with the rights of the sovereign or with English law, they were to become void. Penn was authorized to appoint subordinate officers, including "judges and justices," and to grant pardons. But appeals to the sovereign were to be in all cases lawful. No taxes or imposts of any sort were to be assessed on the people except with the consent of the Proprietary, "or chiefe governor and assembly, or by act of Parliament in England;" but the English "Lawes of Trade or Navigation" were to be inviolably maintained. Penn was obliged to agree to a clause providing

Penn's charter.

that on the petition of twenty persons a preacher or preachers might be sent out for their instruction by the Bishop of London, and that they should be permitted to reside in the province, "without any deniall or molestation whatever." A proclamation of the King, directed to the province, declared that Penn had been entrusted with the powers of government. An address was also issued by Penn himself. He declared that the Governor would not aim to increase his own fortune, and had an "honest mind to do uprightly." "You shall be governed," he said, "by laws of your own making." "I shall not usurp the right of any, or oppress his person." These pledges were honorably fulfilled.

Penn's address.

A cousin of Penn, William Markham, was sent out as Deputy Governor. On August 31, 1682, Penn in person, with a large body of Quaker colonists, in three ships, set sail for his province. The farewell letter which he wrote to his wife and children is full of wisdom and tenderness. Markham had sent back highly encouraging reports of the health of the country, of its fertility, and of the abundance of game found there. Before the coming of Penn, settlers, some of them Quakers from Wales, had arrived in considerable numbers. The site of the capital had been chosen—the peninsula between the Delaware and the Schuylkill. After Penn's arrival, Philadelphia was laid out, and its streets marked out in the rectangular style. At Newcastle, Penn took formal possession of Delaware, and then passed up the river to Chester. Before leaving England he had drawn up the sketch of a constitution. His spirit was democratic. "Any government," he said, "is free to the people under it (whatever be the frame) where the laws rule the people, and the people are a party to these laws; and more than this is tyranny, oligarchy, or confusion. . . . Liberty without obedi-

Penn goes to his province.

Penn's constitution.

ence is confusion, and obedience without liberty is slavery." The first Assembly met at Chester. Penn, in conformity to his purpose to include the Delaware counties under his jurisdiction, had caused them to send to it their delegates. At this Assembly, Penn's Frame of Government, modified in some particulars, and a body of laws were sanctioned. It was provided that there should be a Governor, a Provincial Council, and an Assembly of Freemen. Subsequently, the power to negative laws initiated by the Assembly was conceded to the Governor. Offices were made elective. There was a guaranty of religious freedom, but abstinence from labor on the Sabbath was required. Murder was to be punished with death. Accused persons were to be tried by jury. Indians charged with crime were to have the same right, and in their case half of the jury was to be of their own race. Peacemakers were to be chosen in the several counties to adjust differences of a minor character. There was to be no law of primogeniture. No tax was to be levied without authority of law. Revels, bull-baiting, cock-fighting, stage-plays, lotteries, drunkenness, duelling, profane swearing, and "health-drinking" were forbidden. The care of the poor and the humane treatment of prisoners were provided for. It was ordained that the laws should be taught to the children in the schools. Certain changes at the second Assembly, in the scheme of government, called out a warm protest from one prominent man, Nicholas More. In later times they were sharply criticised by Franklin.

The just and benevolent spirit which dictated all the proceedings of Penn in relation to the colonists was conspicuous in his dealings with the Indians. He won their confidence by himself visiting them in their wigwams. In June, 1683, he held a conference with leading native chiefs at Shackamaxon. At that time

Treatment of the Indians.

he made a considerable purchase of land. In his contracts with the natives he was frank and fair. Consequently they trusted him and loved him. It is true that the character and circumstances of the neighboring Indians were such as to favor the establishment of friendly relations with them. Yet the continued amity between the two races was owing, in no small degree, to the equitable policy of the founder of the colony.

In 1683, there arrived a small company of German Mennonites, most of whom were linen-weavers. A learned young lawyer from Germany, Pastorius, who belonged to a class of devout Lutherans denominated Pietists, and acted in part as the agent of a Frankfort Land Company, began the settlement of Germantown. In conjunction with some others, in 1688, he sent to the Friends' meeting a written protest against the purchase and sale of slaves. Penn was unwearied in his exertions to promote the advancement of the colony. It grew more rapidly in numbers than any other colony had grown except Massachusetts. In 1685, there were upwards of seven thousand inhabitants, somewhat more than one-half of whom were of English extraction. Among the people there were Dutch, French, Scotch-Irish, Finns, and Swedes. At the end of a year and a half one hundred and fifty houses had been built in Philadelphia. In 1684, the number of houses had risen to three hundred and fifty-seven. In 1683, a school was established where the pupils paid moderate fees for instruction. A brisk trade sprung up. There was a beginning of commerce with some of the West India Islands. There was a division of the province into counties and townships. Early in 1684, Penn could say, with pardonable satisfaction: "I have led the greatest colony into America that ever any man did upon a private credit, and the most prosperous beginnings that ever were in it are to be found among us." Religious differences had not created disturbance. The Swedes had their own worship. The Dutch had a church at Newcastle. Quaker meetings had been held as early as 1675. The first meeting at Philadelphia was held in 1683. A little later the Baptists began to establish churches.

Religion.

In 1684, Penn returned to England to advance the interests of his colony there, and to look after the contest respecting boundaries in which he was engaged with Lord Baltimore. The death of Charles II. had the effect to increase Penn's influence at Court. James II. did not forget a dying request of Admiral Penn that he would befriend his son. Penn approved the Declaration of Indulgence by the King, which the most discerning Protestants considered as not only an unconstitutional stretch of the royal prerogative, but also as an element in a plot for their final reduction under the authority of Rome. It should be remarked that the charges of base conduct which were made by Macaulay against Penn sprang from a confounding of names, and are without foundation.

Penn in England.

In Penn's absence the colony was to be governed by the Council, of which Thomas Lloyd, a prudent man, was the President. Turbulent scenes soon arose. The Proprietary system began to be unpopular, as happened in the other colonies where it was established. The Assembly showed signs of impatience under feudal rule, and embarked in various schemes of legislation which engendered strife. Nicholas More, the Chief Justice, was impeached on the charge of partiality and violence, and was expelled from the Assembly, of which he was a member. By order of the Assembly, Robinson, the clerk of the Court, was arrested for refusing to produce his records. The Council would remove neither

Disturbances in Pennsylvania.

of them from office. Penn sent over an earnest remonstrance, occasioned by the animosities and quarrels that prevailed. They had operated, he said, to prevent emigration. His own quit-rents were left unpaid, and only a part of the imposts due to him was collected. The giving of executive power into the hands of five members of the Council, in 1686, having produced little change for the better, Penn appointed Captain John Blackwell Lieutenant-Governor. Blackwell was honest, but was without tact, quarrelled both with the Assembly and the Council, and withdrew at the end of nine months.

A contemporary "Description of Pennsylvania and of its Capital," printed in England in 1698, speaks of Philadelphia as containing many "stately houses, and of brick," "several fine squares and courts." The principal streets, writes the author, take their names "from the trees that formerly grew there." "It hath in it three fairs every year, and two markets every week." Between the principal market-towns, Chester and the others, "the water-men constantly ply their wherries." There is a "great and extended traffique and commerce" with the other colonies, the West Indies, and Old England. All the useful trades and occupations are prosecuted. "Of lawyers and physicians," says the narrator, "I shall have nothing to say, because the country is very peaceable and healthy." He tells us that there are several good schools of learning for youth in Philadelphia. "There are no beggars to be seen, nor, indeed, have any here the least temptation to take up that scandalous, lazy life." The description by this author, who had resided in the colony for fifteen years, is enthusiastic throughout, but rests on a substantial basis of fact.

PART II.

FROM THE ENGLISH REVOLUTION OF 1688 TO 1756

CHAPTER XII.

THE EFFECT ON THE COLONIES OF THE REVOLUTION OF 1688

Result of the Revolution of 1688—King and Parliament—The Colonial Governments—Spirit of the Colonial Houses of Delegates—Navigation Laws—French and Indian Wars—French Explorations—French Claims to Louisiana—Movements in the Direction of Colonial Union.

THE colonies, which had impatiently submitted to the tyranny of Charles II. and James II., did not reap all the benefits which they expected from the Revolution that raised William and Mary to the throne. It is true that they were delivered from the anxiety which they had felt, in common with the Protestants in England, lest the insidious exertions of the sovereign to establish in power the Roman Catholic religion should prove successful. Moreover, the fear that the Anglican prelacy might extend its authority over the Puritan communities on this side of the ocean, at the cost of their ecclesiastical freedom, was now dissipated. William himself was a Calvinist. He had grown up in a church Presbyterian in its polity. The doctrine of Tol-

Effect of the Revolution of 1688.

eration was so far legalized at the Revolution that a reasonable apprehension, which had never been absent since the planting of New England, was now at an end. The Bill of Rights, the great charter of the English Revolution, and other measures which followed the adoption of it, abridged the extent and defined the limits of regal authority. The King was no longer to have the right to suspend laws, or the execution of laws. Standing armies in time of peace, without consent of Parliament, were made illegal. It was ordained that there should be frequent meetings of Parliament. It was settled that control over the public purse should rest with the House of Commons. The "Civil List" was established, which was made up mainly from the hereditary revenues of the Crown; but laws for taxation, and all acts for the appropriation of money for carrying forward the government, must originate in the Lower House, and be passed —if passed at all—by the Lords without amendment. What is especially noteworthy, all grants, the Civil List, of course, excepted, were to be made annually. The House of Commons was rapidly acquiring the complete predominance which, at the beginning of the Hanoverian rule, made the ministers of the monarch its agents, rising to power and falling from power according to the will of the dominant party.

The colonial governments were constituted after the pattern of the government of the mother-country. There was a governor in place of the king—a governor who was appointed in the royal provinces by him—a Council, answering in a general way to the Upper House of Parliament, and a House of Representatives chosen by the people, corresponding to the Commons in England. Whoever studies the colonial history from this date cannot fail to remark the constant striving of the colonial houses of delegates to limit the royal power

The colonial governments.

and to control public affairs, after the model of English precedents as they were shaped by the Revolution. But William chafed under the fetters that were laid upon his prerogative, especially when he found himself embarrassed by them in the prosecution of the great contest in Europe against the ambition and aggressions of Louis XIV. In this protracted conflict William's heart was absorbed. For the sake of the union that was effected between Holland and England, and the advantage thus gained in this European struggle, he was glad to accept the English throne. He wanted to wield the whole strength of the coalition of which he was the head, without being hindered in his operations by the obstructive or dilatory action of Parliament. As regards the colonies, it was not in his thoughts to allow to them the degree of independence and self-government which belonged to Parliament in its relation to the Crown. The king's ministers and Parliament were in agreement on this subject. The antagonism that almost constantly developed itself between the popular branch of the legislature in the colonies, which was bent on exercising a large measure of freedom, and the royal governors and the officials in England to whom the governors were responsible, was an inevitable effect of the opposite ideas entertained by the respective factors in the government. A chronic source of discontent in the colonies was the Navigation Laws. The English merchants were determined to keep the foreign trade of the colonies exclusively in their own hands. These laws were considered by the colonists to be unjust and oppressive, and there was little scruple about evading and disregarding them.

King and Parliament.

Royal governors and colonial assemblies.

Navigation Laws.

Another standing topic of contention, which the history of Massachusetts perpetually brings before us, was the demand, kept up for a long period, and the determined refusal on the part of the local legislature, to appoint a fixed salary for the Governor, in the room of an annual appropriation, the amount of which varied according to the pleasure of the deputies of the people. The motives on both sides were mutually understood, though it was only on certain occasions that they were avowed. The Home Government aimed to make the judgment and conduct of the Governor independent of the popular will; the people were resolved not to surrender the influence which their control over the emoluments of the Governor enabled them to bring to bear upon him. Practically the exclusive control of the local legislature in the whole matter of domestic taxation was conceded. Yet the English laws imposing duties on imports, and the laws relative to post-office arrangements, when these laws were framed, were forms of indirect taxation. One who reads the story of the bickerings and graver disputes between the Home Government and the colonies, from the accession of William and Mary to the beginning of the American Revolution, might naturally imagine that the colonies, or some of them, were consciously aiming all the while at absolute independence of the mother-country. This accusation has often been made. Yet it is wholly untrue. Franklin told Lord Chatham, in 1775, that in all his intercourse with all sorts of people in the colonies, he had never heard a desire to separate from England expressed. John Adams's testimony is of the same general purport. Such proofs, in the absence of contradictory evidence, are conclusive. Minds capable of a prophetic glance might foresee in the distant future, as the result of a natural progress, the development of an American empire. Sir Thomas Browne is one of those who predicted such an event. Bishop Berkeley, in his verses on the march of empire westward, may have had a presentiment of it. But such dreams, if they existed at all on this side of the Atlantic, are something quite different from a practical aim or wish to realize them by a rupture between England and her American dependencies. In the mother-country it was often honestly felt and openly declared that the colonies were prone to complain of reasonable laws and exactions, and showed ingratitude for the protection afforded them. It is true that they owed their exemption from the danger of being subjugated by other European powers to the safeguard afforded by the flag of England. It is true that in the repeated and prolonged wars with Canada, the colonies were aided by the troops and ships of England. But when this fact was brought up, it was replied that the colonies were strong enough to cope with New France, that it was only the bringing over of French forces from abroad that made English assistance necessary, and that for the existence of these intercolonial wars the colonies were not responsible. They sprung out of exigencies in European politics—out of wars of England with the continental monarchies, in which the colonies had no special concern.

It is undeniable that the effect of the English Revolution was to plunge the colonies into costly and desolating conflicts with the French in Canada and their Indian allies. Almost ruinous expenses were incurred, and terrible sufferings were endured, especially by New England and New York, where border settlements, with intervals of comparative quiet, for the greater part of a century were exposed to the murderous inroads of savage foes, instigated and directed by their white superiors. Shortly after the accession of William, England declared war against France. Such a war of necessity included a struggle between the rival nations for dominion in the New World. *French and Indian wars.* *King William's War, 1689-97.*

This contest, the first in the series, went on until the Peace of Ryswick in 1697. Four years later, the second war commenced, which was waged for twelve years, and was brought to an end by the Peace of Utrecht in 1713. Hostilities began anew in 1744, and the Peace of Aix-la-Chapelle, in 1748, by which they were closed, was little more than a truce. The beginnings of the fourth of the intercolonial wars, a war of seven years, which led to the English conquest of Canada, fall chronologically within the compass of the present volume. But the border warfare of the colonies with the French and Indians was not confined within the limits designated above. It often preceded or extended beyond them. Moreover, when armed incursions on one side and the other, and midnight massacres by stealthy bands of savages were, for longer or shorter periods, suspended, there was no certainty that they might not at any time be renewed. There was almost unceasing anxiety and the need of continual vigilance and costly preparations.

Queen Anne's War, 1702-13.

King George's War, 1744-48.

The French and Indian War.

The great obstacle to the spread of New France to the South and West was the enmity of the powerful confederacy of the Iroquois, or Five Nations, to which were added, in 1713, another kindred tribe, the Tuscaroras from North Carolina. When Louis XIV. took the reins of administration in his own hand, a new activity was imparted to French exploration. Courcelles was made Governor of Canada, and the Iroquois for a while abstained from their attacks. The Jesuits and their rivals, the Recollets, a branch of the Franciscan order, were intrepid and unwearied in planting their missionary stations along the borders of the Great Lakes. There sprang up a chain of French forts and settlements as far as the site of St. Louis, on the Mississippi. Father Marquette, accompanied by Joliet, a trader, and five

French exploration.

other Frenchmen, sailed down the Wisconsin, entered the great river, and descended it as far as the mouth of the Arkansas. They returned by the Illinois to Chicago, and to Green Bay by crossing Lake Michigan. In 1680, the companions of La Salle ascended the Mississippi to the Falls of St. Anthony. La Salle himself, who had built a fort, which he called St. Louis, and given to the country on the banks of the Mississippi the name of Louisiana, in honor of the King of France, afterward, in 1682, descended the river to the Gulf. Furnished with a frigate and three other vessels, he sailed from France in 1684, but missed the entrance to the Mississippi, and landed somewhere in Texas. Failing in his search for the river by exploring the country about him, he set out to return to Canada by land, but at the end of three months he was murdered by two of his own men. The men who were left at St. Louis perished. La Salle.

The expeditions of La Salle furnished the basis of the French claim to the whole vast region called by them Louisiana. After the Peace of Ryswick, D'Iberville, a Canadian, was put in charge of an expedition for establishing a settlement at the mouth of the Mississippi. In 1696, he passed a fort which the Spanish had erected three years before, on the bay of Pensacola, and succeeded in planting a company of settlers on the shores of Biloxi. Most of them removed, in 1702, to Mobile, on the bay of the same name, where they formed the first settlement within the present borders of Alabama. In an interval of peace with the Iroquois, a fort and settlement were established at Detroit. French villages were planted between the mouths of the Ohio and the Illinois. Meantime the French abandoned none of their claims in the East. They claimed an exclusive right to fish on the coast as far as the mouth of the Kennebec. Among the Norridgewocks on the Upper Kennebec they

French claim to Louisiana.

founded a missionary station, which was under the charge
of the educated and accomplished Jesuit priest, Sebastian
Rasles. He gained such an ascendency that the tribe was
devoted to the interests of the French. Such, in brief,
were the pretensions of France as regards America in the
early years of the eighteenth century. In numbers and
resources Canada was much weaker than the English
colonies. Much depended on the amount of aid that
might be derived from France. The long English border, with its scattered settlements, furnished the Canadians with great advantages for the sudden incursions
which it was impossible to foresee, and which carried devastation and slaughter into so many peaceful hamlets. It
was a vital matter with the colonists to be united
in using their means of resistance, and in devising plans of attack. Movements in the direction of political union it was therefore the interest of
both the English government and its American subjects
to promote. On the other hand, the colonies had to
guard against schemes of union or consolidation which
would involve the loss of that self-government which they
so dearly prized, and bind upon them more strongly the
fetters of commercial servitude under which they chafed.
Besides, there was a great deal in the slowness of intercourse between the several colonies, and the tenacity of
local ideas and aims, that tended to keep them apart.
Yet it was, in fact, the situation in reference to New
France that gave rise to a series of conventions in which
governors or commissioners from a larger or smaller number of colonies assembled for consultation and to arrange
for combined action. Such congresses, having for their
special business treaty arrangements with the Iroquois,
met at Albany in 1684, in 1694, in 1711, in 1722, in 1748,
and in 1751 ; and a like congress of commissioners from
Maryland, Virginia, and Pennsylvania, met at Lancaster,

Reasons for colonial union.

Pennsylvania, in 1744. In 1709, a convention of several governors was held at New London, to consult in reference to a proposed expedition to Canada. A convention for the same object assembled at the same place in 1711. More significant than previous assemblages of this kind was the congress that met at Albany in 1754, in which Franklin was the leading spirit, and which was intended not only to unite the Five Nations in closer bonds of amity with the English, but also to form "articles of union and confederation with each other for the mutual defence of his Majesty's subjects and interests in North America, as well in time of peace as war." The commissioners were chosen by the Assemblies of the colonies that were represented. In the history of this convention, as elsewhere, it is evident how the sense of the necessity of union for common defence, and for devising and carrying out effective measures for repelling the enemy and for the conquest of Canada, was qualified by the risk to local liberty, and the danger of an increased measure of subjection to England, which it was felt that the schemes of confederation involved.

CHAPTER XIII.

NEW ENGLAND FROM 1688 TO 1756

Board of Trade and Plantations—French and Indian Attacks—Unsuccessful Attempt on Canada—Massachusetts Fails to Regain her Charter—The New Charter of Massachusetts—The Witchcraft Delusion—The Government of Phips— Bellomont—Inroads of French and Indians—Separation of New Hampshire from Massachusetts—Rhode Island under Bellomont—Dudley—Queen Anne's War—Rhode Island under Dudley—Connecticut — Shute — Explanatory Charter of Massachusetts — New Hampshire and Connecticut—The "Great Revival"—Belcher—Connecticut and Rhode Island — Burnet — Shirley—Renewal of Hostilities with France — Capture of Louisburg — The Albany Congress—Military Expeditions—New Hampshire and Connecticut.

THE revolution in Massachusetts which followed upon the news of the revolution in England, left that colony without a legal government. Although the charters of Connecticut and Rhode Island had been given up, they had not been annulled by a judicial decree. But the charter of Massachusetts had been vacated by the verdict of the English courts. It was entirely uncertain whether it would be restored by a new royal grant. In England, a new impetus was given to the commercial interest by the accession of William and Mary. A fresh zeal was consequently awakened in behalf of the enforcement of the Navigation Laws. One consequence was the committing of the whole management of colonial affairs to a new "Board of Trade and Plantations," composed of fifteen members. In the

Board of Trade and Plantations.

ample list of their powers was included the authority and the duty "to scrutinize the acts of colonial legislatures."

While political affairs in the northern colonies were in an unsettled state, there was a neglect to make adequate preparation for the renewed contest with the French. Three months after the accession of William, England declared war against France. Early in 1689, Frontenac, an able and energetic man, was for the second time made Governor of New France. He proceeded to organize three expeditions against the English settlements. One of them, consisting, as usual, of French and Indians, surprised the village of Schenectady by night. There ensued a massacre which lasted for two hours. Sixty persons, of all ages and both sexes, were killed. Thirty persons were carried off as captives. All the houses but two were burned. Another attack, attended with like horrors, was made on the village of Salmon Falls, in Dover. A third party made its way from Quebec to Casco Bay, in Maine, and captured the garrison of the fort there. A little later an assault was made upon Exeter, where a considerable number of persons were killed. An expedition from Massachusetts, under the command of Sir William Phips, in eight small vessels, captured Port Royal, in Acadia, and demolished the French fort at the mouth of the St. John's River.

Frontenac.

French and Indian attacks.

Delegates from the colonies of Massachusetts, Plymouth, Connecticut, and New York met at New York, on May 1, 1690, to concert measures against the enemy. A plan for the conquest of New France was one of the results of the conference. On August 9th, a fleet of thirty-two vessels, containing two thousand men, sailed from Nantasket, near Boston, to make an attack on Quebec. A simultaneous attack was to be made on Montreal by a body of troops from Connecticut

Unsuccessful attempt upon Canada.

and New York, in conjunction with a force of Iroquois Indians. This overland expedition unhappily proved a failure. Owing to a variety of hindrances it advanced no farther than Lake Champlain. Finding Montreal released from peril, Frontenac hastened back from that place to Quebec, and reinforcements for his troops then followed him. Small-pox broke out among the crews of the colonial ships, the ships were damaged by tempestuous weather, and Phips was compelled to return without accomplishing anything, and with a loss of about a thousand men.

Issue of paper money in Massachusetts. One of the worst incidents of this unsuccessful attempt at conquest was the issue by Massachusetts of paper money, in the shape of *bills of credit*, for the payment of the soldiers. They soon fell to two-thirds of their nominal value. This was one of a series of legislative measures of the same kind, which deranged the business of the colony, and drove its government to the verge of bankruptcy. It must be said that the authorities in England, and their official representatives in the colony, set themselves in opposition to these mistaken and ruinous measures, put a check upon them, and finally did much to put an end to them.

Massachusetts was anxious for the restoration of her charter. It had been hoped that, if the Canadian expedition were successful, a favorable impression would be produced in England. This hope, of course, was frustrated. The agent of the colony in London, Increase Mather, was the leading minister of the colony and President of the College. Two others were now associated with him, Elisha Cooke and Thomas Oakes. No efforts were spared by these commissioners to secure favorable action. A bill for the restoration of charters, in which New England was expressly included, passed the Commons, but Parliament was prorogued before it reached the Lords. The General Court in Massachusetts, as a conciliatory measure, opened a little wider the door to citizenship. But as time went on, the adverse party in London grew stronger. There had come to exist in Massachusetts itself a minority, in which were included a portion at least of the later and more wealthy immigrants, that did not care to see the old system of rule re-established, and was willing to leave affairs more under foreign direction. Andros and his fellow-captives, on their arrival in England, did their best to deepen and extend the existing prejudices against the colony. Ratcliffe, the Episcopal clergyman, who had also returned to England, lent what help he could in the same direction. The mercantile class were decidedly averse to the colonial freedom that involved danger to their monopoly. The King himself was not of a mind to lessen his prerogatives. At length, late in 1691, it was settled that there should be a new charter for the province of "Massachusetts Bay." *The new charter of Massachusetts.* Plymouth colony was included in the charter, and from this time ceased to exist as a distinct community. The Governor, Lieutenant-Governor, and Secretary were to be appointed by the King. In the Lower House two deputies were to sit from each town. The Council, the upper branch of the Legislature, was to be appointed from year to year by the General Court, subject to the Governor's approval. The Governor might reject the bills passed by the Legislature. The King, also, at any time within three years, might annul such enactments. Courts of Admiralty were to be constituted by the Crown, and to try cases without a jury. Other courts—except Probate Courts, which were to be constituted by the Governor and Council—were to be established by the General Court. A provision was made for appeals in certain cases to the King in Council. The religious qualification for voters was no longer to continue. A property qualification was substituted for it. This was a very important feature of the new charter. To the General Court was given the right to impose and levy taxes. This provision, with the right conferred on the Court—where the representatives would form the majority—to nominate the members of the Council, were the two features of the charter in which the friends of popular rights had most reason to rejoice. The agents of the colony in England, and the people of the colony, had to bear the disappointment which their inability to recover the old charter inflicted. To Mather was given the privilege of naming the new officers to be appointed by the Crown. At his request, Sir William Phips was made Governor. The old charters of Connecticut and Rhode Island were left untouched.

Phips appointed Governor.

When Phips arrived in the Province which he was to govern, he found the people in the midst of the excitement occasioned by the witchcraft delusion. The reality of witchcraft, or of wicked leagues made by human souls with Satan, was still generally accepted, and the supposed crime was condemned in the legislation of all Christian countries. So great a judge as Sir Matthew Hale, and a divine so kindly and intelligent as Richard Baxter, had no doubts on the subject. With the dawn of the eighteenth century, this old faith began to fade; yet later than the middle of the century another most eminent jurist, Blackstone, and another famous divine, John Wesley, are among those who lent it an undoubting sanction. The date of the beginning of the troubles in Massachusetts on this subject was four years earlier than the arrival of Phips, in the last year of the rule of Andros. Several children in Boston professed to be "bewitched." Increase Mather, some years before, had touched on the subject of witchcraft in a book which he had written. Now his son, Cot-

The witchcraft delusion.

ton Mather, a minister only less prominent than his father, interested himself in these strange phenomena. Cotton Mather was a man of restless temperament, credulous, and fond of praise. But the part which he took in the witchcraft proceedings has been sometimes overstated. If he was superstitious he was not cruel. It ought to be remembered to his credit that when inoculation was first introduced into Boston, he stood by Dr. Boylston against most of the medical faculty, favored the new remedy, and braved public opinion, even when the mob threatened to attack his dwelling. Cotton Mather's "Essays to do Good" was one of the books to which Benjamin Franklin was disposed to ascribe much of the usefulness of his subsequent life. Several years elapsed before the witchcraft prosecutions began in Salem, where Parris, a minister in a part of the town which was afterward called Danvers, was most active in fomenting the delusion. Not less than a hundred persons accused of witchcraft were in jail at the time when Phips assumed his office. He constituted a Special Court to try the cases. It consisted of seven magistrates, with Stoughton, a man of narrow mind, honest, fanatical, and of inflexible obstinacy, at its head. Accusations were made against persons in other towns besides Salem. Among the accused who suffered death by the sentence of the newly created tribunal was one respectable minister, and other persons hitherto held in esteem by their neighbors. Not a few, bewildered by the pressure of accusation and by testimony which they knew not how to rebut, or seeing no other way to save their lives, confessed themselves guilty. Subsequently, when the time of danger was past, confessions thus made were retracted. By the time that the General Court assembled, which was in October, the sway of the delusion was broken. Twenty innocent persons had been sacri-

Cotton Mather.

ficed. Charges had begun to be made against persons of high social standing, and of unblemished reputation. The community was appalled, and the conviction spread that there must be a mistake at the root of these shocking transactions. The Special Court was superseded, and a regular tribunal constituted in its place. After this time, the few who were found guilty were pardoned. A few years later, a General Fast was appointed in the colony, for the errors into which magistrates and people had been betrayed "by Satan and his instruments" in the recent "tragedy," as it was termed. On that day Sewall, who had sat as one of the judges with Stoughton, and was afterward Chief Justice of the colony, arose in his pew in the Old South Church, and stood while the minister read from the pulpit the confession which he had framed of his own accord, and in which he acknowledged and deplored the sin of ignorance that he had committed in connection with the witchcraft trials. There are few more impressive and characteristic scenes in Puritan history than the spectacle of this conscientious and upright man standing before the congregation, with bowed head, and making public confession of errors into which he had unwittingly fallen.

Repentance.

Phips was a native of Maine. He was of a family of twenty-six children by the same mother, twenty-one of whom were sons. Having been apprenticed by his father, who was a gunsmith, to a ship carpenter, he became a seaman. He formed and successfully carried out a plan for fishing up a Spanish vessel, loaded with treasure, which had been wrecked on the coast of Hispaniola. He conveyed the plate and jewels to England, and divided the spoil liberally with the participants in the enterprise. For this achievement he was knighted. Phips was an honest friend of the colony, but was a man of moderate capacity and of a

The government of Phips.

hasty temper. He knocked down in the street, and beat with a cane, one Short, the captain of a frigate who had made a great commotion by undertaking to impress seamen. He had a quarrel with Brenton, who had been appointed, against the will of the merchants, Collector of the port of Boston. Phips was summoned to England. There he continued to be held in esteem, but before it could be decided whether he should resume his office, he died. There was no end to the depredations of the French and Indians. In 1694, Castine was captured, and a part of the English captives were slain. On March 15, 1697, the savages made an attack upon Haverhill. Among their captives was Hannah Dustin. The savages dashed out the brains of her infant, a week old. When far on their way to Canada, she, with her nurse and an English boy, in the night, when her keepers were sound asleep, slew them with their own hatchets, and with her companions made her escape. It was estimated that in the ten years prior to the peace of Ryswick, more than seven hundred Englishmen had been killed, and more than two hundred carried off into captivity. *Inroads of French and Indians.*

In 1697, Bellomont, an Earl in the Irish peerage, was appointed Governor of New York and New Jersey, Massachusetts and New Hampshire. He was made commander of the forces of all the colonies. It was felt in England that energetic measures must be taken to suppress piracy, and to unite the colonies for effective action against France. Bellomont was manly and generous, although of a choleric temper. Privateering, which had flourished during the contest with France, easily ran into piratical depredations, and the seas were infested with lawless freebooters. Bellomont succeeded in seizing the person of Captain Kidd, who, having been entrusted with a commission to *Bellomont.* *Piracy.*

capture piratical vessels, had turned pirate himself. He was sent to England, where he was condemned and executed. To secure the collection of customs, Randolph was appointed, in 1698, Surveyor-General in the northern ports of America. About the same time, a law was passed in England which prohibited not only the exportation of wool, and everything made of wool, to foreign countries from the colonies, but also the transportation of these articles from one colony to another.

It was the policy of English statesmen to weaken, rather than increase, the power and influence of Massachusetts. In 1692, New Hampshire became a separate colony. Samuel Allen, who had bought the claims of Mason, was appointed Governor, with Usher, his son-in-law, to rule in his absence as Lieutenant-Governor. Nothing but the courage of the colonists and their unconquerable perseverance, enabled them to hold their ground under the continual assaults of their Indian foes. Usher had a contest with the people on the titles to the lands, and a quarrel with the Massachusetts Governor, Phips. Usher had made up his mind to lay down his office ; but when Partridge, his successor, arrived, he changed his purpose. The Board of Trade sustained Partridge, who, in 1699, became the Lieutenant-Governor under Bellomont. The question of the land-claims was at length referred to the English authorities in England. Usher was the advocate of Allen's claims, and William Vaughan, a man highly esteemed, represented the colony.

<small>New Hampshire separated from Massachusetts.</small>

In Rhode Island, Samuel Cranston, who was first chosen Governor in 1697, continued in office for thirty years. There was a contest with Phips on the subject of the command of the Rhode Island militia, which had been given to him in his commission. Bellomont was extremely dissatisfied with Rhode

<small>Rhode Island under Bellomont.</small>

Island because of the shelter offered to pirates in Narragansett Bay. In his letters to England he denounced in the strongest language the weakness of the government there, the disregard of law, and the general ignorance and disorder of the people.

The successor of Bellomont was Joseph Dudley. After his departure from Massachusetts he had held for a time the office of Chief Justice in New York. Having returned to New York, he was exceedingly desirous of gaining the appointment of Governor in his native colony, where he had been for five months a prisoner. He was able and industrious, and obtained the support of the dissenting interest in England. Even the Mathers favored his appointment. He received his commission from Queen Anne, and arrived in Boston in 1702. He held the office for thirteen years. During the greater part of this time, he was engaged in a contest with the General Court, or with the lower branch of it. He persisted in his demand, which with equal constancy was refused, that he should have a stated salary. He required, but without success, the rebuilding of the Pemaquid fort in Maine. He obstructed the House in the choice of a Speaker. On the accession of Anne the war with France was renewed, and there followed another long series of Indian attacks upon the border settlements of New England. A signal example of these atrocities, and yet but one among many, was the assault upon Deerfield in the winter of 1704, when sixty persons were killed, and one hundred, including the minister with his wife, were led off as captives through the snows to Canada. The wife fell on the way, from physical weakness, and was killed by an Indian's hatchet. An expedition under Colonel March for the capture of Port Royal, which was organized by Dudley in 1707, and consisted of a thousand men, proved a failure. Three years later a force of New England troops, aided by a regiment of royal marines, captured that place. The next year, another great expedition, led by Hill, an incompetent English commander—an expedition which cost Massachusetts a great outlay of men and money—suffered such disasters on the St. Lawrence as to prevent it from reaching Quebec, while the force that was simultaneously to operate against Montreal could do nothing more than to effect a safe retreat. The opposition to Dudley in Massachusetts was led by an able advocate of popular rights, Elisha Cooke. The Mathers became extremely hostile to the Governor. This was largely owing to disputes relating to the College, in which he withstood them, and the outcome of which was the overthrow of their ascendency. In various ways it appeared that the ancient authority of the clergy was declining. In 1709, Dudley reported that when he arrived the colony contained fifty thousand inhabitants. In 1710, an Act of Parliament established a General Post-Office "in all her Majesty's dominions" in America. Some arrangements had previously been made, at different times, for the carrying of letters. Among the devices occasioned by the disordered state of the currency was a project for a "Private Bank" whose bills of credit were to be based on mortgages of real estate. This futile scheme was crushed, not without considerable loss to its contrivers.

Abortive expeditions against Canada.

Opposition to Dudley.

In New Hampshire a stated salary was granted to Dudley. He found it hopeless, however, to procure obedience to the laws regulating trade. Usher became Lieutenant-Governor in 1704. The Mason claims continued to be a subject of angry contention and of litigation. A liberal offer was made by the province for the settlement of them, but Allen, in whose

New Hampshire.

hands they were held, died before it could be accepted. After the death of his son, which followed, no further attempts were made to enforce the claims, and the people were left to possess their farms in peace. Usher was at variance both with the New Hampshire colonists and with Dudley. When Dudley left his office, he was displaced.

Rhode Island had the same troubles under Dudley as under Bellomont, respecting the suppression of piracy and the command of the militia. He styled the province "a receptacle of rogues and pirates." There was complaint in Massachusetts that Rhode Island did not do her part in the struggle with the Indians. But as the war went on, the contribution of troops from that province became more regular. The monetary troubles in Massachusetts were much aggravated by the large issue of paper money in Rhode Island, which was occasioned by the expenses of the war. There was a school kept up at Newport, but there was no public provision for education. In 1708, the population of Rhode Island numbered seven thousand one hundred and eighty-one.

Rhode Island under Dudley.

Connecticut, fortunate in her situation and in the retention of her charter, was spared many of the ills of her sister colony on the bay. There was a system of education, ordained by law, for the instruction of the people. Yale College was founded in 1700, and chartered the following year. Fletcher, the Governor of New York, who visited Hartford in 1693, to assert practically the right which he claimed to control the militia, signally failed in the endeavor. Serious trouble grew out of the boundary disputes with Massachusetts and Rhode Island. The boundary line on the east was at last determined in accordance with the views of Rhode Island. In the prosecution of the wars, Connecticut is-

Connecticut.

sued paper money, but not in such an amount as to create financial troubles. She made her contributions of men for these contests. This was especially true after the induction of Saltonstall into the office of Governor, who was seventeen times in succession chosen to this place. A native of Massachusetts and a graduate of Harvard, he was trained for the ministry, and became a pastor in New London. By the advice of the clergy he was led to consent to take the office of Governor as the successor of Fitz-John Winthrop. He proved to be a very able and successful magistrate. With dignity of person and manner, and impressive power as a speaker, there were associated the capacity and the firmness of a statesman. It was under Saltonstall's government, in 1708, that a synod was called by the colonial legislature, to meet at Saybrook, for the regulation of the ecclesiastical arrangements of the province. A system of church government, mid-way between simple Congregationalism and the Presbyterian method, was adopted, and was sanctioned by the legislature. In 1714, the last year of Queen Anne's reign, there were about thirty-three thousand people in Connecticut. There were thirty-eight towns and forty-three ministers. Its prosperous and happy condition is indicated by the few events of a startling character that occurred. It approached the happy state ascribed to a people that has no history.

The successor of Dudley in Massachusetts was Samuel Shute. He held his office for a little more than six years. Shute had been a soldier, and had served under Marlborough. William Dummer, a native of New England, was made Lieutenant-Governor. Shute was a dissenter in his religious connection. He was fair-minded, with a soldier's sense of the obligations of law and obedience. But it was inevitable that there should be continual friction in his dealings with the General Court. There were the standing subjects of discussion—the question about a fixed salary for the officials appointed by the King, and the strengthening of the Pemaquid fort. In addition to these points of difference, there was more trouble between the colonists and their English rulers on the matter of the trees reserved for the masts and spars of the royal navy. Trees of a certain height and circumference were held to belong to the King, and it was unlawful to dispose of them in any other way. But this prohibition was nowhere strictly regarded. The King's broad arrow stamped upon them did not restrain the hardy settlers from cutting them down and devoting them to whatever use they pleased. In the dispute about the interpretation of the law on the subject, the people had a champion in Elisha Cooke, the younger. When the Lower House chose him to be their Speaker, Shute declined to ratify their choice. When the Governor failed to please the deputies, they diminished the annual grant for his support. In the war with the Eastern Indians, they would not permit him to erect trading-posts as a means of defence and security. They interfered with his military control by claiming the right to appoint the officers, to remove those who were unsatisfactory to them, and to dictate as to the movements of troops. Despairing of success in this complex quarrel with the General Court, Shute withdrew, and went to England to present his complaints. William Dummer, the Lieutenant-Governor, was left in his place. The House refused to pay the officers whom it did not like, and to vote supplies until they should be removed. Year after year, murders continued to be committed by the Eastern savages. The centre and source of hostile attacks was believed to be the settlement of Rasle. In August, 1724, a force was sent

Shute's conflicts with the Assembly.

Dummer.

Destruction of Rasle's settlement.

up the Kennebec, which attacked and destroyed the settlement. Rasle himself was shot by a soldier. Two years later a treaty of peace was concluded with the Eastern tribes. Jeremiah Dummer and Cooke were employed by the colony as agents in England to oppose Shute. In 1725, an explanatory charter was issued, which affirmed the necessity of the Governor's approval of the choice of a Speaker, and of his sanction for an adjournment of the House for a longer period than two days. This charter abstained from touching the other points in the controversy. After warm debate, on January 15, 1726, the House concurred with the Council in accepting it. Shute was preparing to return to the province, when he was set aside by the accession of George II.

Explanatory charter.

In New Hampshire, the opposition of Vaughan to Shute led to the removal of the former, who was succeeded by John Wentworth, a native of the province. When the Indian wars ceased, the colony grew in numbers and wealth. An important event was the settlement of Londonderry by one hundred families of Scottish Presbyterians from the town of the same name in Ireland—the town so famous for withstanding the siege of the forces of James II. In 1715, there were seven towns in Rhode Island with a population in the aggregate of about nine thousand inhabitants. In a collection of the statutes of Rhode Island there is a law which is thought to belong to the time of Bellomont, excluding Roman Catholics from the privilege of voting and of holding office. In 1724, the franchise was restricted to freemen possessed of real estate to the value of £100, or yielding an income of £2, and to their oldest sons.

New Hampshire.

Rhode Island.

Connecticut, in 1722 and the following year, did not approve of the Indian wars in which her aid was requested by Massachusetts. Her charter was occasionally threatened, but was protected in London by the efforts of Dummer, aided by Sir Henry Ashurst. In 1713, the boundary question with Massachusetts was settled. *Connecticut.*

In the closing part of the seventeenth century the Arminian theology had come to prevail widely in England, in the room of the stricter Augustinian and Calvinistic opinions which had previously held sway among both churchmen and non-conformists. *The "Great Revival."* A tendency to latitudinarian ways of thought in theology was rife in the first half of the eighteenth century. The same phases of opinion silently spread in New England. It was lamented by many that, owing to a variety of influences, there had come to exist a wide-spread decline in religious earnestness, and a corresponding negligence in moral conduct. In 1734, there occurred a remarkable awakening of religious interest in the parish of Jonathan Edwards, at Northampton. He had no sympathy with the current innovations in theology, and was characterized by profound sincerity in his religious convictions. A strong impression was made by his preaching, there was much excitement, and there were many conversions. Similar effects were produced by preachers of a like spirit in other places. In 1739, after a lull in the religious movement, it recommenced. It extended from place to place, and the fire was fanned into a flame by the eloquence of Whitefield, who came into New England from the Southern States in 1740. Whitefield, on his first sojourn in America, had labored *Whitefield.* as a missionary in Georgia. In the course of his seven visits to this country, he repeatedly traversed all the colonies, producing in them, as he produced in England, a great effect by his consecrated spirit and his almost unexampled power as an orator. When he preached, the largest houses of worship were crowded with eager listeners. He addressed in the open air throngs far greater than any building could contain. The result in New England was a large number of conversions, and in many towns a general attentiveness to religion. There were those, however, who deprecated the extraordinary excitement which accompanied the revival. A censorious spirit in relation to worthy ministers who preferred more quiet ways—a spirit which Whitefield, to his regret afterward, did something to encourage—alienated many sincerely religious men. At one time, the Faculties of Harvard and Yale severally issued Declarations adverse to him and to the character of his influence. He was not slow to make reparation for the harm which, in his youthful zeal—for he was only twenty-five when he began his work in New England—he had done by his indiscreet remarks. Among the undesirable consequences of the "Great Revival" was the division in churches of which it was the occasion. The most enthusiastic participants, not satisfied with the preachers who disapproved of the agitation and the outcries which were regarded as "the fruits of the Spirit," broke off from the parishes, and organized "Separatist" meetings. The "Separatist" movement was especially active and mischievous in Connecticut. It was fomented by a fanatical preacher from Long Island, James Davenport. The Connecticut Legislature, in 1742, expelled him from the colony. Other repressive enactments in reference to the schismatical proceedings referred to, were adopted; and a law was passed forbidding any minister to preach within the bounds of a parish without the consent of its

Effects of the Revival. pastor. The estimate of the general character and effect of the Revival varied with the temperament and opinions of those who pronounced upon it. Edwards, and the people in sympathy with him, held that it brought, on the whole, an immense benefit to the communities affected by it, while, at the same time they deplored the extravagances that came in its train. On the other hand, theologians of the type of Dr. Chauncey, of Boston, and President Stiles, of Yale College — more latitudinarian in their type of thought — judged that there was a preponderance of evil, and spoke with regret of "the late period of enthusiasm." There can be no doubt that this religious movement, of which Edwards and Whitefield were the most noted leaders, had a decided influence upon the subsequent ecclesiastical history of New England.

William Burnet was a son of the distinguished Bishop of Salisbury. He was bred to the law. On the accession of George II., he was transferred, in 1728, from the office of Governor of New York and New Jersey to the same station in Massachusetts. His personal excellence, which all acknowledged, could not save him from constant warfare with the House of Representatives during the fourteen months in which he administered the government. Feeling bound to fulfil his instructions, he insisted on the settlement of a fixed salary, which, according to the King's letter, was to be £1,000. The House voted to give him a much larger sum, but refused to be bound for more than one year. The large amounts which were tendered to him he rejected, since he regarded them as bribes to persuade him to forsake his duty. In the course of the controversy he adjourned the Court to Salem, as a place where, unlike Boston, "prejudices had not taken root." His right to do so was called in question. Until the House should yield in the matter of the salary, he refused to concur with its resolves providing for the pay of its own members. Burnet died suddenly from a fever resulting from an accidental overthrow of his carriage

Burnet.

His conflict with the Assembly.

while fording a stream. His only remuneration during his official service was from fees received from passes given to vessels cleared at the Custom-House. This was objected to by the colony, and the custom was afterwards disallowed. While Lieutenant-Governor Dummer was in power, an act was passed relieving Quakers and Baptists from the obligation to pay parish taxes.

Burnet's successor, Jonathan Belcher, was in office eleven years. He was a native of the colony, the grandson of an innkeeper at Cambridge. He had graduated at Harvard, and had resided in England, where he was for a time agent of the colony. He was a man of pleasing manners, but of an intriguing disposition. It was thought that he would be able to manage the fractious and disobedient representatives. But whatever might be the personal traits of the chief magistrate, the representatives were immovable in the resolution to regulate his salary from year to year. This they considered their right by the charter. To give it up would have made the Governor independent of them, but at the same time absolutely dependent on the King. At last, as the result of petitions from the House to the King and to the Commons, the Governor received permission to receive for his support annual grants. In a contest in behalf of these claims to audit public charges before the money which they had granted should be paid out, the Representatives were compelled by the decision of the King in Council, and of the House of Commons, to yield. Their request to the Governor to appoint a day of Fasting and Prayer on account of this afflictive event was refused. When the war with Spain began, in 1739, the House renewed their demand. Consequently only a small number of troops were sent to take part in Admiral Vernon's unsuccessful siege of Carthagena. Belcher was opposed by Dunbar, who was Lieutenant-Governor in

Belcher.

New Hampshire after Wentworth. Belcher favored the union of that province with Massachusetts. He drew on himself the enmity of those who were interested in the Land Bank. But it was chiefly by means of political scheming in England that he was removed from office. The untruth of the charges made against him was established, and he was appointed Governor of New Jersey. There were disputes in New Hampshire between the Representatives and Shute, who refused to ratify their choice of a Speaker. With Burnet there was no trouble. He was allowed a stated salary. *Removal of Belcher.*

In Connecticut, Joseph Talcott, the successor of Saltonstall, remained in office seventeen years, until his death. There was a controversy started by John Winthrop, the nephew of the late Governor, on the question of the distribution of the real estate of persons dying intestate. During the conflict in Massachusetts with Burnet, there was alarm in reference to the charter, and pains were taken to make it understood that Connecticut was not implicated in the policy of the sister colony. In 1729, Baptists and Quakers were exempted from paying for the support of Congregational worship, in case they maintained worship for themselves. Laws were enacted for the punishment and prevention of idleness and vice. An old prejudice against lawyers continued. It was enacted that not more than eleven persons of that profession should be permitted to reside in the colony. *Connecticut.*

In Rhode Island, in 1730, there was a population of seventeen thousand nine hundred and thirty-five, of whom fifteen thousand three hundred and two were whites, the remainder consisting of negroes and a much smaller number of Indians. Cranston, who died in 1727, had been Governor for thirty successive years. His successor, Joseph Jenckes, held office for five *Rhode Island.*

years, and would have retained the station had it not been for his intelligent and upright conduct in refusing to consent to the further issue of paper money. In 1729, there arrived in Newport the illustrious philosopher, Bishop Berkeley. He was a resident there for several years, and while there composed "The Minute Philosopher." Disappointed in reference to his plan for founding a college in Bermuda for training missionaries to the Indians, he returned to England. At Newport he founded a library, and he was a generous benefactor of Yale College.

<small>Bishop Berkeley.</small>

William Shirley, the next Governor of Massachusetts, like Burnet, was bred to the law, and had lived in Boston in the practice of his profession. He was not wanting in talents; he was active and enterprising as well as ambitious. He had early won the favor of the Duke of Newcastle, by whom his fortunes were advanced. Although a determined opponent of the bad financial policy which had so long disgraced the colony, Shirley yielded temporarily to necessity, and took the risk of consenting to a further issue of bills of credit. He proceeded cautiously in respect to the old controversy about the Governor's salary, and when it was evident that the House was not to be moved, it was dropped by the common consent of the Governor and the ministry. On the approach of war between England and France after a long interval of peace, it was necessary for preparations to be made once more against the French and Indians. To Shirley belongs the credit of suggesting the plan for the reduction of the strong fortress of Louisburg. The command of the New England troops—from Massachusetts, Connecticut, and New Hampshire—was given to William Pepperell, a native of Maine, a man in whose abilities and honesty confidence was justly reposed. An English fleet, under

<small>Shirley.</small>

<small>Capture of Louisburg.</small>

Commodore Warren, co-operated in the attack. During the siege a French vessel bringing supplies to the fortress was captured. The expedition was attended with complete success. The fort was surrendered on June 15, 1745. Pepperell was rewarded by being made a baronet. Both he and Shirley were appointed colonels. The English government reimbursed the colonies for their expenditures. The coin thus received enabled Massachusetts to redeem its paper currency. That it was applied to this purpose, in the face of strenuous opposition, was in no, small measure owing to the enlightened views of Shirley, and the earnest exertions of one of the representatives, Thomas Hutchinson, who at a later day became Governor of the colony. The peace of Aix-la-Chapelle, greatly to the sorrow of the colony, included a provision for the reciprocal restoration of all conquests. Louisburg went back into the hands of the French. A riot occurred in Boston, when a British naval officer, Commodore Knowles, undertook to impress seamen. The commotion was so serious that the Governor retired to the castle. The matter was settled by the General Court. The men who had been seized, or the most of them, were given up. In 1749, Shirley, who had now become distinguished, went to England, a part of his errand being to urge the settlement *Shirley in England.* of the boundary between the colonies and New France. The efforts to agree upon a line proved abortive. Shirley was also interested in thwarting the exertions of the French to establish a line of fortresses westward from Crown Point. He returned to Massachusetts in 1753. He entered with ardor into the conflict which was now beginning between the two nations for dominion in America. At the Congress of Com- *The Albany Congress.* missioners, at Albany, which undertook to form a confederation of colonies, Shirley was not present in person.

He believed in the necessity of union, but did not commit himself to the Albany scheme, the particular character of which suited neither the colonies nor the English ministry, although for opposite reasons. Respecting a plan formed by the ministry, Shirley conferred with Franklin. Franklin assured him that the colonies would not be content to be taxed by Parliament while they had no representation in that body.

On April 14, 1755, a council was held at Alexandria, in Virginia, at which were present the commanders, General Braddock and Admiral Keppel. The fruit of this conference was four military expeditions. The first was an expedition to Nova Scotia, in which two thousand provincial troops, under the command of John Winslow, took part. A result of this expedition was the expulsion from their homes of the French Neutrals, or Acadians, a measure decided upon by the British officers, in conformity with a plan which had been considered at a much earlier day in England, as well as among English officials in America. The Acadians were an inoffensive, industrious, pious body of Roman Catholic peasants. It was feared that they might be used as auxiliaries of the French in the great contest which had now commenced. The option was given them to swear allegiance to the British King, or to be driven from their homes. They declined the oath, and were transported, about seven thousand in number, from their loved abodes, to be dispersed in the southern provinces subject to England. About a thousand came to Massachusetts, where they were kindly treated, with the important exception that they were not allowed to have priests of their own. Some wandered as far as the West Indies and Jamaica. Few, if any, ceased to yearn for their old home.

Council at Alexandria.

The expulsion of the Acadians.

Another military expedition, which was designed to attack Crown Point and Montreal, was commanded by William Johnson, an inhabitant of the province of New York, who was considered to have a great influence over the Indians. It was mainly composed of three thousand Massachusetts and Connecticut militia. Baron Dieskau, who had been made Governor of Quebec, moved southward with a force of French and Indians to meet this invading body. On the southern end of Lake George an encounter took place, in which the French were beaten and their leader severely wounded. Among the troops on the victorious side were John Stark, and Israel Putnam, who was a second lieutenant. Among those who fell, in a previous engagement, earlier in the day, was Colonel Williams, who left a bequest which led to the foundation of the college in Massachusetts that is called by his name. *Battle near Lake Champlain.*

A third expedition, against Fort Niagara, at the mouth of Niagara River, where it enters Lake Ontario, was led by Shirley in person. It was substantially a failure. It advanced no farther than Oswego. *Shirley superseded.* Shirley's military ability fell below his own estimate of it and the opinion cherished by others. Before the story of his expedition had reached England he had been appointed to succeed Braddock, as Commander-in-Chief of the English forces in America. But he was soon superseded. He was requested to return to England, the ground alleged being a desire to consult him respecting the operations of the war. He became Governor of the Bahama Islands, but came back to Massachusetts to spend his closing days.

Benning Wentworth, who represented the party in favor of keeping New Hampshire a distinct province, became Governor in 1741. His administration went on smoothly for a number of years. Young Mason conveyed his interest in the Mason claims to a company of twelve, who took such a liberal course in the *New Hampshire.*

disposal of lands as to satisfy the people. Rival claimants who inherited Allen's claims could do nothing. A serious dispute arose between the Governor and the Assembly, which he was accused of packing in order to secure the passage of certain measures. Three years elapsed before the dissension came to an end.

Jonathan Law succeeded Talcott as Governor of Connecticut. The colony sent more than four thousand men to the siege of Louisburg, and the next year contributed a thousand men to the unsuccessful enterprise against Quebec. Connecticut was strongly opposed to the Albany plan of union, in 1754. This was the last year of Roger Wolcott's administration as Governor. He was succeeded by Thomas Fitch. The colony was kind and hospitable to the Acadian exiles. In the struggle with France, in its successive stages, Connecticut had an important part, and was liberal in the bestowal of both men and money.

Connecticut.

Rhode Island, in the war with Spain, and in the subsequent wars with France, was active in the business of privateering. After the siege of Louisburg the colony failed to embrace the opportunity to get rid of paper money. The evils of an inflated currency were of long continuance. Rhode Island had her representatives at Albany in 1754. Her legislature did not commit itself either for or against the plan of union. Into the final war with France, from 1755 to the end, Rhode Island entered with energy, both on the land and on the sea.

Rhode Island.

CHAPTER XIV.

NEW YORK FROM 1688 TO 1756

Leisler's Insurrection—The Assembly called by Sloughter—Fletcher's Ecclesiastical Measures—Bellomont—Cornbury—Trial of Mackemie — Hunter — The "Palatines" — Burnet—Cosby—The Liberty of the Press—Independent Spirit of the Assembly—"The Negro Plot"—Clinton's Struggle with the Assembly—The Albany Convention—Johnson's Victory—Paper Money—Character of the Middle States—Society in New York—Education—Ruling Families.

WHEN the news that James II. was dethroned reached New York, the government, in the absence of Andros, was in the hands of the Lieutenant-Governor, Francis Nicholson, and the Council. Not knowing what to do, and receiving no orders from Andros, who was under arrest in Boston, Nicholson sent to England for instructions. Meantime rumors were scattered abroad of a threatened French invasion. Nicholson's Protestantism was regarded as doubtful, and stories of an intended rising of the "papists," to join hands with the expected foreign foe, passed from one to another. Jacob Leisler, a native of Frankfort, in Germany, had been a soldier before coming to America. In New York he had become a merchant. He was a zealous Protestant, and no doubt put faith in the unfounded tales of a secret purpose of Nicholson and others to strike a blow for the fallen King, or, in some way to bring in by force the religion which James had professed and favored. Leisler was captain of one of the train-bands. Nicholson had too

Leisler's insurrection.

little energy to make any resistance, when he refused to pay the duties on a cargo of wine to the collector, whom he called a "papist," took possession of the Fort, and made himself master of the town. The three councillors who were then in New York, were all Dutchmen, but they were on the side of Nicholson. Most of the common people, however, a large majority of whom were Dutch, were ardent in the cause of King William, credulous as to the wicked intents of the Lieutenant-Governor and his adherents, and lent their help to Leisler. William was proclaimed King. A committee of safety was formed by ten members of an Assembly which Leisler called together in the Fort from a part of the counties. By this committee, he was declared to be Governor of the Fort until orders should come "from their Majesties." Letters to Nicholson, or to "such as may bear rule for the time being," giving them provisional authority, were opened by Leisler and used as a warrant for the extension of his own rule. Thenceforward he claimed to be Lieutenant-Governor by royal commission. He was acknowledged in the town of New York, and his power spread. He arrested and imprisoned any who did not obey him. But in Albany, where Peter Schuyler was Mayor, and was made Captain of the Fort, the people refused to be subject to Leisler. Milborne, his son-in-law, went there with a force, to be used in case of need, to compel obedience; but Schuyler, a cool and resolute man, who was able, if he saw fit, to avail himself of help from the Mohawks, would not yield, and Milborne had to give up his attempt. But when the French inroads began in earnest, and the slaughter at Schenectady took place, the necessity for union was felt to be so pressing, that the Albanians made concessions. Leisler was owned as acting Governor, Schuyler being still left in his office of Mayor. Albany was then a little stockaded

Leisler resisted in Albany.

A compromise.

village, with its two streets crossing each other at right angles. It was, however, even then, a very thriving place, the centre of a profitable trade in furs with the Indians. However arbitrary and violent Leisler was, he was an energetic leader in the warfare against the French. New York held geographically a central place among the colonies, and he showed himself competent to bring the other northern provinces into co-operation with it in the struggle which concerned all.

Colonel Henry Sloughter, a worthless man, was appointed Governor by William and Mary. In consequence of various delays he did not arrive in New York until a year and a half after the date of his commission. Meantime, about six months before his coming, on September 10, 1690, Major Richard Ingoldsby landed with two companies of grenadiers. Since he had no other commission than that of a Captain of Foot, Leisler refused to give up the Fort until the Governor himself should arrive. Ingoldsby assumed a hostile attitude. One day, while the British force was on parade, a collision took place. Shots were exchanged between Ingoldsby's soldiers and the troops in the Fort, and several were killed on both sides. If peace could have been maintained for two days longer, probably no further trouble would have arisen, for two days later Sloughter landed. His Council had been appointed for him in England. It was composed of adversaries of Leisler, two of whom he held in confinement. He had made numerous and bitter enemies. Leisler had no intention to keep possession of the Fort, but Sloughter sent demands for its surrender, in such a form as to show a willingness to put him in the wrong and to occasion some delay. With his principal abettors he was put under arrest, and a special court was constituted to try them on charges of treason and murder, based prin-

Contest with Ingoldsby.

Execution of Leisler.

cipally on the resistance which he had offered to Ingoldsby. Eight of the accused were convicted; two were put to death. The vindictive enemies of Leisler induced Sloughter, in a drunken fit, to sign his death-warrant, and that of Milborne. Both were executed on May 16, 1691. Leisler's dying speech gives convincing proof of his sincerity as a man and a Christian. Parliament, in 1695, after full inquiry, reversed the attainder of Leisler and his associates. In this act it was declared that Ingoldsby had no legal right to take possession of the Fort, and that Leisler was guilty of no fault in connection with the surrender of it to Sloughter. Lord Bellomont, who was one of the committee of Parliament to examine the matter, told Increase Mather that Leisler and his son were "not only murdered, but barbarously murdered." Their destruction was an act of political vengeance done by the "party of aristocrats," as they were styled. It did much to sow the seed of a bitter party contest of long continuance in the colony.

Sloughter was directed in his instructions to give religious liberty to all except Roman Catholics. The General Assembly, which he was authorized to summon, when it met, re-enacted substantially the Bill of Rights of 1683, with the exception that the right of worship according to the "Romish Religion" was denied. It was not on account of this exception that the sanction of the Sovereigns to the act of the Assembly was withheld. Later, in 1700 and 1701, laws were passed expelling from the colony Roman Catholic priests and papist recusants. On the overthrow of James II., and the revival of warfare with France, hostility to the Roman religion was rekindled in all the English dominions. Through the whole period that followed the English revolution, there is witnessed in New York, on the part of the people represented in the popular Assemblies, the

The Assembly.

same contest for self-government as took place in so many other colonies. The only difference is that in New York the popular party were sometimes less ex- acting and less inflexible in their demands than was the case in Massachusetts. The principal subject of controversy had to do with the method of levying taxes and of controlling the disbursement of them. The first Assembly under Sloughter created a revenue for two years. Under later administrations, the term of years was somewhat extended. After 1711, for four successive years, only annual appropriations were voted.

<small>The popular party.</small>

Fletcher, who was the next Governor, had also Pennsylvania and Delaware under his jurisdiction, and there was assigned to him the command of the militia of the Jerseys and of Connecticut. His attempt to assume this last power at Hartford signally failed. He involved himself in a quarrel with the Assembly in reference to the churches. Andros had tried to promote the cause of the Episcopal Church, but his efforts produced no effect. After William's accession that church began to grow. The retention by the Dutch of their own language in religious services retarded the progress of their communion, and was one of the principal causes why, by degrees, it relatively fell behind other religious bodies. Miller, the English chaplain of the Fort, was anxious to have a bishop sent over, and a number of clergymen with him, to take charge of the handful of Episcopalians, and of others who, it was hoped, might be brought to conform to their ecclesiastical system. But this proposal was not seconded. It was a part of Sloughter's instructions that the Book of Common Prayer should be read in the colony. To the vestrymen and church-wardens the right of presentation was to be given. In 1693, an act of the Assembly provided that in four counties that were named

<small>Fletcher.</small>

<small>Seeks to establish Episcopacy.</small>

there should be five ministers, and each county was to raise a specified sum for their maintenance. All freeholders were to vote in the election of vestrymen and wardens. Fletcher insisted that the act must be held to relate to none but Episcopal ministers. This, he contended, was the legal interpretation of the phrase "Protestant minister." The Assembly refused to agree to this construction, and voted that the vestrymen and churchwardens might call, if they chose, "a dissenting Protestant minister." It rejected the Governor's claim to the right "of collating or suspending any minister" in the province. When Trinity Church was established, which was in 1697, Fletcher applied the Act of 1693; but the wardens and vestrymen, instead of being chosen by "all freeholders," were elected by Church of England people alone. It continued to be maintained that none but Episcopal clergymen have any title to a support at the public expense. As a matter of fact, the endowed churches were mostly of that communion. To this extent did the Governor succeed in procuring an establishment of the Anglican Church. Notwithstanding his ecclesiastical zeal, Fletcher was avaricious as well as violent in temper. He sought to enrich himself by fraudulent means. Charges of evil conduct led to his recall.

Bellomont allied himself with the Leislerians. The bodies of Leisler and Milborne were exhumed, and reburied with honors in the Dutch Church. The Assembly passed an act of indemnity for Leisler. Bayard, one of his chief opponents, was arraigned on a charge of treason, based on imputations cast on Bellomont and Nanfan, the Lieutenant-Governor. He would have been convicted but for the arrival of the new Governor, Lord Cornbury, a dissolute spendthrift, who was prospective heir of the Earldom of Clarendon, and first cousin of Queen Anne.

Bellomont.

Cornbury.

He was sent out to keep him out of harm's way, and, if possible, to help him to mend his fortunes. He allied himself at once with the anti-Leislerians. Bayard was released. The law under which he was tried was annulled by the Queen. Cornbury united with his enmity to the popular party a great zeal for the Episcopal Church. He insisted that all preachers should have a license from the Bishop of London. He seized the parsonage of a Presbyterian minister on Long Island, and gave it into the hands of the Episcopalians. Francis Makemie, a Presbyterian minister, was prosecuted for preaching without a license, and for using forms of worship not set forth in the English Prayer-Book. It was pretended that the English acts of uniformity were in force in the province. At the trial, the principles of religious liberty were strongly defended. Makemie made the closing argument for himself. He was acquitted. The law which ordained that a popish priest, if he came into the province of his own accord, should be hanged, was still unrepealed. Cornbury diverted special appropriations of the Assembly to his own use. By his rapacity and profligacy he brought on himself the hatred of all parties. The Assembly, in their contest with him, voted " that the imposing and levying of any moneys upon her Majesty's subjects of this colony, under any pretense or color whatever, without consent in General Assembly, is a grievance and a violation of the people's property." Lovelace, who followed Cornbury, lived less than six months. Then Robert Hunter, a soldier, and a friend of Swift and Addison, became Governor. He was not without excellent qualities. But he found the Assembly resolute on the subject of salaries, and was obliged to acquiesce in a compromise. A great disappointment was produced by the failure of the expedition against Montreal, where Nichol-

His zeal for Episcopacy.

Trial of Makemie.

Hunter. 1710.

son commanded the land-forces, but was obliged to retreat on account of the failure of the British fleet and forces under Walker and Hill. Rumors of an intended insurrection of negroes created such a panic that not less than nineteen blacks were condemned and executed. The British Government took the usual course of preventing the rise of manufactures, but emigration was increasing the population of the colony. A large number of Germans from the Palatinate—hence called "the Palatines"—were brought in, who, as soon as they were set free from the baneful contract system, proved to be industrious laborers. Settlements were gradually extended up the Mohawk valley. Hunter was tolerant in his ecclesiastical policy. He was opposed by the Assembly in his plan for establishing a Court of Chancery which should be independent of the people in its constitution and modes of procedure. But in the adoption of this measure he was sustained in England. When he laid down his office, he parted from the colony with mutual expressions of good-will.

<small>New settlers.</small>

Burnet, the next Governor, obtained the passage of a law forbidding trade with Canada. This was a part of his plan for organizing means for weakening the power of France. But this trade was profitable; the law was unpopular, and in 1729 it was repealed by the British authorities. The Chancery Court was a subject of standing complaint. In his measures against the French, Burnet was useful and efficient. He cemented alliances with the Indians, and established a trading-post at Oswego. The province enjoyed comparative quiet for three years while John Montgomerie was Governor; but this interval of rest terminated, in 1732, at the accession of Cosby. A quarrel immediately sprang up between the Governor and Rip van Dam, the senior councillor, who had administered the

<small>Burnet. 1720-28.</small>

<small>Cosby.</small>

highest office during the vacancy, lasting for thirteen months. The controversy related to the portion of the salary that should be allotted to him for this service. Cosby removed the Chief Justice who was to try the cause, and appointed another in his place. A political contest was the result of this dispute. John Peter Zenger established a newspaper, the *New York Weekly Journal*, on the popular side, against the Governor and his party. *(Contest for the liberty of the press.)* In 1734, not far from a year after its establishment, he was arrested and imprisoned, his paper was publicly burned, and he was prosecuted for libel. When the case was tried, there appeared in court to defend the accused an eminent barrister from Pennsylvania, Andrew Hamilton. His manly and eloquent plea for the liberty of the press moved the jury —despite the efforts of the court to make itself the sole judge of the law—to bring in a verdict of "not guilty." Hamilton received public honors for the service he had rendered. A blow had been struck in the cause of civil liberty. When, in 1736, Clarke, as deputy governor, was in authority, the Assembly, in their response to his address, used plain language. It said to him: "You are not to expect that we either will raise sums unfit to be raised, or put what we shall raise into the power of a Governor to misapply, if we can prevent it; . . . or continue what support or revenue we shall raise for any longer time than one year." *(Independent spirit of the Assembly.)* In 1739, the Assembly insisted on making its appropriations specific, and on naming the officials to whom salaries were voted. It was during the administration of Clarke that what is called the "Negro Plot" occurred. *(The "Negro Plot.")* There were several fires in New York at about the same time. Stories were started that they were kindled by negroes. The people became possessed with the idea that there was a plot formed by the blacks to burn the town. The charge had no better foundation than the testimony of an immigrant woman, bound to service to the keeper of a low tavern. Large rewards were offered to slaves, as well as to whites, for evidence leading to the conviction of any incendiary. The Governor, in a proclamation (May 13, 1741) appointing a day of prayer on account of the war with Spain, referred also to the burning of dwellings by unknown persons, and the consternation occasioned by it The negroes were all put under surveillance. Every effort was made to hunt up proofs and elicit confessions. In accordance with the judgment of the court, thirteen blacks were burned to death, eighteen were hanged, and seventy were transported. The conspiracy was a product of the imagination. In the excitement of the public mind and in the lack of thorough scrutiny into the evidence, this delusion is not without elements of likeness to the witchcraft tragedy in Massachusetts

The next Governor was Admiral George Clinton, second son of the Earl of Lincoln. In the earlier part of his official career, he gave himself up to the influence of the Chief Justice, De Lancey, a shrewd man, the leader of the popular party. He assented to the measures favored by De Lancey, such as the appropriation by the Assembly of money for one year only. He found that his concessions did not aid him in carrying other measures which he wished to have adopted. When he attempted to retrace his steps, and regain the ground which he had given up, he encountered a stubborn resistance. The opposition of the Assembly, no doubt, crippled to a considerable extent military operations. This body refused to send men in aid of the expedition that captured Louisburg. It voted contributions of cannon and money. Indians made an attack on the village of Saratoga, which

Clinton Governor (1741).

His struggle with the Assembly.

they destroyed. Their atrocities led the Assembly to take the extreme course that was taken in Massachusetts; it offered a large bounty for Indian scalps. Clinton, in his political troubles, appealed in vain to the King for help against the encroachments of the Assembly. It was judged that they might be due to his personal defects. When he retired from office, he caused surprise by delivering a commission, as Lieutenant-Governor, to De Lancey. The next Governor, Sir Danvers Osborne, committed suicide a few days after assuming his office. De Lancey presided at the Congress at Albany in 1754. The scheme of union gave certain powers, relating principally to war, Indians, and lands, to a body of delegates from the colonies, with a President and Council appointed by the King. This plan was opposed by De Lancey. William Johnson was made commander of the military expedition to move northward from Albany. Johnson had great influence over the allied Indian tribes. He had learned their ways, and had won their regard by living for a while with the Mohawks. He had married the daughter of Brant, one of their chiefs. Johnson proceeded to build Fort Edward, near the Hudson. There was an unfortunate delay in his movements, owing to a quarrel with Shirley, whom he attacked in his despatches most severely, saying that his conduct "shook the system of Indian affairs." At length he marched at the head of three thousand four hundred men to the southern end of Lake George. There the battle took place in which Dieskau and his forces were beaten. In the early part of the day Johnson was severely wounded, so that the direction of the fight was left to Lyman of Connecticut. Johnson was rewarded by being made a baronet. He was blamed, however, by many, for not following up his victory. He was deterred from doing so by the apprehension, to use

The Albany Convention.

Johnson's victory.

his own words, that the enemy might have "considerable reinforcements near at hand." From time to time, the Assembly of New York made large issues of paper money, and strenuously withstood proposals on the part of the English Government to deprive them of this privilege. They took the ground that there was not coin enough in the province to serve as currency. In 1756, it was concluded to have a permanent English army in America, and the Earl of Loudoun was appointed its general.

<small>Paper money.</small>

Compared with New England, the Middle States had the advantage of a milder climate—a climate that was free alike from the extremes of heat and of cold—and a more fertile soil. The people differed from the New Englanders in being less homogeneous. In the Middle States, except New Jersey, the population had come from different countries, yet there was a steady progress of the English toward the absorption of other elements, or, at least, that complete predominance, as regards language and customs, which finally prevailed. There was an absence in the social life of these communities of the Puritan rigor which marked the institutions and ways of New England; and with this absence, it may fairly be said, there were wanting certain intellectual and moral gains, which were the concomitants of it.

<small>Character of the Middle States.</small>

In New York, the Dutch emigration, for the most part, came to an end with the conquest by the English. But although there were Huguenots in the city of New York, and Palatines on the Hudson, the population of the colony was constituted mainly of the Dutch and the English. By the English, the settlements on the western border of Long Island were early made, and they continued to transplant themselves from New England. The city of New York was so situated that it

<small>Society in New York.</small>

could not fail to become a centre of trade, and such it has always continued to be. The traffic in furs was a principal occupation at Albany. From the banks of the Hudson, and from Albany, settlements were gradually planted westward along the fertile and beautiful valley of the Mohawk. Agriculture was the principal occupation of the inhabitants of the colony. Manufactures, begun with considerable energy by the Dutch, did not flourish. The legal profession in New York attained to no high standing, and the medical profession was in a still lower state. In 1665, a law of the Duke of York was framed to prevent violence in the treatment of patients. The Dutch and the English dissenting ministers were worthy of respect, both for their learning and character. The Dutch clergy held the same theology as their dissenting English brethren, but were less sedate in their ways. They were fond of lively companionship, yet maintained their place as oracles in their villages. Until near the close of the seventeenth century, when the English Church adopted a different policy, toleration was generally practised, the exceptions being in the case of the Quakers, and in that of the Roman Catholics, toward whom the invasions of the French and Indians from Canada, and the influence of the Jesuits there, created a hostile feeling. Under the Dutch rule, schools had been established, and received aid from government; but after the English conquest, the interest in popular education dwindled, and the schools were given up, or fell into decay. The clergy. Education.

Slavery existed in New York, as in the other northern colonies, but in a mild form. There was a certain prevalent antipathy to the blacks, on account of their color, and occasionally, as we have seen, in a time of panic they were cruelly handled; but generally they were well treated. Wealth, even when re- Social classes.

cently acquired, conferred social importance on such as possessed it. But there was an aristocracy in New York of a peculiar cast. Above the ordinary tradesmen and small farmers, were the great Dutch landholders, the patroons, whose vast country estates lay in the neighborhood of the Hudson, and who formed the habit of building, in the city of New York, houses to which they could resort in the winter. These grandees lived in a princely fashion, having spacious mansions, a luxurious table, a great retinue of servants, white and black; celebrating marriages and funerals with feudal magnificence, and administering justice among their numerous tenants. The manors of the Van Rensselaers, the Cortlands, and Livingstons each sent a delegate to the Assembly. Provisions were made of such a character, by will or otherwise, that large manors descended to the oldest son, as if there had been a law of entail. Thus the influence of the ruling families was perpetuated, and their political power was transmitted from father to son. The ordinary farmers were well off, they were never worn out with toil, were quiet and unambitious, and content to live comfortably from the produce of their fertile acres. The farmers of English descent on Long Island had less inertia, and were somewhat more contentious. In the city of New York, the private houses were well built and well furnished, but the public edifices were inferior. There sprung up in that city a more fashionable society than existed in other American towns. Money was freely spent in dress and entertainments. Amusements, such as dancing and card-playing, which were proscribed in New England, were favorite sources of recreation.

CHAPTER XV.

NEW JERSEY FROM 1688 TO 1756

New Jersey after the Revolution—New Jersey a Royal Province—Cornbury and the Assembly—Hunter—Burnet—New Jersey Separated from New York—The Elizabethtown Claimants—The Revival in New Jersey—Social Life.

By the overthrow of the government of Andros, and the English Revolution, the connection of New Jersey with New York was broken off. For ten years the political condition of New Jersey bordered on anarchy; but during this period the Puritans in East Jersey, and the Quakers in West Jersey appear to have managed their affairs through their town organizations, and generally in a safe and orderly way. The authority of the proprietaries was nominally resumed, but they were not very well obeyed. In 1692, Andrew Hamilton was made Governor of both the Jerseys. The dispute with New York respecting customs was opened afresh, and by the decision in a law-suit in Westminster Hall East Jersey won its cause and obtained a separate custom-house. The case was decided during the rule of Basse, Hamilton's successor. The title of the proprietaries was called in question, the people petitioned against it, and it was surrendered by them to Queen Anne, their property in lands being secured to them. The two Jerseys were thus finally united in one province. The form of government which followed, with Cornbury for its first Governor, left the people with

New Jersey after the Revolution.

New Jersey a royal province. 1702.

less liberty than they had been in the habit of exercising. The Councillors were to be appointed by the Crown, and might be removed by the Governor, who was to send his reasons to England for taking such a step. The members of the Lower House must each possess an estate of a thousand acres, and were to be chosen for an indefinite time. A property qualification for voters was prescribed. Religious liberty was conceded to all "except papists." There were regulations for the establishment and maintenance of the Anglican Church, but these proved inoperative by the refusal of the Assembly to make grants for the purpose. No printing of a book or pamphlet was to be allowed without the Governor's special license. The Governor and Council were to be a Court of Chancery. In practice the Governor exercised this function exclusively. There were religious conflicts in New Jersey among three parties—Quakers, Episcopalians, and the Presbyterians and Congregationalists, who acted together. Cornbury, by his mercenary spirit, lost the confidence of all. When the Assembly refused to pass his militia bills and bills for the grant of money, he removed three of its members, and thus obtained a body willing to comply with his wishes. He was confronted by the spirited opposition of Samuel Jennings, the Speaker. He dismissed Lewis Morris, an able man, from the Council. Morris presented the complaints of the colony against him to the English Secretary of State.

<small>Cornbury and the Assembly.</small>

Lovelace, Governor after the removal of Cornbury, died soon after his appointment. With the conduct of Ingoldsby, a rash and violent man, who was left in power after the death of Lovelace, there was no satisfaction. Yet the Assembly voted men and money for the prosecution of the war against New France. The same thing was done under Hunter.

<small>1709.</small>

Bills of credit were issued, according to the custom of the other colonies. Hunter supported the Quakers and the Dissenters, in opposition to the Churchmen. It was maintained that a recent law of England, requiring an oath of officers, jurymen, and witnesses in capital cases, was binding in America. The leader against the Quakers was Daniel Coxe, Speaker of the Assembly in 1716. The Chief Justice was against his view. Hunter took the same ground. He was charged by Coxe and his party with doing an illegal act in calling the Assembly in Amboy, where it had met in the previous year, instead of Burlington. Hunter was successful in the new Assembly, and obtained the grant of a revenue for three years. Coxe failed to produce any effect by his complaints to the Board of Trade. *Hunter.*

Through the early portion of Burnet's administration the old contest on the question of temporary or permanent supplies was waged between between the Assembly, with the usual consequences. Finally, he consented to the issue of forty thousand pounds in bills of credit, and the Assembly continued the revenue act for five years. *Burnet.*

The quiet state of things under Montgomerie gave place to more disturbed relations under Cosby. But in 1738, when the separation of New Jersey from New York was effected, and Lewis Morris, who had been President of the Council, was appointed Governor, hopes of amity between the different branches of the government were confidently cherished. But Morris, although he had been a popular leader, adhered to his instructions. He denied his assent to bills, such as the bills for the disposal of the revenue by the Assembly, which that body insisted on as the condition of voting supplies. No agreement was reached between the conflicting parties. During the brief time *New Jersey separated from New York.*

when John Hamilton acted as Governor, after the death of Morris, the Assembly was in a better mood, and voted £10,000 to equip troops for the Canada expedition. John Reading, another Councillor, held power next, but only for a few months. There was a riot at Perth Amboy, which was one event in a protracted dispute relating to the lands which the "Elizabethtown claimants" held through conveyances from the Indians before New Jersey was a distinct province. These disturbances continued after Belcher became Governor. Appeals were made to the authorities in England, but the controverted points were left undecided, and the claimants remained in possession of their farms. Belcher shrewdly yielded to the Assembly where he saw it was useless to contend, but stood his ground when he deemed it indispensable to do so.

_{1747.}

_{The Elizabethtown claimants.}

_{1747-57.}

The Revival, of which Edwards and Whitefield were the most distinguished promoters, extended into New Jersey. Two brothers, Gilbert and William Tennent, both of whom were forcible preachers, were prominent in evangelistic efforts. The germ of Princeton College, which obtained its first charter in 1746, was a school, or "log college," set up by the father of the Tennents, at Neshaminy, twenty miles north of Philadelphia. The Revival in New Jersey, as in New England, was the occasion of theological and ecclesiastical controversies. Among the Presbyterians, there was a conservative party in which the influence of the Scottish and Irish element prevailed. This party distrusted and condemned the new movement, or the fruits of it. It was called the "Old Side." The "New Side," or the "New Lights," who earnestly favored the Revival, were the founders of the College. David Brainerd, whose biography was written by Jonathan Edwards, labored with

_{The revival in New Jersey.}

zeal and success as a missionary among the Indians at Crosweeksung, near Freehold.

In New Jersey, the Swedish and Dutch elements in the population, compared with the English element, by which they were eventually absorbed, were small. The inhabitants of New Jersey, said Governor Belcher, "are a very rustical people, and deficient in learning." They lived in villages. Their occupation was farming. Some distinction was enjoyed by farmers who were rich enough not to toil with their own hands. There were a few spacious and elegant country-houses. The number of slaves and of indentured servants was small. There were few crimes committed. The New England element gained increasing sway in political and social life. Various New England customs were adopted. For example, the care of paupers was assigned to the lowest respectable bidders at an auction sale. There was early legislation against stage-plays, cock-fighting, card-playing, and other amusements that were specially offensive to Puritans. In towns settled by New Englanders, schools were maintained. The colony was indebted to the Presbyterians and Congregationalists for what was done to promote the education of the people.

<small>Society in New Jersey.</small>

CHAPTER XVI.

PENNSYLVANIA AND DELAWARE FROM 1688 TO 1756

Charges Against Penn—Disorder in Pennsylvania—"The Counties" —George Keith—The Proprietary Displaced—Penn Regains his Province—He Befriends Negroes and Indians—New Charter of Privileges—The Two Parties—Evans—Evans Recalled—Gookin—The Assembly against Logan—Death of Penn—Administration of Keith—Gordon—Anti-Quaker Party—Opposition to the Proprietaries—Franklin—Society in Pennsylvania—Physicians—Tradesmen—Philadelphia—Intellectual Life.

To William Penn the fall of James II. was a disastrous event. James had always been his friend and patron. *Charges against Penn.* In the last years of his reign, Penn had lived at Kensington and had kept up a close intimacy at the Court. It was well known that he was frequently closeted with the King. On the issue of the Declaration of Indulgence, he had led a deputation of Quakers in the presentation to James of an address—which Penn himself probably wrote—conveying thanks and pledges of attachment. When the King fled, Penn remained in London and deported himself in a manly way. Rumors flew in all directions that he was a papist, a Jesuit in disguise who had studied in France at the Jesuit Seminary of St. Omer. Even Tillotson gave credence to these charges until he was convinced of their untruth by Penn's emphatic denial of them. Penn and his brethren might be pardoned for thanking a prince for letting out of prison twelve hundred Quakers, even if he stretched the royal prerogative in doing so. As to the unconstitutionality of the King's Declaration, all that the

Quakers afterward could say was that in their address to him they had expressed the hope that by the concurrence of Parliament his policy of giving freedom to conscience might be made permanent. The Presbyterians and some other non-conforming bodies had in like manner offered their thanks to the King; and similar addresses had been brought to him by Increase Mather from churches and ministers in Massachusetts and Plymouth. But Penn's asseverations of innocence as concerns any sympathy with the tenets of the Romish Church, and of loyalty to William, were discredited by many. What was most painful, many of his Quaker brethren were for a while shaken in their confidence in him. Three times he was brought before the Privy Council, and, after examination, released. He now made extensive and costly preparations to conduct to his colony a large reinforcement of emigrants. But after he barely escaped arrest, on the occasion of George Fox's funeral, on a fourth accusation, which rested on the oath of a worthless perjurer, he gave up the new enterprise and lived in seclusion, although remaining in London.

Meantime Penn's colonial government became a prey to disorder and faction. An able popular leader arose in the person of David Lloyd. The jealousy between the "territories," the Delaware counties, and the province became more inflamed. The deputies of the counties separated from the Assembly and sat as a distinct body, under Markham, the Lieutenant-Governor. In the province itself, party feeling was intense. There were now a great many settlers who were not Quakers. The ascendency of the Quakers was menaced, and even the political privileges which they shared with others were exposed to danger by the movement of George Keith, who had been eminent among them as a preacher and author. This

Disorder in Pennsylvania.

The "Counties."

George Keith.

vehement and vociferous demagogue proclaimed the doctrine that, according to true Quaker principles, members of that sect ought not to hold office as magistrates and take part in executing penal laws. He was arrested for vilifying the magistrates. His imprisonment raised a cry, which made itself heard in England, that the colony was practising the intolerance which it professed to hate. Keith went to England, became an Episcopalian, and enjoyed a benefice. The result of these occurrences was that the rule of the proprietary was displaced, and Fletcher, the Governor of New York, was put in charge of the province. Fletcher remained a short time in Philadelphia, vainly sought to move the Assembly to appropriate money for the common defence on the northern frontier, and addressed rebukes to that body in his own arrogant style. Fletcher had called the Assembly from the counties and the province, and had proceeded without regard to the charter and the system of laws. Through the intercession of certain noblemen, friends of Penn, his innocence was acknowledged, and in 1694 his province was restored to him. Under Markham, the Lieutenant-Governor, the Assembly proceeded to establish its own authority, according to the democratic ideas of its leader. In consequence of strong representations from England, a proclamation was issued by the Governor and Council against illegal trade and the harboring of pirates.

The proprietary displaced.

Penn regains his province.

1696.

On Penn's return to his colony, in 1699, he exerted himself, with his usual humane spirit, in behalf of the rights and interests of negroes and Indians. He formed a treaty with a company of forty chiefs and leading men of the Indian tribes, including a brother of the chief of the Onondagas. Information that Parliament was preparing to abrogate all

He befriends negroes and Indians.

the colonial charters obliged him, in 1701, to return to England. Before leaving, he gave the colony a new charter of privileges. He wanted, if possible, to make the people content, and to appease the continued wrangling between the counties and the province. *New charter of privileges.* The Council was to be an executive body in connection with the Governor. The Assembly was to meet annually, and to initiate legislative measures. The judiciary was left to be regulated by the Assembly. This body was to sit on its own adjournments, and not to be dissolved during the term for which it was chosen. If the Delaware counties should so desire, there were to be two legislatures. This division between the colonies was carried into effect in 1703. Andrew Hamilton, of New Jersey, was appointed Deputy Governor. James Logan, a man of great ability, was made Secretary by Penn, and also agent for the care of the proprietary estates. As time went on, there was a more definite array of parties for and against the proprietary government. Hamilton was constantly in collision with the popular *The two parties.* party. One point for which the Assembly persistently contended was its right to sit on its own adjournments. Evans, the next Governor, a young, hot-headed Welchman, was under the influence of Logan. He wanted to reunite the counties to the province, but now the province would not consent. The Pennsylvania Assembly carried its opposition to an extreme, *Evans.* and sent to Penn himself a very censorious memorial. It was signed by Lloyd, the Speaker, who was the oracle of the popular party. It harshly arraigned the Founder in a series of accusations, beginning with the changes made in the frame of government at the second Assembly, when, in the place of a treble vote in the council, he acquired a negative voice upon legislation. Prominent among the subjects of reproach was the power given to

Evans to prorogue their body without its consent. Penn's calm but plain answer had a powerful effect, and the next Assembly was differently composed and more favorable to the proprietary cause. But Evans roused against himself the whole Quaker interest. He was anxious to organize a militia. In order to stir up contempt for the Quaker doctrine and policy, he caused the whole town of Philadelphia to be suddenly alarmed by the cry that an invading force of Indians was approaching. The principal effect of this foolish manœuvre was to bring disgrace upon himself. He caused a fort to be built at Newcastle, which demanded a toll in gunpowder of every vessel that passed by. He was driven to give up this exaction by a bold act of Hill, a Quaker merchant, who steered his vessel by the fort, and being followed by the leader in command there, contrived to seize him and to deliver him to Lord Cornbury, Governor of New Jersey, who was at Salem, on the Delaware. Cornbury took the side of the captors against Evans. There was a heated controversy respecting the Courts. The bill drawn by Lloyd, the popular leader, to establish a judiciary was rejected in England by the Privy Council. The Assembly, in turn, was determined that Evans should not establish a Chancery Court composed of the Council. The controversy increased in bitterness. The Assembly sought to impeach Logan, who was deemed to be the main pillar of the Governor's party. One source of the unpopularity of Evans was his loose morals. In 1709, Penn was induced by the complaints of the Assembly to recall him.

Evans recalled.

The Assembly was not at all disposed to peace when Gookin, the successor of Evans, arrived. When the Governor called for men and money for the colonial expedition against the French, the Assembly replied that "the raising of money to hire men to fight

Gookin.

(or kill one another) was a matter of conscience to them, and against their principles;" but that they would make a present to the Queen of £500. He had asked for £4,000. When requested to make appropriations for the Lieutenant-Governor's support, they replied with angry reflections on the Secretary, and added that people were not obliged to contribute to the support of an administration that infringed upon their liberties and afforded no redress for their wrongs. As the Governor was instructed not to act without the advice of the Council, the wrath of the Assembly was directed against Logan, who was its principal member. He challenged them to prosecute his impeachment. They arrested him, but he was set free by Gookin. In 1710, Logan went to England, where he was fully sustained. A long and pathetic letter of Penn, in which the sacrifices that he had made for the colony were set forth, and the complaints of oppression were answered, produced a decisive effect. The new Assembly was of a more accommodating spirit. They voted £2,000 for the expedition against Canada. Penn, wearied with the dissensions in the province, with a heavy burden of debt upon him, which was greatly increased by the unfaithfulness of a steward, began a negotiation for the sale of his rights to the Crown, for which he was to receive £12,000. But before the transaction could be consummated, he suffered the first of a series of apoplectic strokes, which enfeebled his mind and disabled him from business. The disagreements of the Governor and the Assembly had been quieted. The views of the latter respecting the judiciary were allowed to be carried into effect. But after an interval, the demonstrations of mutual hostility were renewed. One point of dispute was on the amount of salary that should be voted to the Governor. Another very serious diffi-

The Assembly against Logan.

1711.

1712.

culty arose from his refusal to qualify Quakers for office, unless they took the oath. These and other grounds of opposition to him produced his recall. The strange conduct of Gookin is to be ascribed to mental unsoundness, which did not distinctly reveal itself until after his retirement from office.

Sir William Keith was the next Governor. The next year after he was installed in office, Penn died. The terms of his will occasioned a suit at law which lasted for nine years. It was settled finally that his proprietary rights were left to the three sons of his second wife.

Death of Penn, 1718.

Keith exhibited, from the beginning, a demagogical spirit. He flattered the Assembly and fell in with its wishes. The Council, and Logan, the chief man in it, were practically set aside. The complimentary addresses exchanged between Keith and the Assembly are in amusing contrast with the tone of such documents under the former Governors. The Assembly allowed him to set up a Court of Chancery. He combined with them in the issue of a paper currency, which, although great care was thought to be taken to prevent ill consequences, was the initiation of a policy extremely disastrous in its effects. Keith removed his powerful opponent, Logan, from his offices. But letters were obtained by him from the widow of William Penn, and from the proprietaries, in support of the position taken by the latter respecting the powers of the Council.

Administration of Keith.

In 1726, Keith was superseded by another Governor, Patrick Gordon. But Keith became a member of the Assembly, where his factious and mischievous course lost him the esteem of all parties. The court that he had erected was abolished. In Gordon's time there was a large immigration of Germans. Trade and commerce flourished. When he died, Logan, previously

Gordon.

famous as a conservative leader, was Governor for two years. Under his successor, George Thomas, who had been a planter on the island of Antigua, the boundary dispute with Maryland was settled. It was difficult to avoid controversies in reference to military matters, on account of the peculiar principles of the Quakers. Trouble sprung up between the Governor and the Assembly on the breaking out of war between England and Spain. Thomas gave great offence by enlisting bought or indented apprentices. As in similar conflicts elsewhere, the Governor would refuse his assent to Acts of the Assembly, and by way of reprisal the Assembly would withhold his salary. {1738.}

In studying the history of Pennsylvania in the eighteenth century, it is necessary to bear in mind that the laws framed in this period were often widely diverse in their tenor and spirit from the legislation of Penn. His work, in many particulars, instead of being allowed to bear its proper fruit, was set aside.

The party not in sympathy with the Quakers, and thoroughly adverse to their policy, was growing in strength. On one occasion, in 1742, there was an election riot in Philadelphia, in which sailors from the ships on the Delaware took an active part, but which was supposed to have been stirred up by party leaders. Owing to the spirit that prevailed in the Assemblies, and the strife of factions, the province lent comparatively small aid to the colonial cause in the war with France. {Anti-Quaker party.} {1744}

James Hamilton, the successor of Thomas, was a son of the eminent barrister. He refused his assent to bills which did not secure the proprietaries' right to the interest of loans. He refused to sanction the further issue of paper money. Under the next following Governors, Morris and Denny, in legisla- {Opposition to the proprietaries.}

tive matters, the wheels were blocked by the instructions of the proprietaries to their deputies. But in the case of Denny, a selfish motive was predominant. He repaid the action of the Assembly in relation to his salary by refusing his assent to their bills. As the great war with the French drew near, and partly in consequence of the extension of settlements westward, the relations of the colony with the Indians became at once more important and more critical. Large expenditures for the maintenance of treaties and to prepare for defence became requisite. It was deemed just that the great estates of the proprietaries should be subject, like other landed property, to taxation. This end was not secured until the mission of Franklin to England, in 1757, in behalf of the claim of the colony, substantially accomplished its purpose. In an extended "Historical Review of the Constitution and Government of Pennsylvania from its Origin"—which, if it was written mainly by another hand, was published with his countenance and sympathy—an elaborate attack is made on the proprietary government. Even the proceedings of Penn himself are discussed with unsparing severity.

Benjamin Franklin gradually rose from the position of a printer's boy to be the chief man in the colony. In 1723, at the age of seventeen, he had come from Boston to Philadelphia. By his industry, sobriety, and talents, he acquired a constantly increasing influence. He became the clerk, and then a member, of the Assembly. He originated many plans for the benefit of the community. The foundation of the University of Pennsylvania, and of the American Philosophical Society, was due to him. In 1754, he was the leading commissioner in the convention at Albany for the formation of a union with the colonies.

Franklin.

Bancroft estimates the population of Pennsylvania and

Delaware, in 1754, at one hundred and ninety-five thousand. The two colonies were much alike in their social characteristics. The legislature consisted of one house, and the power of refusing compliance with its acts had fallen into abeyance. Judges, though named by the Lieutenant-Governor, were, like him, dependent on the legislature for their salaries, and these were determined by vote each year. The large variety of products, and the nascent manufactures, made a great difference between Pennsylvania and the Southern colonies. The courts of law, as far as the qualifications of the judges and of lawyers are concerned, were above the ordinary colonial standard. The strongest sects were the Quakers, the Lutherans, and the Presbyterians; but although Sabbath laws were strictly enforced, religious freedom continued to be accorded to all. The smaller degree of control enjoyed by the clergy was a point of contrast both with Virginia and New England. Medical practitioners in Pennsylvania were comparatively well qualified for their profession. In Philadelphia, medical science was early cultivated, and before the expiration of the period which we are considering, a beginning was made in the publication of medical writings. A hospital was founded in 1750, and ten years later medical lectures were given by Dr. William Shippen. Tradesmen were very numerous, and they made their influence felt in the community. The owners of large estates, and wealthy merchants, were not without a certain distinction. There was an aristocratic class in which were represented such families as the Pembertons, the Logans, and the Morrises. The slaves were mostly domestic servants. Slavery was generally condemned by the Quakers. Manumitted slaves, and the large class of indented apprentices, were often offenders against the law, and affected unfavorably the morals of the community. There was a great contrast between Philadelphia and the adjacent district, on the one hand, and the farming class on the western borders of the province, on the other. The latter class were rough and ignorant, lacking in public spirit, and blending superstitious notions with coarse standards of moral conduct. But the intermediate farming class, the Scotch-Irish and Germans in the middle region, were quite different from the frontier population. They were of a much higher grade of intelligence. The Germans, unlike as they might be in manners to the people of English descent, were not deficient either in intellect or in religious sincerity. The Scotch-Irish, however dogmatic and intolerant in their zeal for the Presbyterian creed, cherished the Bible and established schools.

In 1749 there were in Philadelphia eighteen hundred and sixty-four houses, and eleven places of worship. In 1753, it contained fourteen thousand five hundred and sixty-three inhabitants. The city grew rapidly. In 1769 the number of houses was thirty-three hundred and eighteen. In the middle of the century, the simple but comfortable style of living which prevailed was assuming a higher degree of refinement. As wealth was increasing, there was more luxury seen in the structure of the dwellings and in their furniture, and in the style of entertainments. An English theatrical company was licensed in 1754 to act plays not open to censure on the score of indecency, but no building was erected for the purpose until some years later. Even then the project was strenuously opposed.

Philadelphia.

Among the associates of Penn, James Logan was a scholar as well as a politician. He translated Cicero's treatise on "Old Age," and bequeathed his large and well-chosen library to the city of Philadelphia. Andrew Bradford, the first printer, estab-

Intellectual life.

lished, in 1719, the first newspaper in Philadelphia, *The American Mercury*. Fifteen years before, *The News Letter* had appeared in Boston. A group of young mechanics and clerks joined Franklin, then a master-printer, in forming the "Junto," a debating society for the discussion of questions in morals, politics, and natural philosophy. By Franklin's exertions a public library was begun in 1731. In 1743, a Philosophical Society was formed, the predecessor of organizations of the same character which are widely known. At this time David Rittenhouse was a boy eleven years old. In subsequent years he rose to distinction as a mathematician and astronomer. Franklin commenced the publication of "Poor Richard's Almanac," in which he incorporated in telling aphorisms his practical wisdom. It furnished reading even for the class of people who read nothing else, was sold at the rate of ten thousand copies a year, and continued to be issued for about twenty-five years. More and more, Philadelphia became a centre of literature and science. Boston and Philadelphia were at the head of American towns.

CHAPTER XVII.

MARYLAND FROM 1688 TO 1756

The Revolution in Maryland—Overthrow of the Proprietary Government—Intolerance in Maryland — Nicholson—Proprietary Government Restored—Maryland in 1751.

ALL the attempts of Baltimore to retain the government of his province after the accession of William and Mary were of no avail. The circumstance that, although he was a Roman Catholic, he had received no favors from James, who preferred to forward the interests of Penn, did not help him. The Maryland officials were in sympathy with the exiled monarch. Joseph, the President of the Council, hesitated about proclaiming the new sovereigns, an act which New England and Virginia had not delayed to do. The insurrection of Protestants, headed by Coode, mustered a force strong enough to disarm opposition. The State House and records at St. Mary's were surrendered to the "Associators," as they called themselves, and the fort on the Patuxent, to which Joseph and the Council retired, was given up at the demand of Coode, and of his numerous armed followers. They boasted in their address to the King and Queen that they had rescued the government of Maryland from the hands of the enemies of the new sovereigns "without the expense of a drop of blood." The belief that there was a "papist plot," and that an attacking force of French and Indians was on its way to seize the colony, spread among the inhabitants. Coode and some of the other leaders knew that this story was false, but it was believed by those ill-informed. It was a counterpart of the circumstances in New York, with the difference that Leisler was honest, while Coode was a knave. The insurgents were supported apparently by a large majority of the people. The petitions to William and Mary from Coode and his coadjutors, to be delivered from the proprietary rule, represented that the people were the victims of an unbearable tyranny. When later they were called on to specify their grievances, they could allege nothing substantial. But their prayers fell in with what was now the settled policy in England, to make the colonies royal provinces. Moreover, in the great struggle with Louis XIV., on the issue of which might depend the continuance of William's reign, it was felt to be not safe to leave Maryland in the hands of a Roman Catholic ruler. The dangers which England had escaped, from the ecclesiastical connections and purposes of James II., gave new life and vigor to the antagonism to the Roman Church. Little heed was paid to Baltimore's defence of himself and of his government. A suit was begun to deprive him of the province, and William, following the opinion of Chief Justice Holt, that he was not obliged to wait for the slow progress of the legal proceeding, answered the petition of the "Associators," and created a royal government. Early in 1692, Sir Lionel Copley, appointed Governor, arrived in Maryland. For a quarter of a century, Maryland continued to be a royal province. Baltimore was left in possession of the property rights which pertained to him as Proprietary.

Overthrow of the proprietary government.

The most active promoters of the movement for the subversion of the proprietary government were attached to the Church of England, although the members of that Church were a small minority of the population. The principal sufferers by the change were the Quakers, and, in a much higher degree, the Roman Catholics. The religious services of the Roman Catholics were forbidden, and their further immigration into the colony was prohibited. The danger of the restoration of the Jacobite rule in England, which gave rise to the proscriptive measures against Roman Catholics there, had a like effect in Maryland. There was toleration for Protestant dissenters from the Church of England, and gradually the laws which abridged their rights and privileges were partially relaxed. But the first Assembly after Copley's arrival made the Church of England the established religion, and all the inhabitants of the colony were subject to taxation for its support. Puritan intolerance was an episode in the course of the history of Maryland, and lasted only for a few years. It was put down by the restoration of Baltimore to his authority. But the Episcopalian intolerance was of long duration. It created hostile feelings among the people, which paved the way for the course taken by the province in the revolutionary struggle of 1776.

<small>Intolerance in Maryland.</small>

The most vigorous of the royal governors was Francis Nicholson. He was a champion of the Protestant interest. He removed the capital from St. Mary's to the Puritan settlement which was afterward called Annapolis. But he tried to introduce an Act of Uniformity, like that which in England preceded the Act of Toleration. His measure, although passed by the Provincial Assembly, was vetoed by the Crown. The Anglican ministers were often men of profligate lives. The Bishop of London sent out, as "commissary" of Maryland, Rev. Thomas Bray, a man of earnest piety. Yet Bray tried to procure the enactment of a law requiring the Prayer-book to be used in every place of worship in the province. Coode had taken orders in England, but he

<small>Nicholson.</small>

renounced the ministry, and became a noisy advocate of infidelity. What disaffection there was with Nicholson rallied about him as a leader; but he was worsted and driven out of the colony.

The son of Charles, the third Lord Baltimore, renounced Catholicism, and on the death of his father was recognized as Proprietary. But he soon died, leaving an infant son, Charles, the fifth baron of Baltimore. In 1715, the laws of Maryland were revised and formed into a code. *Proprietary government restored.* The growing spirit of freedom was manifested when, in 1722, the lower house passed a series of resolutions, affirming that the common law and such statutes of England as "are not restrained by words of local limitation," together with the acts of the local Assembly, are the standard of government and judicature in Maryland. The upper house and the Proprietary denied their assent to the resolutions. For many years there was not much to disturb the quiet current of political life. Yet there were repeated and partially successful efforts to control the revenues of the Proprietary, and to abridge his prerogatives. In 1751, Frederick, the sixth and last of the Baltimores, inherited the province. He was an unworthy man, addicted to vice. Maryland did not usually exhibit any earnest disposition to co-operate with the other colonies in the warfare against the French and Indians. She sent, however, delegates to the Albany Convention of 1754. When Horatio Sharpe became Governor, in 1753, he set about strenuous efforts to obtain grants of money for the military struggle. The Assembly exacted a compliance with conditions, one of which was apt to be some new measure adverse to the Roman Catholics, whose taxes were doubled, and another was that the burden of public expenses should be shared by the Proprietary, and drawn from his large revenues, amounting to seventy-five hundred pounds annually. Dislike of the proprietary system of government was obviously a principal ground of such proceedings. The policy of the Assembly, except now and then, when there was imminent danger, was one of obstruction. Even Braddock's defeat failed to call out any effective measures of attack and defence.

The population of Maryland in 1751 is estimated to have been about one hundred and forty-five thousand. In this number were comprised a great number of "redemptioners"—immigrants who had been bound to labor for a term of years in order to pay their passage across the ocean, and many thousands of transported convicts. Baltimore was laid out in 1730, but after twenty years was still but a small village.

<small>Maryland in 1751.</small>

CHAPTER XVIII.

VIRGINIA FROM 1688 TO 1756

The Revolution in Virginia—The Governors and the Burgesses—William and Mary College—James Blair—Governor Spotswood—His Dispute with the Burgesses—His Journey over the Blue Ridge—New Immigrants—The Churches—Slavery—The Rich Planters—Dinwiddie—The Ohio Company—English and French Claims—Dinwiddie and the Burgesses—George Washington—An Adjutant-General: A Messenger to the French: At Great Meadows: An Aid of Braddock—Defeat of Braddock—The Retreat—Washington at Winchester—Washington Visits Boston.

THE joy that was felt in Virginia at the accession of James II. had given way to discontent and wrath. He sent over to the colony the captives taken in the Monmouth rebellion. His Governors, Culpepper and Howard of Effingham, came out to make their fortunes. They ruled after the example of their royal master. In the closing days of James's reign there were rumors, as in New York and Maryland, of a popish plot in the colony, and of an impending invasion of French and Indians. Protestant feeling was aroused, the Church of England was thought to be in peril, and there were symptoms of a popular rising. Effingham went back to England in 1688. When he arrived there, James had already fled for France. The Revolution passed by in Virginia without any very marked consequences. Effingham preferred to stay in England; yet he continued to hold his office, and Francis Nicholson, the same from whom Leisler had wrested the government

The Revolution in Virginia.

in New York, was commissioned as his Deputy. For a long time, partly owing to the Bacon rebellion, there was a kind of political apathy, which, however, was in a measure broken up on the approach of the close of the period which we are considering, the eve of the final war with France. Then there were circumstances adapted to provoke a conflict on the part of the Burgesses with the royal Governor. Before that time, the popular house, to be sure, teased the Governors by opposition on many points of no vital importance. The people and their leaders were acquiring a political training, the effects of which were apparent at a later day. One ground why there was less collision between the royal officers and the Burgesses than occurred elsewhere between the Governors and Assemblies, was the fact that in Virginia the quit-rents and other regular sources of the revenues of the King were generally sufficient to carry on the government without the need of large grants of money.

The Governors and the Burgesses.

Nicholson, the Lieutenant-Governor, was ill-tempered and arbitrary. After two years he gave place to Andros, who was commissioned as Governor. He signalized himself, as he had done elsewhere, by his strictness in enforcing the Navigation Acts. He held the office for six years. Then Nicholson returned as Governor. In 1693, mainly by the efforts of Rev. James Blair, a charter was obtained for William and Mary College, which received an endowment from their Majesties, for whom it was named. It was placed at Middle Plantation. It is the second in age among the American colleges, Harvard being the oldest, and Yale being the third in the order of time. The first Commencement of William and Mary was held in 1700, the year in which Yale was founded. In 1698, Nicholson removed the capital from the ruined village of Jamestown to Mid-

William and Mary College.

dle Plantation, which now received the name of Williamsburg, and in honor of the King and Queen was laid out in the form of a W and M combined. Nicholson was an ambitious man, not deficient in courage; but his irascible temper drove him into undignified brawls. Like Andros, he found an antagonist whom he could not manage, in the person of Blair. Blair was a Scotchman by birth, and was ordained in the Episcopal Church in Scotland, but removed to England. He was intelligent, energetic, of a combative disposition, but sincerely religious, and he had at heart the public good. Sent over to Virginia by the Bishop of London to look after the moral and religious interests of the colony, he was appointed, a few years later, the Bishop's commissary, which gave him the highest ecclesiastical authority there, and made him *ex officio* member of the Council. He was indefatigable in the work of obtaining the charter of the College. He was not discouraged by the rough remark of the Attorney-General Seymour, who thought that the money needed for the College might better be spent in the war with France. "The people of Virginia have souls to be saved," said Blair, "as well as the people of England." "Souls!" exclaimed Seymour; "damn their souls! Make tobacco!" In the contest with Nicholson, as with Andros, the influence of Blair in England exceeded the influence of these officials. There was a gain for religious freedom in the extension—not voluntary, but compelled by orders from England—of the benefits of the English Toleration Acts to Dissenters. Non-attendance on church once in a month, or in the case of Dissenters, on one of their own licensed chapels once in the same period, was punished by a fine of five shillings.

James Blair.

In 1704, the Earl of Orkney was appointed Governor. But the office was for him a sinecure. He never set foot in the province. Of the salary of £2,000, £1,200 went into his pockets, and the remaining £800 went to the Lieutenant-Governor. Orkney held his office for forty years. Edward Nott was his first Deputy. Hunter, who was designated as Nott's successor, and whom Dean Swift had thoughts of accompanying in the character of Bishop of Virginia, received another appointment. In 1710, Alexander Spotswood came out as Governor. He was a Scotchman by birth; he had been a soldier, and had received a wound at the battle of Blenheim. He brought with him a concession of the right of *habeas corpus*, and this rendered his welcome the more warm. The constant, but ineffectual, desire of the people was to obtain a recognition of the rights of Virginians to the privileges of Englishmen under the *Magna Charta* and the common law. Spotswood wrote home: "This government is in perfect peace and tranquillity, under a due obedience to the royal authority, and a gentlemanly conformity to the Church of England." But he was soon out of patience with the Burgesses for not appropriating money to carry out his plan of military organization. He sometimes lectured the house like an angry schoolmaster, at one time characterizing its members as a set whom "Heaven has not generally endowed with the ordinary qualifications requisite to legislators." But he fell out, also, with the Council, which in its composition represented the aristocratic tone of the upper class that was growing up in Virginia society. He was in general sustained by the home government, but could not get leave to dismiss the obnoxious councillors. Blair, the commissary, refused to be controlled by him in reference to ecclesiastical affairs. In the Church, the parish vestries insisted on retaining their power, and when it was decided that a minister once inducted into his office could hold it for life, they employed their ministers without any form of induction. Spotswood was interested in the work of christianizing the Indians, and fostered the Indian school at Fort Christanna. He was desirous of extending the Virginia settlements westward, to forestall the French, who were spreading from an opposite direction. With a retinue of companions and attendants, he made an exploring journey over the Blue Ridge. He sent a vessel after a noted pirate on the coast by the name of Teach, and nicknamed Blackbeard. The pirate's head was brought back, fastened to the bowsprit. *His journey over the Blue Ridge.* Spotswood was an able and vigorous man, imperious in his ways and not blessed with tact in dealing with opponents. His letters to the home government abound in indignant complaints against the Council and the Burgesses. Finally the Council succeeded in procuring his removal. His successor, Hugh Drysdale, kept the peace with the Burgesses, and the next Governor, William Gooch, who held his office for twenty-two years, pursued a like conciliatory policy.

Scotch-Irish and German settlers planted themselves in the neighborhood of the Potomac. About 1732, they began to pour over the mountains to the valley of the Shenandoah. The Scotch-Irish erected *New immigrants.* their Presbyterian churches in the region of which Winchester is the centre. The Germans built Strasburg and other towns. They included Lutherans, Mennonites, some Calvinists, and a few Dunkers. In 1737, there came over at one time about one hundred families of Scotch-Irish, from whom the Alexanders, the McDowells, and other distinguished families have descended. A small company of English families settled around Greenway Court, the seat of a nobleman, Lord Fairfax.

After the death of Commissary Blair, the clergy of the Established Church became more loose in their behavior, and more eager for their perquisites, and the character of the vestries and congregations proportionately declined. There were not wanting on the part of the more godly ministers earnest efforts at reform in manners and discipline. The Great Revival made its influence felt in Virginia. The preaching of Whitefield was heard with sympathy by many, but encountered widespread and virulent opposition. The father of Presbyterianism in Virginia was a Scotchman, Francis Mackemie, who was prosecuted by Cornbury in New York. But the real founder of the Presbyterian Church, as an organized and effective body, was the eloquent Samuel Davies, who was settled in Hanover County in 1748, and afterward became President of Princeton College. It was he who obtained in England the declaration from the Attorney-General that the Act of Toleration extended to Virginia. This he had maintained in a noted controversy, in which he contended before a Virginia court against Peyton Randolph, the Attorney-General of the colony.

<small>The churches.</small>

The system of indented servants existed in Virginia, and the treatment of them was regulated by statute. The negroes who were imported from Africa were of different races, and differed much from one another in physical and mental qualities. Virginia made repeated efforts to check this trade, but they were generally discouraged and thwarted by the English government. One of the complaints inserted by Jefferson in the Declaration of Independence is that England had forced upon the colonies this "execrable traffic." The slave population, by its natural increase and by continued importations, multiplied rapidly. In 1714, there were twenty-three thousand. In 1756, they were one hundred and twenty thousand, when the whites numbered one hundred and seventy-three thousand. The laws relating to the slaves naturally became more severe as they increased

<small>Slavery.</small>

in numbers. There were, however, humane legal provisions. They were reckoned as a part of real estate, and one who inherited an estate had the right to buy the slaves connected with it. Negroes who were free were excluded from holding office or being witnesses in any case whatsoever.

There grew up in the first half of the eighteenth century in Virginia a class of wealthy planters. Their estates were large and productive. Besides their servants, there would be numerous tenants or smaller landowners who were more or less their dependents. The Virginia aristocracy lived in ease and plenty. They were hospitable among themselves. They had their horses and carriages. Horse-racing was one of their favorite diversions. In the course of a publication printed in London, in 1724, Hugh Jones, who had been a minister at Jamestown and chaplain of the Assembly, gives us a glimpse of different aspects of Virginia life. "They are such Lovers of Riding," he says, "that almost every ordinary Person keeps a Horse; and I have known some spend the Morning in ranging several miles in the Woods to find and catch their Horses only to ride two or three Miles to Church, to the Court House, or to a Horse-Race, where they generally appoint to meet upon Business, and are more certain of finding those that they want to speak or deal with, than at their Home." There were no manufactures to speak of, and whatever was wanted beyond the products of the soil and of the labor of plain mechanics, was brought from abroad to the planter's door in exchange for his tobacco. Offices of all sorts were in the hands of this patrician class. The towns were very few, so that schools were not established as in other colonies. Intercourse with England might introduce into certain families a fair degree of culture. There were in some of the mansions well furnished apartments.

The rich planters.

The sons could resort to William and Mary for their higher education, and sometimes they were sent abroad to pursue their studies. Under these circumstances there came to exist an opulent, high-spirited class, fond of out-of-door life, and entering with zest into sports and festivities which the leaders in Puritan communities abjured. Printing was forbidden in Virginia when Culpepper was Governor, and the prohibition was continued through the reign of James II. The first newspaper, *The Virginia Gazette*, appeared at Williamsburg in 1736.

Robert Dinwiddie, a Scotchman like his last two predecessors, arrived in the colony as Lieutenant-Governor early in 1751. His coming was simultaneous with a new epoch in Virginian history, and the advent of a crisis in American affairs. A company of merchants and planters, called the Ohio Company, received from the King, in 1749, the grant of a vast tract of territory west of the Alleghanies, in the region of the Ohio. An experienced pioneer, Christopher Gist, was sent out to explore it. He crossed the Ohio, and from the summit of a mountain looked forth on the region now called Kentucky. Dinwiddie was one of the members of the Ohio Company; Lawrence Washington was another. The latter complained that the requirement made of settlers, that they should have a minister of the Church of England, kept back numerous Germans in Pennsylvania and in Germany itself from emigrating to the banks of the Ohio. He contrasts the rapid progress of Pennsylvania, where there was religious freedom, with the condition of things in Virginia. "This colony," he writes, "was greatly settled in the latter part of Charles the First's time, and during the usurpation, by the zealous churchmen, and that spirit which was then brought in has ever continued, so that, except a few Quakers, we have no dissenters. But what has been the consequence? We have increased by slow degrees, except negroes and convicts, while our neighboring colonies, whose natural advantages are greatly inferior to ours, have become populous." But whatever hindrances might retard emigration, it was evident that the English were alive to the importance of taking possession, by actual settlement, of the extensive region west of the Ohio, which the French were now seeking to secure to themselves by building a chain of forts designed to stretch from the lakes to Southern Louisiana. The French claim was based on the discoveries of La Salle. The English claim rested on a treaty with the Iroquois, and especially on the royal grants, according to which Virginia extended indefinitely to the West.

English and French claims.

Dinwiddie was a man of talents. He had risen, partly as a reward for his honesty, from being a clerk in a West India custom-house. His reception would have been more cordial in the province if he had not incurred some odium in his previous station as surveyor of customs in the colonies, and if he had not brought with him the King's negative to certain legislative acts which had been passed with the assent of Gooch. The Assembly remonstrated in vain against this exercise of the royal prerogative. A still greater excitement was kindled when the Governor and Council began to require a fee for annexing the seal to a grant of land, although the warrant of a survey had been sufficient before to establish the title. Peyton Randolph was sent to England by the Burgesses to obtain redress. The Board of Trade decided for Dinwiddie, but advised a compromise. He wrote that his opponents were "full of the success of their party." The spirit of resistance to any enlargement of the royal prerogative, and to the least

Dinwiddie and the Burgesses.

encroachment on colonial privileges, continued to pervade the popular Assembly.

Our interest in Virginia history now begins to gather about one youth whose name will never cease to send a thrill to the heart of every American who knows how to value nobility of character and unselfish patriotism—the name of GEORGE WASHINGTON. He was born on February 22, 1732, in Westmoreland County, of a good family, which had resided there for three generations. His early education was defective except in mathematics; but, as his letters and other writings evince, he took great pains and made constant progress in remedying its deficiencies, especially as regards correctness and propriety of expression. Being a younger brother, it was necessary for him to earn a livelihood. His half-brother, Lawrence, had been with Admiral Vernon, at Carthagena, and had given his name to the estate which George Washington afterward inherited. From him a commission was obtained for George as a midshipman. The unwillingness of his mother that he should go to sea, in which she was supported by the advice of an English relation, put an end to this project. Lawrence Washington married a daughter of Lord Fairfax, and by this means his younger brother, then only sixteen, came to be employed to survey the vast estates of Fairfax beyond the Blue Ridge. During this work, which went on for three years, Washington invigorated his frame, was inured to hardships, became familiar with matters of topography, and conversant with all sorts of people, from the genteel household of the Fairfaxes to the Indians and the rough whites on the frontier.

In 1751, on finishing his task he was appointed one of the adjutant-generals of Virginia, with the rank of major. One of the four military districts, the northern one, was assigned to him by Dinwiddie. The military profession had for Washington a very strong attraction. His first important employment was on a difficult and perilous mission to the French on the Ohio, on which he was sent by the Governor, to present a remonstrance against their encroachments. *An Adjutant-General.* His earliest writing of importance is the journal which records briefly the particulars of this journey. The journey was made with a few attendants, together with Indian guides and some of their chiefs. *A messenger to the French.* It was made in winter, over mountains, through forests, and across rapid rivers, bearing along on their currents broken masses of ice. He traversed a distance of seven hundred and fifty miles. On the way he surveyed the country from high ground, at the confluence of the Alleghany and Monongahela, where their waters unite to form the Ohio. He pronounced the spot on which he stood to be the proper site of a fort, and soon after Fort Duquesne was built there. On his return, in trying to cross the swift and icy Monongahela, on a raft which was made with a hatchet, he barely escaped with his life. He was again in imminent peril from hostile Indians, but, after eleven weeks' absence, arrived in safety at Williamsburg, on January 16, 1754. He now received the command of two companies, and was ordered to go and complete a fort which it was supposed that the Ohio Company had commenced to build. In 1753, the Assembly declined to vote supplies, for the reason that "their privileges" were thought to be in danger. In January, 1754, the Governor succeeded in drawing from them a grant of £10,000, to be used on the frontiers against the French; but their vote was clogged with provisos to ward off the encroachments of prerogative. Washington was made Lieutenant-Colonel of a regiment of three hundred men. On his way to execute his errand he ascertained that the French had got possession of the unfinished fort at the fork of the Ohio. This was the beginning of open hostilities. Virginia declined to take part in the Albany Congress of 1754. Dinwiddie's plan was for two confederations, one for the north and another for the south. The money granted by the Assembly was disbursed by its own committee, and in such a spirit as to excite the disgust of Washington and the other officers. There is no doubt that military operations were checked and embarrassed by the jealousy of prerogative which actuated that body, whatever incidental or remote advantages may have flowed from their policy. Washington attacked a reconnoitring detachment of the French, and its leader, Jumonville, was among the slain. He was obliged by the approach of a greatly superior force from Fort Duquesne to retreat to Great Meadows, and there to surrender a stockade fort which he had built; extorting, however, from the enemy the privilege of marching out his troops with the honors of war. This was on July 4, 1754. The Assembly passed a vote of thanks to himself and his officers, although there was afterward some unjust criticism upon certain articles in the capitulation.

At Great Meadows.

In this early part of the career of Washington, even in his first mission to the French on the Ohio, there are discovered the sound judgment, the self-government, and the courage which were ever distinguishing qualities in his character. With these traits were united an unswerving fidelity to duty and a high sense of honor. In the summer of 1754, Fort Cumberland was built, northwest of Winchester, on the Maryland shore of the Potomac. In the conduct of the war, the power of the Assembly was increased by making their Speaker the treasurer of the colony. This last office the Assembly had filled since 1738. A new military arrangement of Dinwiddie, which made the provincial officers subordinate to officers of the same rank who held a royal commission, led Washington to resign. In February, 1755, General Edward Braddock, who was appointed Commander-in-Chief of all the colonial forces, arrived. He invited Washington to enter his military family as a volunteer, and soon after appointed him an aide-de-camp. A consultation was held with the Governor at Alexandria. There the plan of the campaign was formed. Braddock led his force, which consisted of two thousand one hundred and fifty effective troops, on the way to Fort Duquesne. He was a brave but headstrong soldier, somewhat reluctant to take advice, and ready to break out into vituperation against the colonies on account of hindrances and impediments that he had not expected to find. There were debates between him and Washington on these matters. The General was indebted to the exertions of Franklin for the means of transportation that were furnished him by the farmers of Pennsylvania. The advance of the army was extremely slow, but Washington's counsel was so far adopted that a body of twelve hundred men moved onward under Braddock, the remainder following as a rear-guard. Washington was himself prostrated by a fever, and was still weak when he joined Braddock on the day preceding the battle of Monongahela. The French and Indian force at Fort Duquesne was inferior to that of the English, and if the English commander had been willing to take proper precautions against an ambuscade, the fort would have been easily captured. As it was, on July 9, 1755, he allowed himself to be surprised on the borders of a forest only seven miles from the fort, by a murderous fire from French and Indians, who were concealed behind the trees. The regular troops were thrown into a panic; their methods of warfare were totally unsuited to this exigency; their General refused to let them imitate the foe and make a breastwork of the trees, but sought to rally them in platoons. Braddock, as brave as he was unwise, was mortally wounded, and with difficulty carried from the field. There was a great destruction of life among the officers. In this confused and terrific combat Washington was the only aid who was not wounded. He rode up and down the field, carrying the orders of the General, unhurt, although four bullets passed through his coat, and two horses were shot under him. The young hero, then as always, calm and fearless, was only twenty-three years old. The "dastardly behavior" of the regular troops excited his indignation. On the retreat Braddock died at Great Meadows, July 13th.

The retreat.

A patriotic discourse was delivered by the celebrated Virginia preacher, Davies, before a company of volunteers. In a note to this sermon occur the words: "As a remarkable instance of this, I may point out to the public that heroic youth, Colonel Washington, whom I cannot but hope Providence has hitherto preserved in so signal a manner for some important service to his country." In August, 1755, the Assembly voted £40,000 for military uses. Washington was appointed Commander-in-Chief of the forces, with the liberty to select his own officers. He repaired to Winchester. He found the people in that region in a state of desperate alarm and confusion. French and Indians were committing fiendish outrages along

Washington at Winchester.

the frontiers. The soldiers were extremely ill-behaved, insolent, and insubordinate. He at length persuaded the Assembly to adopt rigorous military regulations. Such was the compassion that he felt for the sufferings of the people that he declared, in a letter to Dinwiddie, that he would willingly submit to be butchered by the savages if he could release them from their sorrows and fears. Captain Dagworthy, at Fort Cumberland, having a royal commission, declined to obey the orders of Washington. The Governor left Shirley, the Commander-in-Chief, to decide the point. Washington made a visit to Boston to consult him on this subject, and on other matters relating to the war. Shirley decided the mooted point in accordance with Washington's views ; and, in compliance with Dinwiddie's request, gave to Washington and his field-officers royal commissions. For a year or two, he had to defend a frontier of more than three hundred and fifty miles in length, with a force of only seven hundred men. But in 1758 he was in command of the advance-guard of the victorious troops who entered Fort Duquesne.

Washington visits Boston.

CHAPTER XIX.

THE CAROLINAS FROM 1688 TO 1756

North Carolina—Conflict of Parties—Indian War—Increase of the Colony—A Royal Province—Immigrants—South Carolina—Archdale—Charleston—Indian War—War with the Yemassees—Hostility to the Proprietaries—End of the Proprietary Rule—Nicholson—The Governor and the Assembly—Indian Troubles—Revolt of Slaves—Trade and Emigration—Glen—Society in South Carolina.

SETTLEMENT in North Carolina, except on the Virginia border, went on very slowly. There were no towns or villages. There were many Quakers in the colony, but when any attention was given to religion, there was much discord. Until 1705, there was no church built, and five years later there was only one clergyman. The scattered settlers were left each to follow his own ways. Organization of every kind was difficult to be secured. Under such circumstances it was not strange that the people should be impatient of the restraints of government, and that disorder should prevail. Runaways from the well-ordered community on the North found a safe asylum. Until 1754, there was no printing-press in the colony.

Social condition.

Philip Ludwell succeeded Sothel. After four years, when he was made Governor of both colonies, and took up his abode at Charleston, the northern province was put under the charge of deputies. The "Fundamental Constitutions" of the English philosophers were now abandoned, and the North Carolin-

1689.

ians were allowed to govern themselves according to the charter. In 1704, Robert Daniel, the Deputy of Governor Johnson, undertook to establish the Church of England, and procured the assent of the legislature, which, also, passed an act requiring oaths to be taken by all officials. This would have the effect to shut out Quakers from holding office. The people now divided into two contending parties. Carey was appointed in Daniel's place, but was soon removed. William Glover became acting Governor, he being President of the Council. Glover was an active Churchman. Carey was the head of the opposing party, who denied the legality of his election. For four years there were two Assemblies and two Governors. When Edward Hyde was sent out by the proprietaries, Spotswood intervened in his favor. Carey, who led an insurrection against him, came into Virginia, but was sent to England to be tried. An Indian war now broke out on the borders. Hundreds of whites on the Roanoke and elsewhere were slaughtered by the savages of the Tuscarora tribe. The North Carolina militia would not obey the call of Hyde, but the Tuscaroras were defeated, and for a time reduced to quiet, by troops from South Carolina. Pollock, made President of the Council, and, as such, acting Governor, described the whole condition of the colony as ruinous in the extreme. Help was again implored from South Carolina, and Colonel James Moore, with a force from that province, inflicted such a defeat upon the Tuscaroras that the bulk of them moved northward and joined the Five Nations. Those that remained made peace. The grounds of their hostility were encroachments on their lands, alleged frauds of traders, and the killing of one of their tribe. Spotswood, the Governor of Virginia, wrote to the Lords Commissioners of Trade (May 9, 1716): "It has been the general

Conflict of parties.

Indian war.

1713.

observation, both in this and the neighboring provinces, that the Indians have rarely ever broke out with the English, except when they have received some notorious injury from the persons trading with them." "Indian traders," he adds, "have been made drunk and imposed upon, and this has provoked a bloody retaliation. They being accustomed among themselves to compound for murder by a payment, count one as the equivalent of the other."

Charles Eden, the next Governor, was qualified for the post. The Carey faction was still active, and there was a growing disaffection with the government of the Proprietaries. The population of the colony was increased in 1690 and in 1707 by the incoming of bodies of French Protestants. Swiss and German colonists settled at Newbern. The Legislature met at Edenton, which was founded in 1715. The progress of the colony was checked by the absence of any town on the coast from which exports could be sent abroad. Virginia rendered a service by interposing to put down piracy. Toleration was enacted, although the establishment of the English Church was continued.

Increase of the colony.

At length the Proprietaries sold their rights to the Crown. The satisfaction of the inhabitants at this change was somewhat chilled by the appearance, as Governor, of Barrington, a worthless profligate, who had before exercised executive authority. He prorogued the Assembly for refusing to establish a permanent revenue and to grant to him the salary which he demanded. He was deprived of his office in 1734. Gabriel Johnston, a Scotchman, held the place for nearly twenty years. The salaries of the Crown officers were expected to be paid from quit-rents, but no satisfactory law for their collection could be extorted from the Assembly. When the Governor set about collecting them

A royal province.

by his own agents, the Assembly resisted the measure, and threw his officers into prison. There were improvements introduced—for example, in the judiciary system. But Johnston's endeavors to promote education do not appear to have been seconded by popular support. During the existence of the royal government, we have accounts of only two schools, one at Newbern, and the other at Edenton. Wilmington became one of the places for the meeting of the Assembly. In 1721, for the first time, a law was passed for the disfranchisement of free negroes. Highlanders and emigrants from Ireland came into the colony, the number of whose inhabitants was still more increased by an emigration into the central and western regions from the western parts of Virginia and Pennsylvania. Dobbs became Governor in 1754. Men and money were contributed for the aid of the more northern colonies at the outbreaking of the war with the French and Indians. But the Assembly kept up a struggle in behalf of popular government, in opposition to the Governor's assertion of prerogative. *Immigrants.*

When Sothel was driven from North Carolina, being a "Palatine," he assumed authority in the southern province, but his misconduct was such that he was obliged to depart. Under Ludwell, his successor, the Proprietaries, finding it impossible to enforce the constitutions, finally gave them up, and left the colony to be governed by the charter. The Parliament became an Assembly. It was conceded that the power of proposing laws should not be confined to the Governor and Council. Smith, who followed Ludwell, succeeded no better than he in allaying strife. Two parties sprang up, that of the Proprietaries and their officers, a party to which the Churchmen adhered, and the party comprised of the Dissenters, a majority of the *1690.* *The two parties.*

people. There was an opposition to the paying of quit-rents. There were disputes about the tenure of lands, the naturalization of Huguenots, and other subjects. It was in Smith's time that rice was brought in from Madagascar. It became the principal product of the colony. As the raising of it was unhealthy for the whites, the effect of its introduction was to promote negro slavery.

Archdale. Joseph Archdale, himself a proprietor, a pious Quaker, who knew how to bridle his tongue, was sent out as Governor, to pacify discontent. He made important concessions. He allowed the number of representatives to be increased. He remitted, on certain conditions, arrears of quit-rents. He paved the way for his successor, Joseph Blake. Yet two years after Blake's coming, the Assembly asked for the privilege of coining money, and petitioned for the removal of duties on exports. In 1697, religious liberty was adopted by laws applicable to all except "papists." A liberal course was pursued in the enactments relating to the Huguenots. In 1700, James Moore was appointed Governor. Prominent party leaders now appear on the stage. One of the foremost was Nicholas Trott, who was at first on the popular side, but was won over by offices, and, with his brother-in-law, Colonel Rhett, became the champions of the Proprietary interest.

Charleston had now become a flourishing town, with a lucrative commerce, handsome houses, the homes of refined and intelligent families. When war

Charleston. broke out between England and Spain, Moore commanded an expedition against St. Augustine. The town was pillaged and the castle was besieged; but the arrival of two Spanish ships compelled the English forces to retire, burning the town behind them. In 1703, a soldier, Sir Nathaniel Johnson, arrived to succeed Moore. The Apalatchees were allies of the Spaniards. Moore was sent out against them at the head of a small body of whites, and a thousand Indians. The Apalatchees, with their Indian helpers, were routed, and their country ravaged. In 1704, Lord Granville, then Palatine, had instructed the Governor, and the faction at his back, to pass stringent laws for the establishment of Episcopacy. A law was enacted which excluded Dissenters from sitting in the Assembly. The Churchmen, on the other hand, were offended by the passage of a law which relegated the trial of ecclesiastical causes to a lay commission. Queen Anne, despite Granville, annulled both of these laws. On this occasion the Board of Trade recommended that the charter itself be annulled. This was not done. It foreshadowed, however, what was to come. The struggle had been a bitter one. Johnson acquired more honor by resolutely meeting and repulsing an attack on Charleston by the French, aided by the Spanish Governor at Havana. Lord William Craven, Granville's successor, was a moderate man. Governor Edward Tynte was conciliating in his temper, but he lived but a short time. Then the brother of the Palatine, Colonel Charles Craven, a man of admirable qualities, ruled the province. Obnoxious laws, adverse to Dissenters, were repealed, but the parish system was introduced, and it was provided that elections should be held, not in Charleston alone, but in the respective parishes. Efficient aid was sent to North Carolina in the war against the Tuscaroras. But the colony had to engage in war with the Yemassees, who had before been friendly, but had been seduced from their friendship by the Spaniards, and were irritated by the traders, who harassed them by demands for the payment of debts. The Yemassees were joined by the Creeks, and the Indian tribes "from Mobile River to Cape Fear" were in commotion. There was a savage massacre of the

Indian War.

War with the Yemassees.

settlers on the borders. The Governor of South Carolina acted with energy. North Carolina sent reinforcements. The savages were beaten, their town was captured, and their fort taken by Colonel Mackay. The Yemassees were driven beyond the Savannah, and took up their abode in Florida.

In 1717, Robert Johnson, a son of the former Governor, Sir Nathaniel, succeeded Craven. From this time the Proprietaries and their officials grew more domineering, and with this change the spirit of resistance in the opposing party kept pace.

<small>Hostility to the Proprietaries.</small>

The expenses of the colony were largely increased by the necessity of paying troops and keeping up garrisons on the border. The Assembly had issued bills of credit, which had depreciated. A royal order came to call them in and cancel them. This was owing to a complaint of the London merchants. To fulfil the order was difficult, partly by reason of another order requiring a repeal of the tax which had been imposed on importations. The pirates had become dangerous, and new expenditures were necessary to suppress their depredations. Johnson was personally admired for his bravery in pursuing one of the marauders, and seizing him after a desperate struggle. But the conflict with the policy which he was the instrument of enforcing, continued. Trott, who was Chief Justice, was the ruling spirit in the conduct of affairs within the province. Directions were sent out to repeal the election law, to which reference has been made, and to repeal other laws deemed by the Assembly to be of vital consequence. One of the Council, Yonge, was despatched to England to carry a remonstrance to the Proprietors. It brought only a disdainful refusal. A Spanish invasion, it was thought, was impending, and grants of money were absolutely necessary. The Assembly pointed to the law for imposing duties. They told the

Governor that the repeal of it by the Proprietors was of no account, and had no validity. The citizens formed themselves into secret associations. The Governor mustered the militia; but they would obey only the Assembly. The Assembly disregarded Johnson's proclamation dissolving them. It resolved itself into a convention, and elected a Governor of its own, James Moore. Opposition was useless. The revolution was successful. A Council was chosen by the Assembly. New legislative acts were passed. Order was taken for laying a report of the proceedings before the Board of Trade and before the King. There was a party, however, still in favor of Johnson. Receiving aid from two English vessels which arrived in the harbor, he proposed to make an attempt upon the forts. He was withstood by the garrisons, and gave up his project when he learned that a provisional royal Governor had been appointed. Francis Nicholson arrived with his commission, on May 23, 1721. The government of the Proprietaries was brought to an end, although the purchase of their rights by the Crown was not consummated until 1729. *End of the Proprietary rule.* *May, 1721.*

The people rejoiced to be rid of the old meddlesome and dictatorial system of rule. Nicholson had profited by his long experience in colonial government, and avoided contention with the Assembly. *Nicholson.* It was now in the highest degree important to bring the Indians on the frontiers into a friendly relation to the English. He set about this task. Much was done for the religious and educational interests of the colony. New parishes were formed, new churches were built, and the London Society for the Propagation of the Gospel sent over clergymen. But when, at the end of four years, Nicholson was succeeded by Arthur Middleton, the old war between the different branches of the Government revived. The Assembly refused to pass a supply bill unless a measure of their own was accepted. In the course of four years the same bill was eight times rejected by the Governor and Council. Six times the Assembly was dissolved and a new election ordered. They claimed to elect their own clerk without the concurrence of the Council; and there were other subjects of controversy.

The Governor and the Assembly.

In pursuance of the pacific Indian policy of Nicholson, Sir Alexander Cumming visited the powerful tribe of Cherokees. Six of their chieftains accompanied Cumming on a visit to England. The Spaniards let Florida be a place of refuge for fugitive slaves. These, as well as the hostile Yemassees, plundered the border plantations. An expedition under Colonel Palmer laid waste the country as far as St. Augustine. A fort was erected in Nicholson's time on the Altamaha River, which the English claimed as the boundary. In 1738, an armed revolt of negroes on the Stono River was discovered in season to be suppressed, and thus an extended massacre of whites was prevented. The negroes had become so numerous as to excite much alarm. German Palatines came over at different times. Swiss emigrants came over in 1732, and settled near the Savannah River. Irish emigrants planted themselves at Williamsburg. The founding of the colony of Georgia served as a means of protection for the frontier. At a later time, new-comers from Virginia and Pennsylvania, and people from the coast, became settlers in the "up country."

Indian troubles.

Revolt of slaves.

Sir Robert Johnson was the first of the royal Governors. Notwithstanding his expulsion from office, he had always been a personal favorite. He was no longer fettered by the directions of Proprietaries. Parliament lightened the restrictions upon the

1731.

commerce of the colony. A bounty on hemp was granted. The people were gratified by the remission of the arrears of quit-rents. The harbor of Charleston was fortified, and ships of war were sent for its defence. The new order of things stimulated the foreign trade. It enticed from abroad the emigration which has just been referred to. The lull in contests of parties, however, could not continue long. The Assembly were at issue with the officers of the Crown in relation to the courts of law. It was determined, moreover, to grant the Governor's salary year by year. Under the Lieutenant-Governor, Broughton, who was in power for two years after Johnson's death, the Assembly had its own way, and made a large issue of paper money. Under Bull, the next Lieutenant-Governor, the colony aided Georgia in an unsuccessful expedition against Florida. Other calamities occurred—the negro insurrection spoken of above, and a disastrous fire in Charleston. There was a standing controversy respecting the Crown lands. James Glen, who began his administration as Governor in December, 1743, was regarded as a friend of the popular interest, but not even he could escape controversies with the Assembly. He was energetic in fortifying the province, and by treaties with the Indians and by other means prepared it to withstand invasion by the Spaniards. In pursuit of these ends, he traversed the colony and made a personal visit to the Cherokees. Troops were sent over from England to garrison the forts on the frontiers. At the beginning of the war with the French and Indians, Glen was not on good terms with the Assembly. He could not obtain a grant of supplies. South Carolina did not take an active part in the war.

Trade and emigration.

1735-37.

Glen.

There was a strong tendency to the division of society into two classes—the slave-owners and their servants.

Commerce prospered, and Charleston became a mart of trade. It became, likewise, a seat of wealth and fashion, where in winter the prosperous planters, who aspired after a certain polish, formed an elegant, pleasure-loving society. In the population of South Carolina the English race was less predominant than was the fact elsewhere. But the intermingling of foreign elements, such was their character, was a source of strength. The various elements conspired to form the foundation of a virile, self-respecting community.

CHAPTER XX.

GEORGIA FROM ITS SETTLEMENT TO 1756

Oglethorpe—His Career—His Plan for a Colony—Grant of Territory—The Settlement—Immigrants from Salzburg—The Colony Reinforced—State of the Colony—Trials—John Wesley—Charles Wesley—Expedition against St. Augustine—Spanish Attack Repelled—Whitefield in Georgia—Surrender of the Charter—The New Government—Social Condition.

UNLIKE the other colonies, Georgia was settled neither from the love of gain nor for the sake of a principle in religion or politics. The motive of its founder was an unselfish philanthropy. Of the leaders in colonization, he was one of the most distinguished and most worthy of respect. James Edward Oglethorpe sprang from an ancient family, which adhered to the house of Stuart down to the fall of James II. Of the early life of James, the third son of Sir Theophilus Oglethorpe, we have scanty information. Prominent as he was, and living to be nearly a hundred years old—living until the colony which he planted had separated from Great Britain and was one of the United States—there is, nevertheless, a remarkable dearth of details respecting his personal characteristics.

Oglethorpe.

We know that his gallantry and nobleness were held in high esteem through all his life. Dr. Johnson appears to have had a great regard for him, and the few glimpses which Boswell affords of Oglethorpe in the company of Johnson are quite important. Once, when the subject of duelling came up, and the question was whether it is right or not, "the brave old General fired up, and said, with a lofty air, 'Undoubtedly a man has a right to defend his honor.'" An incident of his youth is given by Boswell in which Oglethorpe showed equal spirit and tact in repelling an affront. A couplet of Pope refers to him by name:

> "One, driven by strong benevolence of soul,
> Shall fly, like Oglethorpe, from pole to pole."

A year before his death, which was in 1785, Hannah More wrote of him: "He is much above ninety years old, and the finest figure you ever saw. He perfectly realizes my ideas of Nestor. His literature is great, his knowledge of the world extensive, and his faculties as bright as ever. He is quite a *preux chevalier*—heroic, romantic, and full of gallantry."

Even the precise date of Oglethorpe's birth is not determined with certainty. His latest biographer places it on June 1, 1689. His father was an officer in the army, and the son had a strong military taste. Hence he left Corpus Christi College, Oxford, after a two year's residence, to begin his military life. He served at some time, exactly when is doubtful, under Marlborough. His training as a soldier was mainly under Prince Eugene, with whom he was associated as secretary and then as aide-de-camp. He had a share in one of the most memorable military events of that period, the defeat of the Turks before Belgrade and the capture of that place. Returning to England, and inheriting the family estate, he entered Parliament in 1732, and represented the same borough for thirty-two years. He was chairman of a committee of the House of Commons to visit prisons and propose measures of reform. While performing this service, he was struck with compassion for the multitude of poor debtors, many

His career.

His plan for a colony.

of whom were merely victims of misfortune, but, according to the cruel laws of that time, were shut up, it might be, for the remainder of their lives. For their relief, and for the benefit of other classes of deserving poor, he devised the plan of a colony in America, where they might be comfortably established. It was necessary, of course, to compound with the creditors. He secured the co-operation of persons of rank, and other benevolent people; large funds were contributed, a board of trustees was organized, and from the King a grant was obtained of the territory between the Savannah and the Altamaha, where the Carolinians were quite willing that new settlements should be established as a barrier against the incursions of the Spaniards and their Indian helpers. The colony was to be distinct from South Carolina. Freedom of religion was to be enjoyed by all except "papists." For twenty-one years the province was to be governed by the corporators and their successors. Then such a form of government was to be established as the King should ordain, and thereafter all its officers were to be appointed by royal authority. Arms as well as tools were to be furnished to the settlers. Grants of land in tail-male were to be made to them. For traffic with the natives a license was to be required. The introduction of spiritous liquors and of negro slaves was absolutely prohibited. Arrangements were to be made for the cultivation of the mulberry; and there was a provision for the breeding of silk-worms. On one face of the seal of the colony, silk-worms were engraved in different stages of their labor, to serve as a symbol of what it was hoped would be a leading industry among the colonists, and also as a suggestion of the unselfish spirit that should prevail—the motto being inscribed, *Non sibi, sed aliis.* Great care was taken, by means of a committee and by other agencies, to choose the emigrants and to

Grant of territory.

exclude applicants of unworthy character. On November 17, 1732, a company of one hundred and thirty persons, led by Oglethorpe himself, arrived at Charleston.

The settlement. Accompanied by Colonel William Bull, the leader proceeded to the Savannah River and made choice of a site for the settlement on an adjacent bluff. The neighboring Indians, whose chief was an old man, Tomo-chi-chi, showed themselves friendly. The colonists were brought to the place, the town, named Savannah, was regularly laid out, and the houses were built. The superintendence and personal exertions of Oglethorpe carried forward the work in an orderly style. From a convention of chiefs in May, 1733, a title was acquired to the territory described in the charter. The convenience, as well as the rights of the Indians were thoughtfully secured in the stipulations. The influence of Tomo-chi-chi, then and afterward, was invaluable. As the immigrants increased in number—among whom were Italians from Piedmont to manage the silk industry—several other villages and plantations were formed on the Little Ogeechee and the Great Ogeechee, and elsewhere. The House of Commons appropriated to the trustees £10,000, the fruits of the sale of the island of St. Christopher. In

Imm'grants from Salzburg. 1734, a company of Protestants, who had been driven out of Salzburg for embracing the reformed faith, came over, bringing their ministers with them. Happy in their new home, they finally settled on the Savannah, near the junction of Ebenezer Creek with that river. Between them and the town of Savannah, a company of pious Moravians, with their pastor, Spangenberg, planted themselves. Early in 1734, Oglethorpe returned to England, taking with him Tomo-chi-chi, with a select number of Indian companions, all of whom were duly impressed by the magnificence of London, and gratified by the presents which they received. It was essential to provide for defence against attacks that might be expected from the Spaniards in Florida. On the Altamaha, sixteen miles above the island of St. Simon, a chosen company of brave Highlanders, with women and children, founded the settlement of New Inverness, in the district which they named Darien. These were joined subsequently by additional emigrants from Scotland. In February, 1736, Oglethorpe returned with a company of two hundred and two persons, among whom, besides the English, were German Lutherans and Moravians. He was accompanied by two young clergymen, John and Charles Wesley, whose names were one day to become famous in the religious history of both England and America. By this new accession of colonists it was made possible to build the town of Frederica, on the island of St. Simon, which was planned as a military town, and, with the water-battery in front of it, proved to be, as it was intended to be, a kind of citadel for the security of the other settlements, and a bulwark against Spanish invasions. While the houses were building, the colonists were safely sheltered in bowers of palmetto leaves. In 1737, Oglethorpe secured a commission as colonel. He was appointed to the chief command of the South Carolina as well as the Georgia troops. *The colony reinforced.*

So far everything had gone smoothly. Georgia had been signally exempt from the sufferings through which nearly all the other colonies at the beginning had to pass. But now there were days of trial. The culture of silk proved an absolute failure. There was no profit to be made from the vine. The hot climate engendered fevers and other diseases. The land allotted to the settlers was far from being all productive. There was a demand for the introduction of ardent spirits, which the colonists could not be prevented from procuring—although not without *State of the colony.* *Trials.*

much trouble and expense—from South Carolina. There was a still louder demand for the introduction of negro slaves, who could so much more easily endure the burden of labor in that climate. Why, it was said, should the people be deprived of an advantage which was enjoyed in the sister colony? Then there was a desire expressed to have a fee-simple title to their lands, and a regular constitution and body of laws. The Wesleys were the occasion of new and peculiar troubles. John Wesley was at that time unripe in his spiritual life.

John Wesley.

He afterward said of himself that he was not then "converted." The fact is that he was a ritualist and an ascetic in his religious ideas. He was so high in his churchmanship that, much to his regret in later times, he refused the communion to an excellent man because he had not been baptized by an Episcopally ordained clergyman. The number of services that he appointed was so great that they became burdensome and distasteful. He was unwearied in labor, which his iron constitution enabled him to bear; but he undertook to be a censor of individuals as well as of the community as a whole. He became involved in a love affair with a young woman to whom he taught French, and this led to further complications. Her uncle, Thomas Causton, first magistrate of Savannah, and keeper of the public stores, became his enemy. Finally, Wesley was indicted, one of the accusations being that he had unjustifiably denied the communion to Causton's niece, who had married a Mr. Williamson. Wesley thought it best to withdraw from the colony. Accompanied by a few persons he fled from Savannah, and after various dangers and privations succeeded in reaching Charleston.

Charles Wesley.

His brother, Charles Wesley, was equally unacceptable at Frederica, and in about a year returned to England. Oglethorpe was absent for a while in Eng-

GEORGIA FROM ITS SETTLEMENT TO 1756

land to obtain troops for the contest with the Spanish, which he saw to be impending. On coming back to Savannah he removed from office Causton, who, besides being arbitrary and tyrannical, turned out to be a defaulter. Oglethorpe did what he could to quiet the disturbances at Savannah. He brought home with him some regular troops, together with six hundred men whom he himself raised.

Oglethorpe visited the Creeks and Cherokees to keep them from being drawn to the side of the Spaniards. He aided in putting down the negro insurrection in South Carolina, which they had stirred up. He now determined to anticipate attack from the side of the Spaniards by capturing, if possible, their stronghold, St. Augustine. *Expedition against St. Augustine.* Preparations were elaborately made. In May, 1740, he moved upon the Spanish capital with a force of English and Indians, numbering about two thousand men. There was to be a joint attack by the land forces and by the English fleet under Vernon. A combination of adverse circumstances caused the expedition to result in a failure. Among the occasions of the disaster was the tardy action of South Carolina in sending its aid in men and munitions of war, the failure of the fleet to co-operate in the attack at the seasonable time, the ill-behavior of the Indians, and the success of the Spaniards in bringing in through the Matanzas River reinforcements, with provisions and munitions. The chief benefit of this abortive attempt was its effect in putting the Spaniards for a considerable time on the defensive. During the next two years Oglethorpe was engaged in fortifying Frederica, and in making all possible preparations to meet an attack which he felt sure would be made upon the colony. *Spanish attack repelled.* In June, 1742, a Spanish fleet of fifty-one vessels, with five thousand men on board, appeared off the island of St. Simon. To meet the assault Oglethorpe had a few armed sloops and a guard schooner, and a force of about six hundred and fifty men. His military skill and courage were assisted by a lack of spirit in the invaders, and by dissension among them; but his complete success could only have been gained by a competent and heroic general. Thenceforward Georgia was delivered from the danger of a Spanish conquest.

In 1741, a number of malcontents who had left Georgia, published at Charleston a clever, but spiteful pamphlet, respecting the colony which they had abandoned. Not without justice they accuse Causton of haughtiness and cruelty. But they direct their shots against the trustees, and do not spare Oglethorpe, who is personally addressed in a satirical preface, and is charged with being overbearing and despotic. He was a soldier, accustomed to prompt obedience, and it would appear that in the trying circumstances in which he was placed he gave way to occasional gusts of temper. But nothing more serious can truthfully be alleged against him. This caustic pamphlet describes the decline of the colony in population, and so far it is correct. Whitefield first visited Georgia in 1740. He was regarded with much more favor than Wesley had been. He founded an orphan-house ten miles from Savannah, for the building and support of which he gathered contributions in his wide evangelistic journeys. As already stated, on one occasion he emptied the pockets of Franklin, although Franklin did not approve of the location chosen for the institution, in a distant and sparsely settled colony. Whitefield tells us that he found Georgia almost deserted, except by such as would not go away. The thing most complained of was the exclusion of rum and negroes. On this matter the colonists were importunate in their petitions, with which the trustees, much influenced by Whitefield and by Habersham, an inhabitant of the colony, at last complied. It was also granted that lands should be held in fee-simple and disposed of at the will of the owners. Oglethorpe returned to England in 1743. He did not again visit Georgia. The President and Assistants of the county of Savannah were made the rulers of the entire province. The first Provincial Assembly, which had no power to legislate, but only to advise, met in 1751. The government of the trustees had become more and more obnoxious. The trustees, in turn, were willing to relinquish their cares and responsibilities. The formal surrender of their charter to the Crown took place on June 23, 1752. The new government of Georgia resembled in general that of the other royal provinces. But the Governor's powers were large. He exercised the rights of a chancellor, besides presiding in the Court of Errors. He collated to all vacant benefices, and had charge of the probate of wills. He could suspend any member of the Council. This body was appointed by the King, to hold office during the King's pleasure. There was a property qualification for electors and for members of the Lower House. The principal privilege of the Assembly was the exclusive right to originate bills for grants of public money. The first of the royal Governors was Captain John Reynolds. Georgia was not represented in the Albany Congress of 1754. *Surrender of the charter.* *The new government.*

When the royal government was established, the population of the colony consisted of about twenty-three hundred whites and about one thousand negro slaves. The benevolent motives of the trustees had not availed to give prosperity to the colony. Their interference with industry and production was well-meant, but harmful. The cultivation of cotton was just beginning. Under the royal government, the exportation *Social conditions.*

of rice, indigo, lumber, and skins became profitable. It had been impossible to build up a town life, and the estates were generally small. There were no manufactures. Among the settlers, as might be expected, in view of their previous history, there were some who disappointed the hopes of those who sent them out, and the servants of the colonists were much worse. The farmers were fond of fishing and hunting, and horse-racing came into vogue. Laws were passed against gambling and betting. There was a rigorous slave-code, and the enactments indicate the fear that prevailed of negro revolts. Education was left in the hands of itinerant school-masters, who are said to have been often addicted to intemperate habits. The Church of England was established, and the people were taxed for the support of it. But the Dissenters were numerous. There were laws for the observance of the Sabbath, and to enforce attendance on church. The only literary productions were controversial pamphlets respecting the government of the trustees and the proceedings of Oglethorpe. But these were written by immigrants, and there was no printing-press in the colony. A new and brighter epoch in the history of Georgia opens at about the time of the American Revolution.

CHAPTER XXI.

LITERATURE IN THE COLONIES

The Writings of John Smith—Sandys—Whitaker—Early New England Writers—Winthrop—Mather's "Magnalia"—Hubbard—Prince—The New England Divines—Their Ideas of Providence—Absorption in Religion and Theology—The Bay Psalm Book—Anna Bradstreet—"The Day of Doom"—Franklin and Edwards—Legists.

LITERARY activity in the American colonies, so far as printed publications are concerned, for a period was necessarily confined to strictly practical ends. The books which the colonists read, so far as they could find leisure to read, they brought over with them, or imported later. Yet in the mother-country there was an eager curiosity to be gratified respecting the new world, and its strange, dusky inhabitants. Especially was there occasion to put in print in England descriptions designed to promote an interest in schemes of colonization, or to repel calumnies that were scattered abroad concerning the behavior of the settlers. The earliest writer who appeared in this department of authorship, in truth the first in order of time of all American writers, was John Smith. His accounts are trustworthy, except the tales of personal adventure where he allows himself to mingle ingredients of fiction with the authentic record. His enthusiasm lends a degree of fascination to his narratives, and in his spirited "Letter of Remon- *The writings of John Smith.*

strance to the London Proprietors" he writes with point and vigor. As Drayton composed an ode to the Virginia colonists before they set sail, so it is interesting to know that another English poet of no inconsiderable merit,

<small>Sandys.</small> George Sandys, sojourned for a while at Jamestown in its early days, and finished there his translation of the "Metamorphoses of Ovid." The pious missionary, Alexander Whitaker, two years after he came

<small>Whitaker.</small> over, wrote the "Good News of Virginia," in which, in a clear style, and in a tone of Christian sincerity, he sets forth the condition and unfolds the wants and claims of the new colony. Among the few Virginia writings of the seventeenth century, the "Burwell Papers" deserve to be mentioned. They were discovered in manuscript about a hundred years after they were composed. They present a well written account of the rebellion of Bacon, of whom the anonymous author was an adherent, together with a poem of high merit, praising his virtues and deploring his death. Several productions of Virginia authors of a later day are not without worth. Beverley's "History of the Colony," the first edition of which was printed in 1705, was written in a racy style, and is marked by a considerate treatment of the Indians. In 1747, Stith published a work of much higher authority, which brought down the history of the colony to 1624. William Byrd, a man of fortune, witty

<small>Byrd.</small> and accomplished, a typical Virginia gentleman of the better class, who lived in affluence, and possessed the best library in the South, wrote a journal of expeditions in which he took part for fixing the boundary between Virginia and North Carolina. His work, which was printed from the manuscript in 1841, is an intelligent and lively account of the region and the people which he had occasion to observe.

The first of the New England descriptive and historical

narratives was "Mourt's Relation," a journal by William Bradford and Edward Winslow of the first twelve months of the history of the Pilgrim emigrants. The narrative was continued in Winslow's "Good News from New England," which was published in 1624. Morton's "Memorial," which was issued at Cambridge in 1669, was derived largely from Bradford's "History." The "History" of Bradford, which was first printed in 1856, from the recovered manuscript, is the work of an educated man who writes with all the charm of an artless chronicler. John Winthrop, on his voyage from England, composed "A Model of Christian Charity," in which he describes the unselfish temper that was required for the success of the colony of which he was the leader, and thereby, without intending it, delineated his own character. His "History of Massachusetts" is a diary in which he records, although with many breaks, the events which concerned himself, his family, and New England, from 1630 until his death in 1649. It is an historical monument of inestimable value. On its pages are reflected the sagacious and dispassionate mind, and disinterested temper of the founder of Massachusetts. Mason, the hero of the Pequot war, wrote the story of it, and long after the close of Philip's War a spirited account of it was published by a son of Captain Benjamin Church, from notes of his father. In 1702 was issued the "Magnalia" of Cotton Mather, a church history of New England from 1620 to 1698. Its learning, of which there was a pedantic display, was profuse. But while it is an important source of knowledge, there is a lack of accuracy, and the leading characters, especially the ministers, are extolled without stint. An important part of the value of the work at the present day is the picture which it presents of the intellectual

Early New England writers.

Winthrop.

Mather's "Magnalia."

character of the author himself, an eminent divine of the second generation—somewhat inferior to the first—of Massachusetts Puritans. William Hubbard, minister of Ipswich, related the history of the Indian wars, and a history of New England down to 1680, which did not see the light until 1815. "The History of New England," by Thomas Prince, the first volume of which was printed in 1736, although written in the dry form of annals, was the fruit of careful researches, and is distinguished from preceding works by its superior correctness.

<small>Hubbard.</small>

<small>Prince.</small>

The mental activity of New England, as it has already been remarked, was concentrated chiefly on theological and religious themes. The ministers were well-educated; they collected what, for the time, were large libraries, at a cost bearing sometimes a great proportion to the total amount of their property; and they were hard students. Their favorite authors were the same as those cherished by the Puritan divines in England. Cotton had pored over the fathers and schoolmen. In reply to the inquiry why he studied late at night, he replied that he loved to sweeten his mouth with a piece of Calvin before he went to sleep. Besides their sermons, of which many were printed, they composed elaborate treatises—such as the writings of Hooker, Cotton, and Richard Mather—on church polity. These divines and their contemporaries did not differ in the qualities of their style from the Puritan clergy in England, with whom, in general ability, they stood on a level. The same remark may be made of the controversial publications composed by New England ministers, such as those which emanated from Cotton and Roger Williams, in their debate on the question of the right and expediency of State interference in matters of religion. The quaint, and frequently long, titles of books and pam-

<small>The New England divines.</small>

phlets were conformed to the fashion that existed in those days in the mother-country. Without considering in detail the contents of the sermons and other writings of the New England ministers in the seventeenth century, it will be understood that they taught the Calvinistic doctrines. With regard to one article in their religious belief and teaching a few words may be said. They were not peculiar in cherishing a faith in the universal Providence of God. It was a tenet which they held practically, applying it to all events, large and small, that occurred within the range of their experience. But, as was characteristic of much religious teaching elsewhere, they pushed to an unwarrantable extent their interpretation of the dealings of Providence, ascribing to a special divine judgment for particular offences, real or imaginary, whatever calamities might happen to men — whether it were themselves personally, their neighbors, or the community at large — even when such calamities could not be connected in the line of cause and effect with transgressions that preceded them. This habit of pronouncing on the meaning of Providence as regards the details of life often led to uncharitable and even ludicrous judgments. It scarcely needs to be added that the religious teachers of New England shared in certain superstitions which belonged to the age, and were not peculiar to them. They made much of signs and omens. Increase Mather's two discourses, in 1683, on comets, were occasioned, as the copious title explains, by "the late blazing stars," and related what massacres, fires, plagues, tempests, and other horrors had followed upon the appearance of like celestial phenomena at previous times in the world's history — all ending with a solemn rebuke to the inhabitants of Boston, to whom the skies had been the vehicle for conveying the divine threats. Mather's teaching is but one

Their ideas of Providence.

of any number of illustrations that might be presented of a prevalent mode of belief.

There was a class of Puritans in England who at the same time that religion had the supreme place in their thoughts retained a profound sympathy with liberal studies in the broad sense of the phrase. It is only needful to mention the name of Milton, the noblest exemplar of the class referred to. But Puritanism, it has already been remarked, tended to part company with the characteristic moods and influences of the Renaissance. Such an effect of an intense absorption in theology was manifest, it should be said, wherever Protestantism was a living power. In New England this tendency prevailed, with nothing to check it. Its early inhabitants were pioneers in a wilderness, compelled to extort their subsistence from a niggardly soil, and to contend for life against wily and savage foes. "Chill Penury," even by itself, according to the poet, is enough to freeze

<blockquote>"The genial current of the soul."</blockquote>

Absorption in religion and theology.

It is true, as we have said, that the study of the Greek and Latin classics was always highly valued. But the Renaissance spirit stopped at this limit. What has been called the "play-element" in the human mind — that element which gives birth to the higher forms of imaginative literature and art — was dormant. So long did the divorce between the understanding and the æsthetic nature continue, that when, at the close of the last century and in the first half of the present, the latter asserted itself, the change carried in it a revolt against the old faith. Thus, in part at least, is this revolt to be accounted for. Among the Puritans of old, as among the English people of that time, there was a fondness for rhymes — a jingle of words which was often rather a jangle. Such was the character of the metrical Psalms, the "Bay Psalm-Book," which the fathers of New England used in their public worship, and which was the product of the combined exertions of a number of divines. Among the verse-makers of New England in the seventeenth century there is one name which has a higher place than the rest. Anne Bradstreet was a voluminous author of poems. Her productions were printed in 1650. "Among all this lamentable rubbish," says Mr. Tyler, in speaking of them, "there is often to be found such an ingot of genuine poetry as proves her to have had, indeed, the poetic endowment." No other poem had the popularity which was enjoyed by the "Day of Doom," a theological epic of Michael Wigglesworth, a preacher at Malden, who died in 1705. It is the *Dies Iræ* of New England; it embraces a description of the terrors of the final judgment. Its circulation is said to have been as great, proportionately, as that of "Uncle Tom's Cabin" in our time. Yet its prosaic texture and uncouth rhymes, together with its harsh theology, render it now simply an object of curiosity.

The "Bay Psalm-Book."
Anne Bradstreet.
"The Day of Doom."

In truth, in the colonial period prior to the middle of the last century there were only two authors who rise above a merely provincial rank. These were Benjamin Franklin and Jonathan Edwards. Franklin was born in 1706, and Edwards in 1703. They illustrate respectively the two sides of the New England character; the one, its strong understanding, sagacity, and thrift; the other, its profound religious spirit, and the deep interest felt in the problems and truths of religion. Franklin had the genuine eighteenth-century spirit. His philosophy was empirical; he was bent on improving the condition of society on the material side; his inventiveness went out in this direction. His ethical maxims were prudential. He was a typical burgher. He

Franklin and Edwards.

wrote in a simple, engaging style. His essays on scientific matters were lauded for their clearness and precision. Edwards from his early youth was a metaphysician. He delighted in exploring the most abstruse questions in philosophy and theology. He was a master of logical art. He was at once speculative and deeply religious in his mental habit. He was a most acute disputant, and he discoursed from his own enraptured experience on the reality of spiritual light. His writings have exerted a powerful influence on thought, both in America and in Great Britain. He was the founder of a school of theologians in whose hands Calvinism has undergone important modifications. Perhaps no other man has so strongly affected American religious life.

It was not until the epoch of the American Revolution was approaching, that, in connection with the political questions which then arose, there sprang up in the colonies a class of able legists, whose discussions, continued through the period of the formation of the Federal Constitution, are important contributions to political science.

Legists.

APPENDIX

I.

CHRONOLOGICAL TABLE

	A. D.
Columbus discovers San Salvador, Cuba, etc.	1492
Discovery of North America by John Cabot	1497
Vasco da Gama doubles the Cape of Good Hope	1497
Columbus discovers the mainland of South America	1498
Gaspar Cortereal visits the Newfoundland coast	1500
Second voyage of Cortereal	1501
Florida discovered and named by Ponce de Leon	1513
Invasion of Mexico by Cortez	1519
Verrazano sails directly west to America	1524
Pizarro sails from Panama for the conquest of Peru	1524
Cartier's voyage to Canada	1534
De Soto's expedition from the coast of Florida	1539
Coronation of Queen Mary	1553
Coronation of Queen Elizabeth	1558
French settlement in Florida	1562
Frobisher's first voyage to the N. W.	1576
Sir H. Gilbert's first expedition	1578
Sir H. Gilbert's second expedition	1583
Amadas and Barlow sent out by Raleigh	1584
Raleigh's first colony	1585
Raleigh's second colony	1587
Defeat of the Spanish Armada	1588
Weymouth's voyage	1602
Gosnold's expedition to Massachusetts	1602
The London and the Plymouth Companies chartered	1606
Settlement of Jamestown	1607
Emigration of the Scrooby congregation to Holland	1608
Founding of Quebec by Champlain	1608

APPENDIX

	A. D.
Enlarged charter of Virginia	1609
Hudson discovers Manhattan and the Hudson River	1609
Block explores the Connecticut River	1614
Dutch West India Company formed	1618
Settlement of Plymouth by the Pilgrims	1620
The Council for New England incorporated	1620
Settlement of New Netherland begins	1621
Massacre in Virginia by the Indians	1622
Virginia charter annulled	1624
John Endicott arrives at Salem	1628
Grant of New Hampshire to John Mason	1629
Settlement of Winthrop and his company	1630
The Maryland charter issued to Cecilius Calvert	1632
Settlement of Maryland	1634
Settlement of Connecticut	1635
The Council for New England resigns its patent	1635
Roger Williams in Rhode Island	1636
Establishment of Harvard College	1636
The Pequot War	1637
Settlement of New Haven	1638
Planting of Exeter (N. H.) by Wheelwright and others	1638
Grant of Maine by charter to Gorges	1639
Union of New Hampshire and Massachusetts	1641
Founding of Montreal	1642
Beginning of the Civil War in England	1642
New England Confederation formed	1643
Patent of Providence given to Roger Williams	1644
Execution of Charles I	1649
Coddington in power in Rhode Island	1651
Subversion of the Proprietary government in Maryland	1654
Battle at Providence, Maryland	1655
Quakers in Massachusetts	1656
Proprietary government restored in Maryland	1658
The Restoration : Charles II., King of England	1660
Grant of Carolinas by Charles II	1663
New charter of Rhode Island	1663
Conquest of New Netherland by the English	1664
Union of New Haven and Connecticut	1665
Settlement of Elizabeth (N. J.)	1665
Locke's Constitution for Carolina	1669
Frontenac at Quebec	1672

APPENDIX

	A. D.
Recovery of New York by the Dutch	1673
Marquette's explorations	1673
New York restored to the English	1674
King Philip's War	1675
Rebellion of Bacon in Virginia	1676
Division of New Jersey into East and West	1676
Charter to William Penn signed	1681
La Salle on the Mississippi	1682
Penn's "Frame of Government"	1682
Charter of Massachusetts annulled	1684
Virginia a royal province	1684
Death of Charles II.; accession of James II	1685
New England colonies under a Governor and Council	1686
New York under a Governor and Council	1686
Andros demands the Connecticut charter	1687
The East Jersey Proprietors surrender their patent	1688
Landing of William of Orange in England	1688
Revolution in Massachusetts; Leisler in power in New York; Coode's successful rising in Maryland	1689
King William's War	1689–97
Execution of Leisler in New York; Provincial charter of Massachusetts; the annexing of Plymouth to Massachusetts; the New York Bill of Rights	1691
The witchcraft delusion in Massachusetts	1692
Maryland a royal colony	1692
First class graduates at William and Mary College	1700
Penn grants a new charter; Yale College chartered; West Jersey Proprietors surrender their rights of government	1701
Union of the Jerseys	1702
Queen Anne's war; "the War of the Spanish Succession"	1702–12
Separate Assemblies in Pennsylvania and Delaware; war in South Carolina with Apalatchees	1703
War in North Carolina with the Tuscaroras	1711
Treaty of Utrecht; Acadia given to the English	1713
Death of Queen Anne; accession of George I	1714
War in South Carolina with the Yemassees	1715
Subversion of Proprietary rule in South Carolina	1721
Charter of the Carolinas surrendered by the Proprietors	1729
The settlement of Georgia	1733
The "Great Awakening" in New England begins	1734
Georgia threatened by the Spaniards	1736

	A. D.
War of England with Spain	1739
Invasion of Florida by Oglethorpe	1740
Negro plot in New York	1741
Invasion of Georgia by the Spaniards	1742
King George's war	1744–48
Capture of Louisburg	1745
Foundation of Princeton College	1746
Washington a messenger from Dinwiddie to the Ohio valley	1753
Charter of King's College in New York	1754
Washington attacks Jumonville; surrenders Fort Necessity	1754
Braddock's defeat	1755
Declaration of war by England and France	1756

II.

BIBLIOGRAPHICAL NOTE *

"Winsor's Narrative and Critical History of America" is in eight large octavo volumes. It is not a consecutive narrative, but a collection of distinct historical and bibliographical essays. The historical essays are of unequal value. Some of them—for example, those of the Editor on "New England (1689-1763)" and on other topics, those of Mr. Charles Deane on the "Voyages of the Cabots," and on "New England," the essay of Professor F. B. Dexter on "The Pilgrims' Church and Plymouth Colony," that of Mr. F. D. Stone on "The Founding of Pennsylvania"—are of great value. The volumes are furnished with numerous maps, portraits, and fac-similes of autographs and of extracts from MSS. Vol. viii. (1889) contains an index, but this does not supersede the more full indexes of the several preceding volumes. The bibliographical information is minute and exhaustive. The work traverses the main parts of American history. It treats with much detail of the early voyages and discoveries. These volumes are an invaluable guide for the student.

"Bancroft's History of the United States" (6 vols., author's last revision, 1888) is founded on protracted, unwearied investigations. There was the utmost painstaking in the choice of the phraseology, in order to secure at once vividness and exactness. The outcome of long and diligent researches is frequently condensed in a few carefully chosen words. The work is generally accurate. There are faults of style. The manner is rhetorical, and interspersed in the narrative are episodes of ornate disquisition. The later revised editions omit the foot-notes. Hence the earlier issues are still valuable to the historical inquirer.

Hildreth's "History of the United States" is based on conscientious studies. The author had a legal training, and was bent

---

* This Note makes no pretension to the character of a complete bibliography of the subject. It is a selection of titles, to which are added short comments, such as may be useful to younger students.

on being impartial. The style is clear, and virile to the verge of bluntness. As regards the colonial era, the work is void alike of the attractions and the dangers of a sympathetic narrative.

Bryant and Gay's "History of the United States" (in four large volumes) is an illustrated work. The narrative is graphic and detailed.

Frothingham's "Rise of the Republic of the United States" (1 vol.) opens with a concise review of movements in the direction of union among the colonies.

Of Doyle's "English Colonies in America" three volumes have been published, one of which relates to Virginia, Maryland, and the Carolinas, and the other two are upon the New England Colonies. Mr. Doyle is an Englishman. He draws his knowledge of the subject from the original sources, and writes with ability and independence of judgment. An American student finds it interesting and instructive to look at our early history from an English point of view.

Lodge's "Short History of the English Colonies in America" relates the history of each colony separately down to 1765. The chapters on the condition of the several colonies in 1765, rest upon extensive researches, and are extremely interesting. The outlines of the political history of each colony, although the author, in reference to these chapters, makes "no pretence to original research," are written in an enlightened spirit.

Thwaites's brief history, "The Colonies, 1492–1750," is a very condensed narrative. It exhibits much care in its composition. It is furnished with good maps, and references to books on the several topics.

Doyle's short "History of the United States" (1 vol.), edited by President F. A. Walker, is a good epitome, but is of necessity meagre in its treatment of the colonial period.

There are two other works of note, of an earlier date, by British authors. The one is "Political Annals of the Present United Colonies, from their Settlement to 1763," by George Chalmers (Book I., London, 1780). Chalmers had investigated the subject, and writes in a dispassionate tone. He thinks that the government of Massachusetts under the patent was against English law, and condemns the treatment of theological dissentients. "The History of the United States of North America, from the Planting of the British Colonies until their Assumption of Independence," by James Grahame, in the Boston edition (4 vols., 1845), has prefixed to it a memoir of the author by Josiah Quincy. Grahame had a warm attachment to America. He studied its history with ardent interest. He is in full sympathy with the principles of the Puritans, and defends their treatment of religious dissentients.

Among English histories, Gardiner's "History of England, from 1603 to 1643," and his volumes on the "History of the Civil War in England," are to be especially commended.

B. P. Poore's "Collection of the Federal and State Constitutions, Colonial Charters, and other Organic Laws of the United States" (2 vols., pp. 2102), is extremely useful to the student of colonial history. Force's Collection of Historical Tracts (4 vols.) contains various early writings relating to the colonies, north and south.

Three volumes of the Calendars of State Papers from the British Record Office, relate to America and the West Indies: They are Vols. I., V., and VII., of the Colonial Series. They contain very valuable materials for the historian. In respect to Vol. I., the Editor, Mr. Sainsbury, says: "The history of the province [Virginia] can nowhere be so fully and so authentically illustrated as in these rarely consulted State Papers." In Vol. V. (1661-1668) we have documents pertaining to the contests with Massachusetts in that eventful period, to the fugitive Regicides, Berkeley's administration in Virginia, to Carolina, New York, etc. In Vol. VII., are the "Shaftesbury Papers" relating to the Carolinas, documents about the relations of Massachusetts and Maine, etc. There is much in Vols. V. and VII. on the sending of convicts, and emigrants spirited away, to Virginia. In the "Domestic Series" of the Calendars are interesting documents connected with the voyages, in the sixteenth century, of Hawkins, Gilbert, Drake, and others.

The best history of American literature is that by Tyler (2 vols.). Richardson's work is shorter (1 vol.), and Beers's very short, but excellent. Extracts from the early writers are given in Stedman and Hutchinson's "Library of American Literature."

Palfrey's "History of New England" embraces five volumes, the last of which is posthumous. In the recent literature it is the principal authority on the subject. Dr. Palfrey was an able and accomplished man, eminent both as a scholar and a writer. He spared no pains in the study of the documentary sources at home and abroad. The full marginal references in the work enable the reader to test the author's correctness. The objection is often made that in his exposition of Puritan history—of Massachusetts history in particular—Palfrey lacks impartiality, is too apologetic. There may be ground occasionally for this criticism; yet he was not in sympathy with the Puritan theology, and his historical opinions grew up spontaneously, in the process of his studies and reflections. A writer so well qualified for his task, and so thorough in the performance of it, is not likely to be soon superseded.

Mr. John Fiske, in his readable volume on "The Beginnings of New England; or, The Puritan Theocracy in its Relations to Civil and Religious Liberty" (1889), by his philosophical views of history in general, and his more catholic tone, furnishes an agreeable antidote to various intemperate assaults upon the fathers of New England. Mr. Fiske's volume carries the history as far as 1688. Bacon's "Genesis of the New England Churches" (1 vol., 1874) is a work of much value. Weeden in his "Economic and Social History of New England" (2 vols., 1890) has brought together, under different heads, a large, miscellaneous collection of facts on the subject to which it relates.

One of the best of the State histories is Belknap's "History of New Hampshire," of which the first volume appeared in 1784, and the second and third in 1791-2. Barry's "History of Massachusetts" (3 vols., 1855-57) is more complete than any other, but is not a strong book. Baylies's "History of New Plymouth, 1608-1682" (2 vols., 1866), is a full account of the Pilgrim Colony. The "Memorial History of Boston," edited by Mr. Justin Winsor, an extended work in four volumes, is very instructive, not only in reference to Boston, but, also, respecting the Colony and State. The first volume is devoted to the early and colonial period. Lodge's "Boston" (1891), in the Series of Historic Towns, has much to say on colonial matters. The best history of Rhode Island is that of Arnold (2 vols., 1859-60). "The Life of Roger Williams" has been written by Knowles, Elton, and Gammell (1845). Trumbull's "History of Connecticut" (1 vol., 1797, 2 vols., 1818) is thorough and trustworthy. The brief "History of Connecticut," by Johnston (1 vol., 1887) in the Commonwealth Series, propounds some untenable views concerning the constitution of the Connecticut colony. Bacon's Historical Discourses (1 vol., 1839), on the early history of New Haven, is the fruit of careful researches. The same is true of the Life of Hooker, by G. L. Walker, in the Makers of America Series.

APPENDIX 329

The original authorities relating to the history of New England are to a large extent accessible in modern editions. Arber's edition of John Smith's writings includes his "Description of New England" (1616), and his "New England's Trials" (1622). Bradford's "History of the Plymouth Colony" was edited by that learned scholar in American history, Mr. Charles Deane (1856). Morton's "New England's Memorial" is found to have been largely borrowed from Bradford. Young's "Chronicles of the Pilgrim Fathers" (1844) contains Winslow's "Journal of the Plymouth Colony" (1622), and his "Good News from New England" (1624). Of early writings unfriendly to New England, Morton's "New English Canaan," has been edited by Mr. C. F. Adams, Maverick's "A Description of New England," by Mr. Charles Deane, and Lechford's "Plain Dealing in New England," by Mr. J. H. Trumbull. In all these editions, the notes added are highly important. Winthrop's "Diary," or "History of Massachusetts," is a work of priceless worth. Mr. Savage's edition of it (1853) contains illustrative notes of much importance. The publication by the Massachusetts Historical Society of Sewall's "Diary," puts us in possession of a picture of Massachusetts—and indeed of New England—at the end of the seventeenth and in the early years of the eighteenth century, which is parallel in interest with Winthrop. In connection with Winthrop's Diary should be mentioned his Life and Letters (1869), by Mr. R. C. Winthrop. A brief, but interesting, "Life of Winthrop," by J. H. Twichell, is in the Makers of America Series. Hubbard's "History of New England" was based on Winthrop and Morton, from which he borrowed largely. Poole's edition (1867) of Edward Johnson's "Wonder-working Providence of Zion's Saviour in New England" (1654) is enriched with accurate editorial notes. Certain peculiarities of the early ecclesiastical system are clearly explained by Mr. Poole. Governor Hutchinson's "History of Massachusetts Bay," of which the first volume reaches down to 1691, was composed by one who had access to original sources, some of which are no longer extant. Mason's "History of the Pequod War" is in the Collection of the Massachusetts Historical Society, Third Series, vol. iii. The story of King Philip's War is given by Hubbard, "Present State of New England," etc. (1677), and in Church's (well-named) "Entertaining Passages Relating to Philip's War" (1716), edited by H. M. Dexter (1865). Mr. J. H. Trumbull's "The True Blue Laws of Connecticut and New Haven, and the False Blue Laws," etc. (1876), exposes the inventions in Peters's "History of Connecticut" (1781), which are still occasionally cited as facts.

The writings of Roger Williams have been issued by the Narragansett Club. Of special consequence are his publications in the debate with Cotton on religious liberty: "The Bloudy Tenent of Persecution," first printed in 1644, and his Rejoinder to Cotton's Answer. The discussion of Williams and Cotton was closed by Cotton's "A Reply to Mr. Williams, his Examination," etc. This writing, which is very important to the understanding of the causes of the banishment of Williams, was ably edited by Professor J. L. Diman (vol. ii. of the Narragansett Club Series). "The Treatment of Intruders and Dissentients by the Founders of Massachusetts," is instructively considered by Dr. G. E. Ellis in a volume of Lowell Lectures (1869). "As to Roger Williams," by Dr. H. M. Dexter, is by an author learned in New England history. Among the writings on the Antinomian Controversy we have "John Wheelwright, his Writings," etc., by Charles H. Bell, A.M., printed for the Prince Society, Boston, 1876. It contains Wheelwright's famous Fast-Day Sermon, and his vindication of it.

Very important documents are the "Records of the Massachusetts Government from 1629 to 1684" (6 vols., edited by Shurtleff); the "Colonial Records of Connecticut" (15 vols., edited by J. H. Trumbull and C. J. Hoadley); the "Colonial Records of New Haven" (2 vols., edited by C. J. Hoadly); the "Rhode Island Colonial Records" (10 vols., edited by J. R. Bartlett). The collections of the Historical Societies of Massachusetts, Rhode Island, Connecticut, and New Haven contain very valuable materials for the history of New England.

The "History of New York, down to 1732," by William Smith, was first printed in London in 1757. (Later editions, Philadelphia, 1792; Albany, 1814.) Posthumous continuation to 1762 (New York, 1829). Smith was one of the leaders of the dissenting element in New York. The "History of New York," by J. R. Brodhead (1st vol., revised ed. 1872, 2d vol., 1871), extends over the period from 1609, the date of the discovery, to 1691. It is an elaborate work, founded on exhaustive researches, and written with great care. The author is fully appreciative of the merits of the Dutch, and shows a lively antipathy to the New England Puritans. A good popular "History of New York," by Ellis H. Roberts (2 vols., 1887), is in the Commonwealth Series. Mr. Roosevelt's "New York" (1891), in the Historic Towns Series, is an interesting volume. An account of the early Dutch writings respecting New York is given in Winsor's "Narrative and Critical History," vol. iv., p. 409 seq. The "Documents Relating to the Colonial History of New York," in eleven quarto volumes, contain a mass of valuable materials procured by Mr. Brodhead in Europe. Four volumes of "Documents Relating to the History of the Colony from 1604 to 1799" were published in 1849–54. Several additional volumes of Documents have been edited by Mr. Fernow. The collections of the New York Historical Society are important.

Samuel Smith's "History of the Colony of Nova Cæsarea, or New Jersey, to 1721" (1 vol., 1765 ; 2d ed., 1877), is derived partly from sources not now accessible. The "New Jersey Archives" is intended to embrace in its series of volumes all colonial documents of importance. Whitehead's "East Jersey under the Proprietary Governments" (2d ed., 1875) was first issued as vol. i. of the "Collections of the New Jersey Historical Society." It is prepared with much care. Earlier writings on New Jersey history are noticed in Winsor, vol. iii., p. 449 seq.

Proud's "History of Pennsylvania, from 1681 to 1742," is a meritorious work. It was published in 1797–98. Burden's "History of Friends in America" (1850–54) is by a Quaker, and contains the history of Pennsylvania. Watson's "Annals of Philadelphia" is full respecting the life of the early settlers. A number of extremely valuable collections of documents have been issued by Mr. Samuel Hazard : "Annals of Pennsylvania" (1609–82), "Votes of the Assembly," "Colonial Records," "Pennsylvania Archives," and "Duke of York's Laws." The titles are given in full in Winsor, vol. iii., p. 510. The most important of Penn's writings relating to the colony is the "Letter from William Penn" (1683). Two other early publications are also of great interest, "The Planter's Speech," etc. (1684), and Budd's "Good Order Established in Pennsylvania" (1685). Gabriel Thomas's "Description of Philadelphia and of the Province" was printed in London in 1698. He came over in 1681. Extracts are given in Watson's "History of Philadelphia," vol. i., p. 66 seq. An epitome and partial translation of the "Description of Pennsylvania," by Pastorius, the leader in the settlement of Germantown, is in the "Memoirs of the Historical Society of Pennsylvania, vol. iv., part 2, p. 83 seq. Of much worth are the "History of the Quakers," by Sewel (the first edition in 1722), and that by Janney (4 vols., 1860-67). Janney is the author of the best "Life of Penn" (1852). An "Earlier Life," a standard work, is by Clarkson. "Penn's Collected Writings" have passed through several editions since the first issue in 1726. The "Memoirs of the Pennsylvania Historical Society" present much information on the early history. For further bibliographical statements on the subject, see Winsor, vol. iii., p. 495 seq.

Chalmers in his political "Annals of the Present United Colonies" (London, 1780) goes over the early history of Maryland. Bozman's "The History of Maryland, from 1633 to 1660," is founded on wide researches, and is an accurate work. Burnap's "Life of Leonard Calvert," in Sparks's American Biography, gives an outline of the history of the colony to 1647. Scharf's "History of Maryland" (3 vols., 1879) is copious, and brings the narrative down to the present time. "Maryland," in the Commonwealth Series, is from the pen of Mr. William Hand Browne, who is also the author of the "Lives of George Calvert and Cecilius Calvert" in the Makers of America Series. Both of these works are instructive. Mr. Browne writes in warm sympathy with the founders of Maryland, and is convinced of the injustice of Penn in relation to the boundary dispute. On the question of Maryland toleration, the motives and extent of it, there are many controversial publications. It was taken up in the discussions of Manning and Gladstone, in 1875. On this subject, what Rev. E. D. Neill has written in his "Terra Mariæ," etc. (1867), in his "English Colonization of America," and in other writings, is important. Other references on this topic are in Winsor (vol. iii., p. 561 seq.).

Among the early documentary writings on the history of Maryland the following are of special interest: "A Relation of Maryland" (1635), written under the supervision of Baltimore. "Extracts from Original Letters of the Jesuit Missionaries" (with notes by Dr. Dalrymple) were published by the Maryland Historical Society in 1874 and 1877. Baltimore's pamphlet, "The Lord Baltimore's Case," etc., appeared in 1653, and the answer to it, "Virginia and Maryland," etc., in 1656. The volumes of "Maryland Archives," published by the State, and edited by Mr. Browne, throw much light on its early history.

The early work of Beverley, the "History of Virginia" (1705), is vivid in its descriptions of natural objects and of the Indians.

Keith's "History of Virginia" (1738) leans on Beverley. The first accurate work, which is valuable at present, on the subject, is Stith's "History of the First Discovery and Settlement of Virginia" (1747). Charles Campbell is the author of a "History of the Colony and Ancient Dominion of Virginia down to 1783," a work of considerable merit. E. D. Neill's work, "English Colonization in America in the Seventeenth Century"—which is the title of the later English edition—is founded on the original "Records of the Virginia Company." "Virginia" (1883), in the Commonwealth Series, is by John Esten Cooke. Mr. Cooke carries the narrative down to the present time. He presents many interesting details. He defends, on insufficient grounds, the Pocahontas story. On the ecclesiastical history of Virginia, Dr. F. L. Hawks's "Contributions," etc. (1836), and Bishop Meade's "Old Churches," etc. (1855), are to be mentioned. McConnell's "History of the American Episcopal Church" (1890) is written in a lucid, racy style, and brings out interesting facts.

"The Genesis of the United States," by Alexander Brown (2 vols., 1890), is a thorough account, based on documents, some of which had not before been used, of the inception and early history of the Virginia colony. He prints from the Simancas MSS. the correspondence of Philip II. and his successor with the Spanish ambassadors in England, as far as it has to do with the Virginia Company and its colony.

John Smith's "A True Relation of Virginia" covers the interval from April 26, 1607, to June 2, 1608. In "Purchas his Pilgrimes" (1685–90), vol. iv., is an account, by George Percy, of the voyage of the first emigrants to Virginia until their landing at Jamestown. The "Relatyon of the Discovery of James River," by Captain Newport, with the brief supplemental descriptions of the country and the natives, is printed in the collections of the "American Antiquarian Society," vol. iv. (1860). In the same volume are Edward Maria Wingfield's "A Discourse of Virginia," which covers the interval from June 22, 1607, to May 21, 1608. In 1624, John Smith published his "Generall Historie," which was a compilation including in it his prior publications on America, except the "True Relation." "Good Newes from Virginia," by Whitaker, the clergyman, was issued in 1613. Hamor, who had been Secretary of the Virginia colony, in his "True Discourse of the Present State of Virginia," carries the narrative down to June 18, 1614. The "Proceedings of the First

Assembly in Virginia" were published (in 1 vol.) in 1874, under the title "The Colonial Records of Virginia." Hening's "Statutes at Large," etc. (13 vols.), is a comprehensive collection of the statutes of Virginia. They exhibit incidentally the state of society.

A contemporary account of "Bacon's Rebellion," by "T. M." is printed in Force's Tracts, vol. i., No. 8. A valuable account in MS., from the time of Bacon's rebellion, which was found in the Burwell Papers, is given in the "Collections of the Massachusetts Historical Society," vol. xi.

For other documentary materials respecting Virginia, the reader is again referred to Winsor, vol. iii., p. 153 seq.

The "History of North Carolina," by Francis L. Hawks, D.D. (1858), rests upon original researches. Moore's "History of North Carolina" (2 vols., 1880) is a work of more popular interest. Carroll's "Historical Collections" (2 vols.) contain early printed writings relating to South Carolina. In the first volume is Hewitt's "History of the Rise and Progress of the Colonies of South Carolina and Georgia" (first published in 1779). Ramsey's "History" (1670–1808) appeared in 1809. Of much value are the two publications of Mr. Rivers, "Sketch of the History of South Carolina to 1719" (1856), and "A Chapter in the Early History of South Carolina" (1874). Documents in the English archives have been used by Doyle in his "English Colonies in America" (Virginia, Maryland, and the Carolinas). For a discussion of the sources of the history of the Carolinas, see Winsor, vol. v., p. 354 seq.

Respecting Georgia, Hewitt's work is less full than upon South Carolina. Stevens's "History of Georgia" (down to 1798) was written at the request of the Georgia Historical Society. White's "Historical Collections of Georgia" brings together a mass of documentary material. The latest and best work on the subject is the "History of Georgia," by C. C. Jones, Jr. The collections of the Georgia Historical Society are important. Among the Lives of Oglethorpe the "Memoir," by Robert Wright (London, 1867), is specially to be commended. Mr. Henry Bruce's "Life of Oglethorpe," in the Series of Makers of America, is an interesting, but discursive narrative, in which are brought together the details, as far as they are known, of Oglethorpe's career.

The series of works by Francis Parkman, under the general title of "France and England in North America," embrace "The

Pioneers of France in the New World," "The Jesuits in North America," "Frontenac," and other volumes. They are the result of a faithful study of original documents. The narratives are drawn up with great ability and judgment. The extensive work of the Jesuit Father, Charlevoix, on the History of New France (1744), has been translated in six volumes by Dr. Shea (1866-1872). For a full bibliography relating to the whole subject, see Winsor, vol. iv.

On the subject of the Physical Geography of America, Professor J. D. Whitney's "United States" is excellent. To be highly commended, also, is Professor N. S. Shaler's essay on the "Physiography of North America" (in Winsor, vol. iv., Introduction).

INDEX

ACADIANS, expulsion of the French, 238
Adams, John, on New England, 165; 210
Adolphus, Gustavus, 183
Albany, founded, 180; named, 189; Colonial Congress at, 237
Albemarle Colony, 79. *See* Carolina.
Albemarle, Duke of, 76
Alexander, Pokanoket chief, 154
Alexander VI., Pope, his bulls giving "the Indies" to Spain (1493), 14
Alexandria, council at, 238
Algonkins, spread of the race, 7; attacked by the Governor of New Netherland, 184
Allen, Samuel, purchaser of Mason's claims, 224; 226
Almanac, Poor Richard's, 271
Amadas, Philip, 26
American Philosophical Society, 268
Ames, William, theologian, 116
Amsterdam, New, on Manhattan, founded by the Dutch, 180; Dutch Church organized in, 181; described as it was in 1647, 184; in the hands of the English, 189; in the hands of the Dutch, 190; restored to the English, 191. *See* New Netherland and New York.
Amyraut, Moïse, theologian, teaches Penn, 200
Andros, Sir Edmund, Governor of New England, 160, 161; at Hartford, 162; his government overthrown, 164; Governor of New York and the Jerseys, 191, 192; 197; 219; 220; Governor of Virginia, 278
Anne, Queen, 225
Apalatchees, the, war of South Carolina against, 296
Archdale, Joseph, Governor of South Carolina, 296

Argall, Captain Samuel, Deputy-Governor of Virginia, 41, 42
Argyle, Earl of, 198
Aristotle, 13
Arlington, Lord, 52
Arundel, Lord, 29
Ashley River Colony, 79, 80
Ashurst, Sir Henry, 231
Assemblies, Colonial, their conflicts with royal governors and other officials, 209. *See* the several Colonies.
Atherton, Captain Humphrey, 145
Avalon, Lord Baltimore's first colony, 63
Averroes, 13
Aviles, Melendez de, 21
Ayllon, Vasquez de, 17

BACON, FRANCIS, 39
Bacon, Nathaniel, Jr., his rebellion, 53 *seq.*; the "Burwell Papers" concerning, 318
Balboa, Vasco Nuñez de, discoverer of the Pacific, 17
Baltimore, the town, 276
Baltimore, Lord. *See* Calvert.
Baptists in Rhode Island, 143; 234
Barclay, Robert, Governor of New Jersey, 197
Barlow, Arthur, 26
Barneveldt, Jan Van Olden, 179
Barrington, Governor of North Carolina, 294
Barrowe, Henry, Independent preacher, 89
Basse, Jeremiah, Governor in New Jersey, 255
Baxter, Richard, 163, 220
Bayard, Nicholas, 246
Belcher, Jonathan, Governor of Massachusetts, 234, 258, 259
Bellomont, Earl of, Governor of New York and of Massachusetts, 223, 224, 244, 246

Bennet, Richard, 49, 71
Berkeley, Bishop George, 210, 236
Berkeley, Lord, 190, 194, 196
Berkeley, Sir William, Governor of Virginia, 48 seq.; describes Virginia, 51; 55; organizes a government for Albemarle, 77
Bermuda, 41
Berry, John, Deputy-Governor in New Jersey, 196
Beverley, Robert, 314
Biloxi, 213
Blackstone, Sir William, 220
Blackwell, Capt. John, 206
Blair, Rev. James, Bishop's Commissary in Virginia, obtains a charter for William and Mary College, 278; his interview with Seymour, 279; his differences with Spotswood, 280
Blake, Joseph, Governor of South Carolina, 296
Block, Adrian, his voyage of exploration, 179
Boston, founded, 112
Boswell, James, on Oglethorpe, 303
Boylston, Dr. Zabdiel, 221
Braddock, General Edward, Washington's relations to him, 238, 239; his defeat and death, 290
Bradford, Andrew, 270
Bradford, William, his early life, 90; 94; Governor of Plymouth Colony, 97; 149; 181; his "History," 315
Bradstreet, Simon, Governor of Massachusetts, 151
Bradstreet, Anne, 318
Brainerd, David, 258
Branford, settled, 145
Bray, Rev. Thomas, Bishop's Commissary in Maryland, 274
Breda, Peace of, 190
Brewster, William, at Scrooby, 90; his death, 99; his library, 99, 149
Brooke, Lord, 131
Broughton, Lieutenant-Governor in South Carolina, 301
Browne, John, 105
Browne, Robert, Independent preacher, 89
Browne, Samuel, 105
Browne, Sir Thomas, 210
Bull, William, Lieutenant-Governor in South Carolina, 301, 306
Burdet, George, preacher at Dover, 124

Burghley, Lord, 89
Burnet, William, Governor of New York, of Massachusetts, 233, 248, 257
Burwell Papers, 314
Byllinge, Edward, 198
Byrd, William, 314

CABOT, JOHN and SEBASTIAN, their voyages, 15, 16
Calamy, Edmund, 120
Calvert, Cecilius, second Lord Baltimore, 63, seq., 205. See Maryland.
Calvert, Charles, third Lord Baltimore, 73, 272, 273, 275. See Maryland.
Calvert, Charles, fifth Lord Baltimore, 275
Calvert, Frederick, sixth Lord Baltimore, 275
Calvert, George, first Lord Baltimore, 62 seq. See Maryland.
Calvert, Leonard, Governor of Maryland, 66, 68 seq.
Calvert, Philip, 72
Cambridge, Harvard College established there, 141; the synod of, 141
Campbell, Lord Neill, 198
Canada, attempts on, 217, 226. See New France.
Canonchet, Sachem of the Narragansetts, 155
Carleton, Sir Dudley, 180
Carolinas, The, 76 seq.; Grant by Charles II., 76; the Albemarle and Clarendon settlements, 77; the "Constitutions," 77; civil disturbances in North Carolina, 79; South Carolina settled, 80; Huguenots in South Carolina, 80; Social Condition in North Carolina, 292; "Constitutions" given up in North Carolina, 293; Indian War, 293; North Carolina a royal province, 294; Scotch and Irish immigrants, 295; Two parties in South Carolina, 295; Archdale, Governor, 296; War against the Apalatchees, 297; War against the Yemassees, 297; End of Proprietary rule, 299; Revolt of Slaves, 300; Trade and immigration, 301; paper money, 301; Society in South Carolina, 301.

INDEX 339

Carr, Robert, 189
Carteret, Sir George, New Jersey granted to him, 190; contest with Andros, 191; grants "Concessions," 194; 196, 197
Carteret, James, Governor of New Jersey, 196
Carteret, Philip, Governor of New Jersey, 195, 196, 197
Cartier, Jacques, discovers the St. Lawrence, 20
Cartwright, George, 189
Carver, John, Governor of the Plymouth Colony, 94
Castine, 223
Causton, Thomas, 308, 309
Cecil, Robert, Earl of Salisbury, 39
Champlain, Samuel de, Governor of New France, 23
Charles I., King of England, 48, 108, 121, 139, 150, 181, 200
Charles II., King of England, 49, 52, 149, 151, 152, 157, 187, 196, 199, 201, 205, 207
Charles V., Emperor, 23
Charleston, S. C., the settlement there, 80; a seat of wealth and fashion, 302
Charlestown (Mass.), the settlement there, 111, 112
Charter Oak, legend respecting it, 162
Charters, of Virginia, 32, 39, 42, 44, 45; of Maryland, 64, 74; of the Carolinas, 76, 200, 204; of Plymouth, 95; of Massachusetts, 102, 158, 219, 230; of Rhode Island, 136, 145, 151; of Connecticut, 150; of New Hampshire, 100, 158, 230; of New Jersey, 190, 196; of Delaware, 201; attack on the New England charters by the English ministry, 157
Chatham, Lord, 210
Chauncey, Dr. Charles, 233
Cherokees, the, 300
Chester, named by Penn, 202
Chicheley, Sir Henry, Governor of Virginia, 56
Christiaensen, Hendrick, 178
Christiana, Fort, built by the Swedes in Delaware, 183
Church, Colonel Benjamin, in the contest against Philip, 155, 156; his history of the war, 315
Church of England, in England, 85, 100; in Virginia, 34, 50, 60, 279,

280; in relation to Massachusetts, 121, 161; in New York, 190, 245, 247; in Maryland, 68, 273; in South Carolina, 81, 297; in New Jersey, 256
Cibola, search for, 18
Clarendon Colony, 77. *See* Carolinas.
Clarendon, Earl of, 76, 188, 190
Clarke, John, 124, 143, 144, 151
Clayborne, William, 48; his contest with Maryland, 66 *seq.*
Clinton, Admiral George, Governor of New York, 250, 251
Coddington, William, 124, 143, 144
Coligni, Caspar de, 21
Colleges, Harvard, 169; William and Mary, 278; Yale, 227; Princeton, 258
Colleton, James, Governor of South Carolina, 81
Colonial union, reasons for, 214; conventions for, 214
Colonization, incentives to, under James I., 31 *seq.*
Columbus, 13, 15
Colve, Anthony, Governor-General in New York, 191
Conant, Ryer, 100, 102
Congregational Church, the first in Massachusetts, 104
Congregationalism in Virginia, 48; in New England, 113
Congregationalists, expelled from Virginia, received in Maryland, 69
Congress at Albany, 237 *et passim.*
Connecticut, early settlers, 126; Hooker and colonists with him, 127; government established, 128; New Haven founded, 129; its government, 129; fiction of Blue Laws, 130; Saybrook joined to Connecticut, 131; the Pequot War, 132; complaint against Massachusetts, 142; death of Hooker and Haynes, 149; charter from Charles II., 150; New Haven annexed to Connecticut, 150; hiding of the charter, 162; observance of Sunday, 172; sumptuary laws, 173; founding of Yale College, 227; the Saybrook platform, 228; "Separatists," 232; extension of religious freedom, 235; part in the siege of Louisburg, 240
Coode, John, 74, 272, 274

Cooke, Elisha, 218, 226
Cooke, Elisha, the younger, 229, 230
Cooper, Lord Ashley, Earl of Shaftesbury, 76
Copley, Sir Lionel, Governor of Maryland, 74, 273
Copping, John, an independent preacher, 89
Cornbury, Lord, Governor of New York and New Jersey, 246, 256, 264
Coronado, F. V. de, 18
Cortereal, Gaspar, 16
Cortes, Hernando, 17
Cosby, William, Governor of New York, of New Jersey, 248, 257
Cotton, John, 116 seq., 136, 148, 149, 166, 316
Courcelles, Daniel de Remi, 212
Covenant, the Half-way, 148
Coxe, Daniel, 257
Cranfield, Edward, Governor of New Hampshire, 158
Cranston, Samuel, Governor of Rhode Island, 224, 235
Craven, Charles, 297
Craven, Lord William, Governor of South Carolina, 297
Creeks, the, 297
Cromwell, Oliver, Lord Protector, 71; one of the commission for managing the colonies, 135; proposes to the Massachusetts people to emigrate, 142; favors the independents, 143; sends an expedition against New Netherland, 188
Cromwell, Richard, 49, 149, 199
Culpepper, John, 79
Culpepper, Lord, Virginia given to, 52; Governor of Virginia, 56, 277
Cumberland, Fort, 288
Cumming, Sir Alexander, 300

DAGWORTHY, CAPTAIN, 290
Dale, Sir Thomas, Governor of Virginia, his system of martial law, 40
Daniel, Robert, Deputy Governor of North Carolina, 293
Darien, 307
Davenant, Sir William, appointed by Charles II. Governor of Maryland, 70
Davenport, James, 232
Davenport, John, protects the regicides, 129, 130; his part in the founding of New Haven, 150; removes to Boston, 151
Davies, Samuel, 282, 290
D'Aulnay, 139
De Gourges, Dominic, 21
D'Iberville, 213
De Lancey, James, 250, 251
De Monts, 22
De Soto, Ferdinand, ascends the Mississippi, 19
Deerfield, massacre at, 155, 225
Delaware, Dutch settlers in, 180, 182; 185; Swedish settlers, 183; granted by the Duke of York to Penn, 201; a separate assembly in, 263
Delaware, Lord, Governor of Virginia, 40
Denny, William, Governor of Pennsylvania, 268
Detroit, fort built at, by the French, 213
Dieskau, Baron, 239, 251
Dinwiddie, Robert, Governor of Virginia, 284, 285, 288
Dixwell, John, one of the Judges of Charles I., 150
Dobbs, Arthur, Governor of North Carolina, 295
Dongan, Thomas, Governor of New York, 191, 192
Dorchester Company, 100, 102
Dover, N. H., founded, 124
Doyle, J. A., 107
Drake, Sir Francis, 24, 27
Drummond, William, 55, 77
Drysdale, Hugh, Governor of Virginia, 281
Dudley, Joseph, Governor of Massachusetts, 158, 159, 160, 161, 225, 226, 227
Dudley, Thomas, Governor of Massachusetts, 109, 122, 148, 160
Dummer, Jeremiah, 230, 231
Dummer, William, 228, 229, 234
Dunbar, David, 234
Duquesne, Fort, battle near, 287; taken by the English, 289
Dustin, Hannah, 223

EAST NEW JERSEY, division line, 196; purchased by Penn and others, 197; Scotch immigrants, 198; union with West Jersey, 198. See New Jersey, and West New Jersey.
Eaton, Theophilus, 103, 129, 130, 149

INDEX

Eden, Charles, Governor of North Carolina, 294
Edenton, 294
Edward VI., King of England, 23, 86
Edward, Fort, 251
Edwards, Jonathan, the "Great Revival," 231; as a writer, 319
Eliot, John, 151; befriends the Christian Indians, 156
Elizabeth, Queen of England, 24, 87
Elizabethtown claimants, the, 258
Endicott, John, Governor of Massachusetts, 102 seq., 146
Esopus Indians, the, 187
Eugene, Prince, 304
Evans, John, Governor of Pennsylvania, 263, 264
Exeter, planted, 124; attacked by the Indians, 217

Fairfax, Lord, 282, 286
Fairfield, founded, 145
Fendall, Josiah, Governor of Maryland, 72
Fenwick, George, 131, 134
Ferrar, Nicholas, 44
Fitch, Thomas, Governor of Connecticut, 240
Fletcher, Benjamin, Governor of Pennsylvania, of New York, 227, 245, 246, 262
Florida, discovery of, 16; French colonists in, 21; Spanish settlement in, 22
Fox, George, 79, 146, 261
Francis I., King of France, 20
Franklin, Benjamin, 210, 215, 221, 238, 268, 271, 289, 310, 319
Frederica, 307
Frobisher, Martin, 24
Frontenac, Count de, Governor of New France, 217, 218
Fuller, Samuel, 105

Gama, Vasco da, doubles the Cape of Good Hope, 15
Gardiner, Lion, 131
Gardiner, S. R., 106
Gates, Sir Thomas, Governor of Virginia, 41, 42
Geography, Physical, of North America, 1 seq.
Georgia, 303 seq.; its settlement, 306; increase of colonists, 307; condition of the colony, 307; expedition against St. Augustine,
309; Spanish attack on, 309; Whitefield in, 310; surrender of its charter, 311; new government, 311; social condition, 311. See Oglethorpe.
Gibbons, Major Edward, 69
Gilbert, Sir Humphrey, 25, 26
Gilbert, Captain Raleigh, 83
Gist, Christopher, 284
Glen, James, Governor of South Carolina, 301
Glover, William, Governor in North Carolina, 293
Goffe, William, one of the Judges of Charles I., 149
Gomez, Stephen, 17
Gondomar, 46
Gooch, William, Governor of Virginia, 281
Gookin, Charles, Governor of Pennsylvania, 264, 265
Gookin, Daniel, 156
Gordon, Patrick, Governor of Pennsylvania, 266
Gorges, Sir Ferdinando, 29, 33, 82, 123, 125, 135
Gorton, Samuel, 137, 138, 140, 143
Gosnold, Bartholomew, 28, 34, 35, 36
Governments, the form of the colonial, 208 seq.
Granville, Lord, 297
Great Meadows, 288. See Washington, George.
Greenwood, John, independent preacher, 89
Grenville, Sir Richard, 27
Grotius, Hugo, 179
Guilford, settlement of, 130

Hakluyt, Richard, 24
Hale, Sir Matthew, 220
Hamilton, Andrew, Governor in New Jersey, 198, 249, 255, 263
Hamilton, James, Governor of Pennsylvania, 267
Hamilton, John, 257
Harvard College, founded, 169; and the Mathers, 226
Harvard, John, 170
Harvey, Sir John, Governor of Virginia, 48
Haverhill, attacked by the Indians, 223
Hawkins, Sir John, 21, 57
Haynes, John, Governor of Massachusetts, of Connecticut, 116, 128, 149

342 INDEX

Heath, Sir Robert, 76
Henrico, college founded at, 41
Henry IV., King of France, 22
Henry VII., King of England, 23
Henry VIII., King of England, 23, 85
Henry, Prince of Portugal, promotes maritime discovery, 13
Heyes, Pieter, plants a Dutch colony in Delaware, 182
Higginson, Francis, 103
Holyman, 123
Hooker, Thomas, 116 *seq.*, 127, 132, 149, 316
Howard, Lord, of Effingham, 56, 277
Hubbard, William, 316
Hudson, Henry, discovers Hudson River, 177
Humphrey, John, 109
Hunt, Rev. Robert, 35
Hunter, Robert, Governor of New York, 247, 257
Hutchinson, Ann, 117 *seq.*, 124, 135, 184
Hutchinson, William, 124
Hutchinson, Thomas, Governor of Massachusetts, 237
Hyde, Edward, 293

INDEPENDENTS, their tenets, 88; persecuted, 89; favored by Cromwell, 143
Indians, the, 6; classification of, 7; their traits and manners, 7, 8; occupations, 8; tribal arrangements, 9; religion, 10; their moral qualities, 10; their number, 11; massacre by, in Virginia, 45; seized by slaves, 57; in New England, 95; Christian converts among, 156; hated, 157. *See* the several colonies.
Ingle, Captain Richard, 68 *seq.*
Ingoldsby, Major Richard, 243, 256
Insurrection in New York, Leisler's, 241
Inventions in the fifteenth century, 12
Iroquois, the, 191, 192, 212
Isabella, Queen of Castile, 14

JAMES I., King of England, 30 *seq.*, 46, 101
James II., King of England, 159, 162, 163, 164, 192, 199, 205, 207
Jamestown, planted, 35; burned, 54

Jeffreys, Sir Herbert, Governor of Virginia, 56
Jenckes, Joseph, Governor of Rhode Island, 235
Jenings, Samuel, Governor of West Jersey, 198, 256
Jesuits, their missions in Canada, 212
Johnson, Dr. Samuel, 303
Johnson, Lady Arbella, 112
Johnson, Isaac, 109
Johnson, Sir Nathaniel, Governor of South Carolina, 293, 296
Johnson, Robert, Governor of South Carolina, 298, 300
Johnson, Sir William, 239, 251
Johnston, Gabriel, Governor of North Carolina, 294
Joliet, Louis, Jesuit Missionary, 212
Jones, Hugh, 283
Joseph, William, 272
Jumonville, 288

KEITH, GEORGE, 261
Keith, Sir William, Governor of Pennsylvania, 266
Keppel, Admiral, 238
Kidd, Captain William, 223
Kieft, William, Governor of New Netherland, 134, 183, 184
Knowles, Sir Charles, 237

LA SALLE, his explorations, 213
La Tour, 139
Lake Champlain, battle near, 239
Lane, Ralph, Governor of Raleigh's Roanoke Colony, 27
Las Casas, 56
Laud, William, 108, 110, 121, 123, 125, 129
Laudonnière, 21
Law, Jonathan, Governor of Connecticut, 240
Lawrie, Gawen, Governor of East Jersey, 197
Legists, colonial, 320
Leisler, Jacob, leader in a revolution in New York, 193, 241; 242, 243, 244
Leon, Ponce de, discovers Florida, 16
Literature in the colonies, 313 *seq.*
Lloyd, David, 261, 263, 264
Lloyd, Thomas, 205
Locke, John, frames the "Constitution of Carolina," 77

INDEX 343

Loe, Thomas, 199
Logan, James, Secretary of Pennsylvania, 263, 264, 265, 266, 270
London Company, chartered, 32; new charter, 39; annulling of the charter, 45; grants a patent to the Pilgrims, 91
Londonderry, New Hampshire, its settlement, 230
Lothrop, Captain, 155
Loudoun, Earl of, 252
Louis XIV., King of France, 199, 209, 212
Louisburg, capture of, 236; restored to the French, 237
Louisiana, French settlements in, 213
Lovelace, Lord, Governor of New York, 190, 247, 256
Ludwell, Philip, 80, 292, 295
Lyford, John, 97, 100
Lyman, General Phineas, 251

MACAULAY, LORD, his mistake regarding Penn, 205
Mackay, Colonel, 298
Maine, the Popham colony, 83; Gorges' settlements in, 125; not in the New England Confederacy, 135; annexed to Massachusetts, claim of Gorges purchased by Massachusetts, 146, 158; 225
Makemie, Francis, 247, 282
Maltravers, Lord, 76
Manhattan, 180; purchase of, 181
Markham, William, Governor of Delaware, of Pennsylvania, 202, 261, 262
Marquette, Father James, 212
Mary, Queen of England, 86
Maryland, 62 *seq.*; grant to Baltimore, 63; charter, 64; religious toleration, 64; Clayborne's settlement, 66; the first colonists, 66; the legislature, 67; revolution and counter-revolution, 68; non-conformists in, 69; act of religious freedom passed, 70; overthrow of Baltimore's government by the Commissioners, 70; Puritan ascendency in, 71; Baltimore restored to power, 71; slavery in, 72; overthrow of proprietary rule in, 74; society in, 74; the revolution at the accession of William and Mary, 272; overthrow of the proprietary government, 273;

Episcopalian intolerance in, 274, proprietary government restored, 275; population, 276
Mason, John, 100, 123, 157
Mason, Captain John, 133
Massachusetts, the first settlers, 102; the great emigration to, 110; sufferings of the Colony, 111; the General Court, 112; its theocratic system, 113; Congregationalism in, 113; dissentients in religion, 114 *seq.*; the charter threatened, 122; the Pequot War, 132; her conduct in the Confederacy, 136; address to Parliament by, 141; love of independence, 141; Maine annexed to, 146; the Quakers in, 146; "intolerance," 147; Royal Commission, 152; annulment of charter, 158; middle party in, 159; 216; issue of paper money, 218; fails to regain its charter, 218; new charter, 219; the witchcraft delusion, 220; New Hampshire separated from, 224; Indian atrocities in, 225; expedition against Canada, 226; explanatory charter, 230; the "Great Revival," 231
Massachusetts Company, chartered, 102; its transfer to New England, 109. *See* Massachusetts
Massasoit, Chief of the Pokanokets, 154
Mather, Cotton, 221, 225, 226, 315
Mather, Increase, 163, 218, 220, 225, 226, 316
Maverick, Samuel, 152
May, Cornelius Jacobsen, Dutch Director in New York, 180
Mayas, the, 6
Mayflower, her voyage, 92; compact made in her cabin, 93
Mennonites, the, 204
Mexicans, the, 6
Miantonomo, Chief of the Narragansetts, 137, 138
Michaelius, 181
Middle States, their characteristics, 252
Middleton, Arthur, Governor of South Carolina, 299
Milborne, son-in-law of Leisler, 242
Milford, Conn., settled, 130
Miller, Rev. John, 245
Miller, Thomas, 79
Minuit, Peter, Dutch Director in New York, 181, 182

Mohawks, the, 132, 133, 191
Mohegans, the, 132, 133, 137, 138
Monk, General George, 76
Montgomerie, John, Governor of New York and New Jersey, 248, 257
Moore, Colonel James, Governor of South Carolina, 293, 296, 299
More, Nicholas, 203, 205
Morris, Robert H., Governor of Pennsylvania, 267
Morris, Lewis, Governor of New Jersey, 256, 257
Morton, Thomas, 96, 121
Mound Builders, the, 6

NANFAN, Lieutenant-Governor of New York, 246
Nantes, edict of, 22
Narragansetts, the, 132, 133, 137, 138, 145, 155
Narvaez, Pamfilo de, 17
Nassau, Fort, 180
Navigation acts, English, history of, 50; made stricter under Charles II., 149; source of chronic complaint, 209; enforced in New York, 191; in Massachusetts, 224; in Virginia, 278
Negro Plot, in New York, 249
New England, the Popham Colony, 83; John Smith in, 83; the Council of, 84; motives of the permanent settlement, 85 seq.; towns in, 99; Council of, surrenders its charter, 123; Confederacy of, 133; how treated under the Commonwealth, 136; acts of the Confederacy, 139; death of eminent founders, 149; visit of the Royal Commission, 152; attack on the New England Charter by Charles II., 157; royal government in, 159; the revolution in 1689, 164; society in, 165; of pure English stock, 165; government and laws, 165; town organization, 167; the ministry, 168; education in, 169; social distinctions, 170; religion, 171; sumptuary laws in, 173; employments, 175; Board of Trade and Plantations, 216; attacks of French and Indians, 223; expeditions against Canada, 226; "the Great Revival," 231; writers in, 314 seq.; absorption in religion and theology, 318. See the several New England Colonies, et passim.
New France, rise of, 22 seq.
New Hampshire, Mason's grant, 100; Exeter and Dover founded, 124; a distinct royal province, 158; again united to Massachusetts, 158; again separated, 224; Londonderry founded, 230; Mason claims settled, 239
New Haven, its settlement, 129; government, 129; population, 130; annexed to Connecticut, 150
New Jersey, grant to Carteret and Berkeley, 190, 194; its constitution, 194; settlement at Elizabeth, 195; divided, 196; annexed to New York, 198; a royal province, 255; separated from New York, 257; the Elizabethtown claimants, 258; the Revival, 258; social life, 259. See East New Jersey, West New Jersey
New Netherland, Hudson's discovery, 177; the "New Netherland Company," 179; settlement on Manhattan, 180; the patroons, 181, seq.; Van Twiller's controversy with Connecticut settlers, 183; trouble with the Indians, 184; under Stuyvesant, 184; treaty with Connecticut, 185; New Sweden conquered, 185; relations to Connecticut, 187; conquered by the English, 189; surrendered to the Dutch, 190; restored to the English, 191. See New York.
New Sweden, settled, 183; conquered by the Dutch, 185
New York, surrender of New Netherland to the English, 189; recaptured by the Dutch, 190; regained by the English, 191; described by Andros, 191; "charter of liberties," 191; a royal province, 192; Leisler's insurrection, 193, 241, seq.; Assembly's Bill of Rights, 244; struggle for self-government, 245; Fletcher establishes Episcopacy, 245, 246; Cornbury's intolerance, 247; German immigrants, 248; contest for the liberty of the press, 249; the Albany Congress, 251; paper money, 252; society, 252; the clergy, 253; education, 253; so-

cial classes, 253, 254. *See* New Netherland.
Newcastle, Duke of, 236
Newport, 124, 136
Newport, Captain Christopher, 34, 35
Nicholas V., Pope, 14
Nicholson, Francis, Lieutenant-Governor in Virginia, Governor of Maryland, Deputy-Governor in New York, Governor of Carolina, 193, 241, 242, 247, 274, 277, 278, 299, 300
Nicolls, Colonel, 152, 189, 190, 195
North Carolina. *See* Carolina.
Norton, Rev. John, 151
Nott, Edward, Deputy-Governor in Virginia, 280

OAKES, THOMAS, 218
Oglethorpe, James Edward, 303 *seq.*
Oglethorpe, Sir Theophilus, 303
Ohio Company, the, 284
Oldham, John, 100, 127
Orkney, Earl of, Governor of Virginia, 279
Osborne, Sir Danvers, Governor of New York, 251
Oxenstiern, Swedish Chancellor, 183

PACIFIC, its discovery, 17
Palfrey, John G., 106
Parris, Samuel, 221
Pastorius, F. D., 204
Patroons, in New York, 181 *seq.*
Penn, William, 73, 196, 197, 199 *seq.*, 260, 261, 262, 264, 265, 266. *See* Pennsylvania
Penn, Admiral Sir William, 190, 200, 205
Pennsylvania, grant to Penn, 200; Delaware obtained from the Duke of York, 201; Penn's charter, 201; his address to the colonists, 202; arrival of Penn, 202; his constitution, 202, 203; emigration to, 204; religion in, 205; domestic strife, 205; description of, 206; party feeling in, 261; the proprietary displaced, 262; restored to Penn, 262; he befriends the Indians, 262; new Charter of Privileges, 263; the two parties in, 263; dissensions, 264 *seq.*; opposition to the proprietaries, 267 *seq.*; society, 269; population, 269; physicians, 269; tradesmen, 269; intellectual life, 270
Pennsylvania, University of, 268
Penry, John, Independent preacher, 89
Pepperell, Sir William, 236, 237
Pequot War, the, 132 *seq.*
Pequots, the, 132, 133, 153
Peruvians, the, 5
Philadelphia, founded, 202; legal and medical science in, 269; population and social life in, in 1749, 270
Philip II., King of Spain, 21, 177
Philip III., King of Spain, 45
Philip, King, war of, 153 *seq.*; 154, 155, 156
Phips, Sir William, 217, 218, 220, 221, 222, 223, 224
Pilgrims, at Scrooby, 89; in Holland, 90; preparations to emigrate, 91; voyage to New England, 92; first winter at Plymouth, 95; purchase of land, 97. *See* Plymouth Colony.
Pineda, his voyage of discovery, 17
Pinzon, 14
Plato, 13
Plymouth. Mass., decline of the town, 145
Plymouth Colony, arrival of the Pilgrims, 92; compact framed, 93; agreement with the merchants, 94; the patent, 95; form of government, 96; purchase of the stock and land, 97; growth and character, 98; number of "Praying Indians," 98; spirit of the colony, 140; King Philip's War, 153; annexed to Massachusetts, 219. *See* Pilgrims.
Pocahontas, 37
Pokanokets, the, 154
Pollock, Colonel, Acting Governor of North Carolina, 293
Popham Colony, 83
Popham, George, 83
Popham, Lord Chief-Justice, 29, 33
Port Royal, Captured by Phips, 217
Portsmouth, R. I., settled, 124; incorporated in Providence Plantations, 136
Poutrincourt, 22
Powhatan, 36, 37
Presbyterians in England, 88; in New Jersey, 218; in New York, 247; in Pennsylvania, 270; in Virginia, 282

Prince, Thomas, 316
Princeton College, 258
Pring, Martin, his explorations, 29
Printz, Swedish Governor, 183
Providence, R. I., founded, 115
Providence Plantations, charter of, 136
Puritanism, rise and progress in England, 87 *seq.*
Putnam, Israel, 239
Pym, 135

QUAKERS, in Virginia, 50; in Maryland, 73; in North Carolina, 79; in Massachusetts, 146, 151; 234; in New York, 186; in New Jersey, 196, 257; their tenets adopted by Penn, 199; in Pennsylvania, 202; Anti-Quaker Party in Pennsylvania, 261, 267
Quebec, founded, 23

RALEIGH, SIR WALTER, 25; his first colony, 27; his second colony, 28
Randolph, Edward, 157, 159, 160, 164, 224
Randolph, Peyton, 282, 285
Rasles, Sebastian, 214, 230; destruction of his settlement, 229
Ratcliffe, Philip, 121, 160, 219
Ratcliffe, John, Governor of Virginia, 34, 36, 37
Reading, John, 258
Recollets, the, in Canada, 212
Reformation, the English, its progress, 85
Regicides, the, in New England, 150
Renaissance, the characteristics of the, 12
Revolution of 1688, its effect in England, 208; in the colonies, 208 *seq.*
Reynolds, Captain John, 311
Rhett, Colonel William, 296
Rhode Island, Roger Williams founds Providence, 123; settlement of Newport and Portsmouth, 124; not a member of the Confederacy, 135; charter granted to Williams, 136; contest of Coddington and Clarke, 143; union under Williams's charter, 145; new charter obtained by Clarke, 151; Bellomont's complaints against, 224; laws limiting the franchise, 230; part in the first war with France, 240

Ribaut, Jean, 21
Richards, John, 158
Rigby, Alexander, 146
Rittenhouse, David, 271
Roanoke, the first colony, 27; the second colony, 28
Roberval, Lord of, 20
Robinson, John, 90, 97, 179
Roche, Marquis de la, 22
Rolfe, John, 41, 57
Rudyard, Thomas, Governor of East Jersey, 197
Russell, Rev. John, 150
Ryswick, Peace of, 213

SAGAS, the Norse, 13
St. Louis, 212
St. Mary's, Maryland, planted, 67
Salmon Falls, massacre at, 217
Saltonstall, Gordon, Governor of Connecticut, 228
Samoset, a Wampanoag Indian, 95
Sandys, Sir Edwin, 33, 44, 46
Sandys, George, 314
Saratoga, destruction of, 250
Sassacus, a Pequot chief, 133
Savannah, planted, 306
Say and Sele, Lord, 131, 135
Saybrook, 131; synod of, 228
Sayle, William, Governor in South Carolina, 80
Schenectady, massacre at, 217
Schuyler, Peter, 242
Scott, John, 187
Scrooby, the congregation at, 90
Sewall, Samuel, Chief Justice in Massachusetts, 120, 222
Sharpe, Horatio, Governor of Maryland, 275
Shippen, Dr. William, 269
Shirley, William, 236, 237, 239, 291
Shute, Samuel, Governor of Massachusetts, 228, 229, 230
Skelton, Samuel, Governor of Massachusetts, 103
Sloughter, Col. Henry, Governor of New York, 243, 244, 245
Smith, Thomas, Governor of South Carolina, 295
Smith, John, 35, 36, 38, 40, 83, 179, 313
Sothel, Seth, Governor in North Carolina, 79, 295
South Carolina. *See* Carolina.
Southampton, Earl of, 29, 47
Spangenberg, August Gottlieb, Moravian Bishop, 306

INDEX 347

Spotswood, Alexander, Governor of Virginia, 280, 293
Standish, Miles, 95, 121
Stark, John, 239
Stephens, Samuel, Governor in North Carolina, 79
Stiles, Ezra, President of Yale College, 233
Stirling, Lord, 188
Stith, a Virginia historian, 314
Stone, Rev. Samuel, 116, 127, 132
Stone, William, Governor of Maryland, 69 seq.
Stoughton, William, 221
Stratford, Conn., planted, 145
Stuyvesant, Peter, Governor of New Amsterdam, 142, 184 seq.
Swanzey, massacre at, 155
Swedish settlement in Delaware, 183

TALCOTT, JOSEPH, Governor of Connecticut, 235
Tennent, Gilbert, 258
Tennent, William, 258
Thacker, Elias, an Independent preacher, 89
Thomas, George, Governor of Pennsylvania, 267
Tillotson, John, Archbishop, 260
Tobacco, its cultivation in Virginia, 41; made legal currency there, 43
Tomo-chi-chi, 306
Toscanelli, 14
Tribes of North America, their languages, 5
Trott, Nicholas, 296, 298
Tuscaroras, the, 212, 293
Tynte, Edward, Governor of South Carolina, 297

UNCAS, Chief of the Mohegans, 137, 138, 145
Usher, John, 224, 226

VACA, CABEZA DE, 18
Van Dam, Rip, 248
Van Rensselaer, 182
Van Twiller, Wouter, Governor of New Amsterdam, 183
Vane, Sir Henry, 117, 124, 135, 136, 144
Vassall, William, 140, 143
Vaughan, William, 224
Verhulst, William, Dutch Director in New Amsterdam, 180
Vernon, Admiral Edward, 234, 286, 309

Verrazano, John, 20, 28
Vespuccius, Americus, 15
Virginia, 30 seq.; the first charter, 32; the superior council, 33; the colony, 34 seq.; dissension, 36; complaints by the company, 38; new charter, 39; code of martial law, 40; the third charter, 42; method of government altered, 42; House of Burgesses constituted, 42; slaves introduced, 43; growth of the colony, 44; written constitution, 44; Indian massacre, 45; annulment of the charter, 45; parties in the colony, 47; effect of the annulling of the charter, 48; nonconformists expelled, 49; submits to the Commonwealth, 49; recognizes Charles II., 49; its condition in 1671, 51; grant to Arlington and Culpepper, 52; Indian troubles, 53; Bacon's rebellion, 53; again a royal province, 56; negro slavery, 57; social life, 58; tobacco culture, 58; condition in 1681, 59; aristocracy in, 60, 277 seq.; revolution, 277; new immigrants, 281; the churches, 282; slavery, 282; the rich planters, 283

WAR, the French and Indian, 211
Ward, Nathaniel, 148, 166
Warren, Admiral Sir Peter, 237
Warwick, Earl of, 131, 135
Washington, George, his birth and education, 286; a land surveyor, 286; an Adjutant-General, 287; a messenger to the French, 287; at Great Meadows, 288; an Aid of Braddock, 290; in the battle at Monongahela, 290; in command at Winchester, 290
Washington, Lawrence, 284, 286
Wentworth, Benning, Governor of New Hampshire, 239
Wentworth, John, 230
Wesley, Charles, 307, 308
Wesley, John, 220, 307, 308
West, Joseph, 80
West India Company, in Holland, 179, 181
West New Jersey, division line, 196; sold to Penn and others, 196; union with East New Jersey, 198. See New Jersey, and East New Jersey.

Weston, Thomas, 96
Weymouth, George, 29
Whalley, Edward, 149
Wheelwright, Rev. John, 118 *seq.*
Whitaker, Rev. Alexander, 41, 314
White, Rev. John, 102
Whitefield, George, 231, 310
Wigglesworth, Michael, 319
William and Mary, King and Queen of England, 150, 164, 207, 210, 216, 217
William and Mary College, 278
Williams, Col. Ephraim, 239
Williams, Roger, 114 *seq.*, 123, 124, 132, 136, 137, 143, 144, 145, 316
Willoughby, Sir Hugh, 23
Wilson, John, First Minister of Boston, 111, 151
Wingfield, Edward Maria, 35, 36, 37
Winslow, Edward, 315
Winslow, John, 238
Winthrop, John, 69, 109, *seq.*, 121, 122, 135, 137, 138, 146, 169, 315

Winthrop, John, the younger, 131, 145, 150, 187, 228
Winthrop, John, nephew of the first John Winthrop, 235
Witchcraft, "The Salem," 220
Wolcott, Roger, Governor of Connecticut, 240
Wollaston, Captain, 96
Wyatt, Sir Francis, Governor in Virginia, 44, 48

YALE COLLEGE, founded, 227
Yeamans, John, Governor in the "Clarendon" Colony, 77
Yeardley, George, Governor in Virginia, 42
Yemassees, The, 297, 300
Yonge, Francis, 298
York, Duke of, James, 152, 158, 187, 196, 197, 201

ZENGER, JOHN PETER, 249
Zuñiga, Spanish ambassador in England, 45

THE A

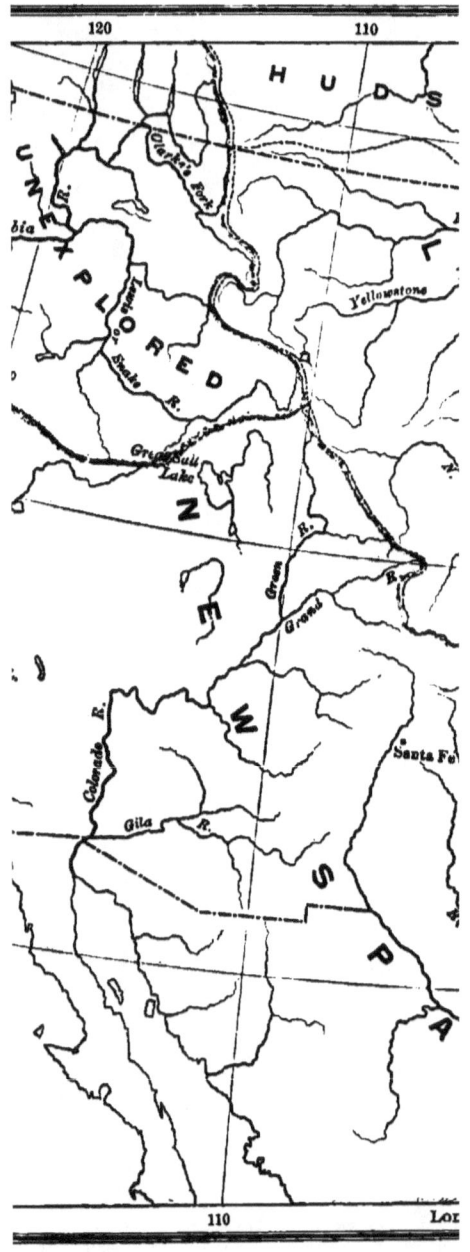

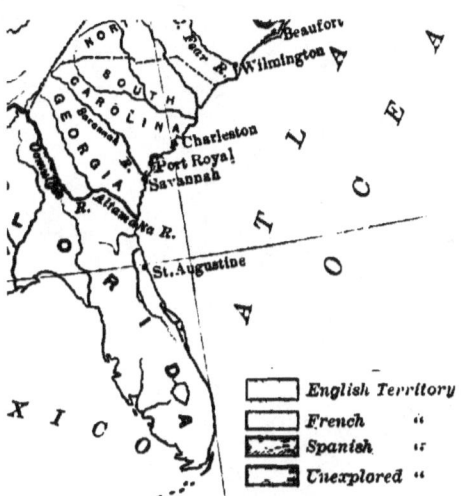

www.ingramcontent.com/pod-product-compliance
Lightning Source LLC
Chambersburg PA
CBHW032041220426
43664CB00008B/813